J. A. K. THOMSON

CLASSICAL
INFLUENCES
ON
ENGLISH
PROSE

LONDON
GEORGE ALLEN & UNWIN LTD

FIRST PUBLISHED IN 1956

PRINTED IN GREAT BRITAIN

in 12 point Bembo type

BY PURNELL AND SONS LTD
PAULTON (SOMERSET) AND LONDON

PREFACE

THE present volume is planned on the lines of my *Classical Influences on English Poetry*, but diverges at one point. In that, quotations were printed in Latin; in this, with a few exceptions,* they are not. If they had been, the book would be too large and expensive to suit its purpose, which is to indicate, not elaborate, the relation of English to classical prose. The writer hopes that the student will not be deterred by the translations from comparing them with the originals, to which a reference is always given.

J. A. K. THOMSON

* The exceptions, which are four in number, are translated in the Appendix.

CONTENTS

PASSAGES FROM QUOTED
GREEK AND LATIN AUTHORS

AMMIANUS. *History* (Rerum gestarum libri) XXI · 16 · XXVII · 3 · 12.

ANTIPHON. *D. Caede Herodis*. 20–28.

APULEIUS. *Metamorphoses* III · 29 · V · 1 · IX · 12, 13.

ARISTIPPUS. From Diogenes Laertius.

ARISTOTLE. *Rhetor*. II · XX (1393b). *Nic. Eth.* I̅V̅ · II (1123b–1125a). *Pr. Anal*. 1 · II (24b).

AUGUSTINE. *Confess*. VIII · 12. *D. Civ. Dei* X · 9.

BION (Borysthenita). From Clement of Alexandria, *Strom*. 712.

BOETHIUS. *D. Cons. Phil*. I̱ *Prosa* I. I̱I̱ *Prosa* VII.

CAESAR. *Bell. Civ*. II · 41 § 5; 42. *Bell. Gall*. V · 12–14; VII · 77.

CICERO. *D. Officiis* I̅I̅I̅ · 1; IX; XIV. *D. Divin*. I̱ · XXVII · 57. *D. Nat. Deorum* I̱ · XIX; XXVI. *D. Senect*. XXI. *Tusc. Disp*. V̱ · XXIII · 64–66. *Somn. Scip*. 5. *Pro Plancio* XXVI · 64f. *Pro Murena* XXIX, XXX, XXXI. *Philip*. II · 30, 31; *ad finem*. *Orator* XXXIX. *Epist. ad Fam*. IX · 26. *Epist. ad Att*. II · 19 · 2–4.

CURTIUS RUFUS. *Vit. Alex*. VIII · IX.

DEMOCRITUS. From Natorp.

DEMODOCUS. From Bergk.

DEMONAX. From 'Lucian' *Vit. Demon*.

DION (PRUSENSIS). *Venator ad fin*.

EPICTETUS. *Discourses* 16, *De Providentia*.

ERASMUS. *Colloquies: Naufrag.; Charon; Diversoria. Epis. ad Francisc*. *Fragm. Papyr Erot*. p. 7–10.

GELLIUS. *Att. Noct*. VI · 14.

HELIODORUS. *Aethiop. ad init*.

HERODOTUS. II · 10–12; 121. III · 39–44; 109; 139, 140. V · 101, 102; 105. VI · 12; 86; 125. VIII · 65; 137.

HORACE. *Serm*. I̱ · V.

LIVY. *Praefatio*. I̱I̱ · XII; XXXII · 8–12. V̅I̅I̅ · IX, X · X̅X̅I̅X̅ · XXXII. X̅X̅X̅I̅V̅ · V

'LONGINUS'. *D. Sublim*. XVI; XXXIV.

LONGUS. *Daph. et Chloe* IV.

LUCIAN. *Dial. Mort*. 14. *Charon* 15, 16. *Vera Hist*. I · 5, 6; II · 20; 32, 33.

LYSIAS. *D. Caed. Erat. ad init.*

MACROBIUS. *Comm. Somn. Scip.* I · XXIII. *Saturn.* II · 3 · 2.

MARCUS (AURELIUS). *Medit. ad fin.*

MORE. *Utopia* I · 26.

PETRONIUS. *Sat.* I · III. *Cen. Trim.* 28 · 6–29 · 9; 48; 59.

PHOCYLIDES. From Bergk.

PLATO. *Apol. ad finem. Gorgias* 485a–486b. *Laches* 183c–184a. *Phaedo* 65d–66b; 97b–98c. *Protag.* 314c–315b. *Resp.* 359d–360b; 414d–415c. *Symp.* 215, 216; 222c–f.

PLINY (JUNIOR). *Ep.* VI · 16 and 20. VII · 27. VIII · 8. IX · 26.

PLINY (SENIOR). *Nat. Hist.* II · 1; V · 1; 8 ; VIII · 1; X · 2.

PLUTARCH. *Alexander ad init. Moralia, De Superstitione.*

QUADRIGARIUS. *Fragm.*

QUINTILIAN. *Inst. Orat.* X · 85.

RHETORICA AD HERENNIUM. (Nobbe) IV · 50–57.

SALLUST. *Catil.* 14, 15.

SENECA. *Ep.* XLI; CVII. *Nat. Quaest. Praef.*; I · 7. *D. Tranquil. Animi* VII. *Apocol.* 5. *Medea* 374f.

SUETONIUS. *Nero ad fin.*

SULPICIUS. *Cic. Ep. ad Fam.* IV · 5.

TACITUS. *Agric.* 46. *Hist.* I · 49; III · 84, 85. *Ann.* I · 7; 11, 12; 9, 10; 61; XIV · 39.

THEOPHRASTUS. *Char.* XII; XIV.

THEOPOMPUS. *Fragm.*

THOMAS (AQUINAS). *Summa Theol. Quaestio* 49.

THUCYDIDES. *Hist.* II · 22, 23.

XENOPHON. *Anab.* IV · 7. *Cyrop.* V · 1 · 9f.

INTRODUCTORY

THERE is a kind of prose which may be recognized in almost every period of English literature—which may be read in the 'Anglo-Saxon Chronicle', in Tyndale, in Latimer, in Bunyan, in Defoe, in Cobbett and others—simple, idiomatic, giving an impression of naturalness, of being racy of the soil. This, it may be thought, is English prose in its native purity. It seems to be unaffected by any influence from classical literature. Whether it is wholly unaffected is a point that admits of argument. But it need not be argued here. One has only to put this further question: 'Is every other kind of prose to be excluded from the canon?' That would mean excluding the greater part of our generally accepted literature. We should have to say that Hooker does not write English prose, nor Donne, nor Taylor, nor Browne, nor Milton, nor Johnson, nor Gibbon, nor Burke, nor Landor, nor Ruskin and fifty more. Now whoever takes that view it cannot be the historian of literature. He must not follow one line of development and neglect another. It is not for him to pass judgement upon styles but to account for them, for all of them. To account for most of them he is led back to the prose of classical antiquity, since he finds that they are mixed styles, blending in different ways and proportions the vernacular virtues with the classical. It is possible to isolate these classical elements; indeed to do that is the main purpose of this volume. But they should not be studied, for they cannot be understood, in isolation. They are inwoven in our literature as the result of a process which has operated in the general mind of Europe. English literature is that part of European literature which is written in English.

European prose like European poetry begins among the Greeks. Since prose is an artistic arrangement of words, we are not concerned with inscriptions (of laws or ordinances), or genealogies, or records of business transactions, or treaties, or liturgies—all of which may come first in point of time among the written memorials of a race. These are not, unless by accident, literature. But long before these, long before writing was invented, the art of story-telling was practised in human communities. Prose has its origin in oral narrative, which is an artistic arrangement of words that, written down, become literature. Writing them down, however, is not the simple process one might imagine. A reader cannot be addressed exactly as if he were a listener. The *diseur* conveys a great deal by look and gesture; the writer has to do without these aids. Therefore, if he is not to lose much of that dramatic vividness which counts for so much in good story-telling, he must do in words what the speaker does by gesture. Without speaking he must give the effect of speech. The written story must preserve the qualities of oral narrative: simplicity, directness, vividness, dramatic force, above all clearness. In some forms of literature, such as the prophetic or apocalyptic, obscurity has great power over a simple audience. But not in a story; they will not tolerate obscurity in that. Here chiefly is where the art of the story-teller finds scope. It is notoriously hard to get a distinct account of any complex experience from people whose minds have not been trained in this form of expression. They ramble and repeat themselves, they do not begin at the beginning, they assume that you know what they know and don't know what they don't. If, however, a simple man is given time to relate over and over again the story of some event he witnessed or shared in, he will at last, as he discovers what his auditors will listen to and what not, gradually get his narrative shaped into its most telling form. This is what happened to the traditional stories of the Greeks. They were told better and better, or at least more effectively, as time went on. Colourless details fell away, the edge of the narrative was sharpened, no room was left for the smallest obscurity, the slightest ambiguity. But, as some men are naturally better than others at telling a story, the art which at first was hardly conscious became fully conscious in them. They learned their business, and there arose a class of professional story-tellers. It was at a comparatively late period and no doubt with reluctance that they put the stories (their stock in trade) into writing. The transposition had become inevitable, and it involved the artistic problem I have indicated. The problem was solved by Herodotus, completely solved, and for that reason we may say that the history of European prose begins with him.

The art of Herodotus was narrative. But prose need not, even for a primitive audience, be always narrative; even a primitive audience has sometimes to be convinced. The Greeks, an argumentative race, gradually worked out a style adapted, as the narrative style is not, to produce conviction in the listener. To persuade you must argue, and to argue you must oppose one statement to another. This leads to a form of sentence different from that which is normal in simple narration. The man who seeks to prove a case must employ conditional and complex sentences. He cannot just go on making a series of affirmations or assertions. He must draw conclusions from premisses, which he has induced his auditor or reader to accept.

It is therefore for the purposes of this volume convenient to divide prose into *narrative* and *argumentative*. Under the former division will fall not only the legend, the anecdote, the short story, but history, biography, the romance, the novel. Under the latter will fall oratory, philosophy and the literature of science. It is not so easy to place satire, the letter, the 'character', the literature of travel. They may accordingly be treated with greater independence. Since the history of ancient prose is largely an account of how the different genres came to be invaded by rhetoric, the clearest as well as the most logical procedure will be to deal first with prose of the narrative kind in all its branches and developments. About this procedure there is nothing scientific; it is merely a convenient arrangement of the diverse material.

CHAPTER ONE

SIMPLE NARRATIVE

S IMPLE narrative is ·found in its purest form, as we might
expect, in stories that have long been told among simple
people or that are told in the manner of such stories. This is the
earliest and as it were the original form of prose. It does not
follow that it is the easiest, nor have practised writers found it
so. To be clear and simple, to know what to put in and leave
out, to be colloquial without being trivial—to be this and more
than this is rare and perhaps increasingly rare. Yet the old
story-teller very often had the qualities which enabled him to
succeed in all that, even if his art is at least partly instinctive. In
classical literature the art must be described as entering with
Herodotus, because of all the story-tellers his work alone has
survived. Yet it is enough for our purpose, since he provides
many consummate examples of the traditional story told in the
traditional way. One of these I will give at once, translating it,
as I propose to translate the others, as nearly as possible word
for word, since fidelity to the structure of the Greek is
essential to the stylistic argument on which our conclusions
must depend. To translate Herodotus into a modern idiom
is to falsify the impression which he made on the ancients
themselves.

This Alexander was seventh in descent from Perdiccas, who won
the lordship of the Macedonians in the way I shall tell. Among the
descendants of Temenus there were three brothers, Gauanes and
Aeropus and Perdiccas, who escaped from Argos to Illyria, whence
passing into the upper parts of Macedonia they came to the city of
Lebae. Here they served for wages in the household of the king, one
feeding horses, the other kine, but the youngest, Perdiccas, the
meaner cattle. Now the queen cooked their victuals with her own

hands—for in olden days even kings were poor, and not only the common people—and, whenever she baked, the loaf of the serving lad Perdiccas swelled to double its size. Because this never failed to happen she told her lord. And he as soon as he heard it believed that the thing was out of nature and portended some serious matter. And he summoned these servants and commanded them to be gone out of his country. But they answered that they ought to get their wages before they departed. Then the king, hearing mention of wages, pointed to the sunshine, which was pouring into the house by way of the chimney, and said: 'There is the wages ye have earned; I give you that.' (God willed this to his destruction.) Now Gauanes and Aeropus stood confounded when they heard these words, but the lad said: 'O King, we accept thy gift'; and he scored out the image of the sun into the floor with a knife he had, and wafted the sunshine into his bosom, and so departed, he and his brothers. But after they had gone one who had been there explained to the king what the lad had done, saying that it was for a purpose that the lad had taken what was given. When the king heard this he was seized with anger and sent horsemen after them to kill them. Now in this land there is a river to which the descendants of these men offer sacrifice as their saviour; for after the Children of Temenus had crossed over it, this river rose so high that the riders were not able to pass it. But the brothers came to another part of Macedonia and settled close to the gardens which are called the Gardens of Midas the son of Gordias, wherein grow without art of man roses each having a hundred leaves and in perfume excelling all others. In these gardens also Silenus was taken, as the Macedonians tell.*

Herodotus is able to work this story into the texture of his main narrative, because when he comes to describe the part played in the Persian wars by the royal house of Macedon, which claimed to be of Greek descent, it is natural to relate the legend on which the claim was founded. But a legend it is, almost a fairy tale, and so Herodotus can tell it in the traditional manner. And certainly, in that manner, it could not be better told. But now let us advance a stage nearer history and see how

*Herodotus VIII. 137.

he manages a tale which is halfway between fact—for evidently something did happen—and awestruck fancy.

Dicaeus the son of Theocydes, an Athenian then in exile and held in honour among the Persians, said that at this time, when Attica was being wasted by the footmen of Xerxes and was empty of its inhabitants, it came to pass that he was with Demaratus the Lacedaemonian in the Thriasian Plain when they descried a pillar of dust, such as thirty thousand men might raise, moving from Eleusis. And as they wondered who were the cause of the dust, anon they heard the sound of voices, and it seemed to him that it was the ritual chant to Iacchus. Demaratus was ignorant of the rites that are performed at Eleusis and asked him what sound was that. And he said: 'Demaratus, it cannot be but that some sore evil will fall upon the host of the King. For, no men being left in Attica, surely these are immortal voices proceeding from Eleusis to take vengeance on behalf of the Athenians and their allies. Now if this sign descend on Peloponnesus, the King himself and his land army will be in jeopardy; but if it turn toward the ships at Salamis, the King will be in peril of losing his fleet. This is that festival which the Athenians hold yearly in honour of the Mother and the Maid, when every Athenian or other Greek that desires it receives initiation; and the sound thou hearest is the chanting of the initiates.' Demaratus answered: 'Hold thy peace and tell this to no other man; for if these thy words be carried to the King, thou wilt lose thy head and I shall not be able to save thee, I nor any other man. But keep quiet, and the gods will deal with this host.' That was his counsel.

Then the dust and the cry became a cloud, and the cloud rose high and moved to where the Greeks were stationed by Salamis. And so they knew that it was the fleet of Xerxes that was doomed.*

This is not some 'Once upon a time' story but a piece of historical evidence, however mistakenly interpreted. Accordingly there now enters into the telling (which in other respects is done in the style of the Perdiccas legend) a tendency to put the case to the reader as something which Herodotus would like

*VIII. 65.

him to believe, being disposed to believe it himself. The tale is told not quite objectively and for its own sake but as an argument in favour of a belief in signs and omens. Hence the clauses are a little more closely articulated, as happens when a man is marshalling evidence.

But now consider the following passage:

When the Ionians had come with this fleet to Ephesus they left their ships at Coresus in the land of the Ephesians and marched up from the sea in a great company, taking men of Ephesus to guide them. They marched along the banks of the river Caÿster, and then leaving this crossed the mountain Tmolus and came to Sardis and took it, no man opposing them. All of it they took except only the castle; but the castle was defended by Artaphrenes himself, having under him no small force of men. What prevented the Ionians from sacking the city after they had taken it was this. Of the houses in Sardis the greater part were framed of reeds, and those that were indeed built of bricks had their roofs thatched with reeds. One of these was set on fire by a soldier, and immediately the fire went from house to house and began to devour the whole town. And because the town was burning in this manner the Lydians and as many of the Persians as were in the city, being cut off on every side, as the fire was consuming the parts about them that were nearest, and they had no way by which they could pass out of the town, ran together into the market place and to the river Pactolus, which flows through the midst of the market place carrying down for them gold dust from Tmolus, and then joins the river Hermus, and so into the sea. Here then crowding into the market places and up to the Pactolus the Lydians and Persians were forced to fight. But the Ionians, seeing some of the enemy defending themselves and others running up to them in great numbers, became afraid and withdrew to the mountain Tmolus, and from there when night had fallen they went back to their ships.*

Here is something which may be called history, being an episode in the Persian wars. Remark how the style, while never

*V. 100, 101.

losing its original character, while still reading like a story told not written, has tightened its framework until it is now capable of supporting the new burden laid upon it. We see the traditional manner of the old story-tellers developing in the hands of this master towards a style in which a true history could be written. But it is development not change. From first to last it is the simple narrative style that we find in Herodotus, with here and there a touch of 'rhetoric' so slight as to make no real difference. But the art died with him. In what then consists his importance for the historian of literature? In two things: first, he gave to later writers the groundwork of a narrative style; secondly, he made history an art. Without him it might have remained, what it evidently was to his contemporary Hellanicus, a mere record of year-to-year occurrences without artistic design in structure or expression. Records of that nature are common in the early history of nations as soon as they have learned to read and to write. But (so far as Europe is concerned) it was only in Greece that they got beyond the chronicle stage. If history is now a branch of literature that is due to Herodotus.

When more than half a century after Herodotus it occurred to Plato to introduce into his Dialogues an occasional myth so great an artist could not but feel that the myth ought to be related in language which should have some tincture of the traditional style which had been so exquisitely used by Herodotus. For the myth was or purported to be a traditional story, and therefore by every canon of Greek art must be related in the traditional way. No doubt when the myth (as often happens in Plato) had a significance too profound for a common audience the style, without changing its fundamental character, had to suggest a meaning which did not lie on the surface, as in Herodotus it always lies; and in this way the simplicity becomes in a manner deceptive. But when the story Plato has to tell is straightforward he can tell it almost in the Herodotean style; almost but not quite, for the *audience* (and of course the dialect) is different. So there is a touch of archaism in his simplest story, such as that which I now quote. It is the story of the Ring of Gyges.

They say that he was a shepherd in the service of the king who ruled over Lydia at that time. After an earthquake and rainstorm the ground was rent in the district where he fed his flocks, and a chasm appeared. Seeing and wondering at this, he went down and beheld, among other wonders that the story tells of, a hollow bronze horse with windows in it, through which he saw when he stooped a dead man, who seemed of more than human proportions; from whom he took nothing but a gold ring which the corpse had upon its hand, and came out again. Now when the shepherds met according to their custom that they might make their monthly report to the king about their flocks Gyges came too, wearing the ring. Well, when he had sat down with the rest, he happened to turn the bezel of the ring towards himself, to the inside of his hand; whereupon he vanished from the sight of those who were sitting by him, and they began to speak of him as though he were not there. Gyges wondered at this and, again feeling the ring, turned the bezel outward; whereupon he became visible. Observing this he made trial of the ring to see if it possessed such a power, and found that when he turned the bezel inwards he became invisible, and visible when he turned it outwards. Thus taught of experience he contrived to be one of those who carried the report to the king; and came and had to do with the queen, and with her aid attacked him and slew him, and so seized the throne.*

The story could not be told in simpler language. But its simplicity has not the naïve character of the genuine folk story. That naïveté has been lost, and, so far as Greek literature is concerned, perhaps lost for ever. Now let us see how Cicero tells the story. I will translate his Latin to facilitate comparison with Plato.

After the earth had gaped as the result of heavy rains Gyges went down into the gap and (as stories tell) perceived a bronze horse, in whose sides were doors. Opening these he saw the body of a

*Resp. 359d–360b.

dead man of exceptional size and on its finger a ring, which he drew off and put on his own—I should have said that he was one of the king's shepherds—and then repaired to one of their meetings. There turning the bezel of the ring inwards he was seen by nobody, while he himself saw everything; when he turned it round to its proper place he became visible again. So making use of the advantage conferred on him by the ring he violated the queen, with her aid slew the king his master and made away with those who, he thought, stood in his way; nor did anyone see him commit these crimes. Thus profiting by the ring he soon rose to be king of Lydia.*

This is rather a résumé of the story than the story itself, and as such it is clear and succinct. But the antique charm has gone out of it. And that is what happened to the oral narrative; it kept its original quality in Herodotus but lost it afterwards. In certain directions its capabilities were brilliantly developed, but they were new directions; nor could the old be found again. When centuries after Herodotus Arrian told the story of how Nearchus sailed from the Indus to the Persian Gulf he felt that so marvellous a tale should be written in the style of Herodotus. But the result is pastiche and one is surprised that so sensible an author should have attempted it. It is a curious illustration of the force of tradition in Greek literature. Yet if the charm of a native simplicity now eluded authors it was less their fault than that of their readers, who had become too sophisticated to like or even perceive it. What they wanted was rhetoric, and rhetoric was what they got.

The character of Latin prose was largely determined by that of Greek. If it had been allowed to develop on lines of its own it might have produced its own Herodotus. But it was born too late for that; the Greek models on which it formed itself had already acquired a rhetorical structure. One may learn something here by considering a passage from the early annalist Claudius Quadrigarius. It recounts the legend of how Manlius braved and slew a gigantic Gaul.

*De Offic. III. ix. 38.

Cum interim Gallus quidam nudus praeter scutum et gladios duos torque atque armillis decoratus processit, qui et viribus et magnitudine et adulescentia simulque virtute ceteris antistabat. is maxime proelio commoto atque utrisque summo studio pugnantibus, manu significare coepit utrisque, quiescerent. pugnae facta pausa est. extemplo silentio facto cum voce maxima conclamat, si quis secum depugnare vellet uti prodiret. nemo audebat propter magnitudinem atque immanitatem facies. deinde Gallus inridere coepit atque linguam exertare. id subito perdolitum est cuidam Tito Manlio, summo genere gnato, tantum flagitium civitati adcidere, e tanto exercitu neminem prodire. is, ut dico, processit neque passus est virtutem Romanam ab Gallo turpiter spurcari. scuto pedestri et gladio Hispanico cinctus contra Gallum constitit. metu magno ea congressio in ipso ponti, utroque exercitu inspectante, facta est. ita, ut ante dixi, constiterunt: Gallus sua disciplina scuto proiecto cunctabundus; Manlius, animo magis quam arte confisus, scuto scutum percussit atque statum Galli conturbavit. dum se Gallus iterum eodem pacto constituere studet, Marlius iterum scuto scutum percutit atque de loco hominem iterum deiecit; eo pacto ei sub Gallicum gladium successit atque Hispanico pectus hausit. ubi eum evertit, caput praecidit, torquem detraxit eamque sanguinulentam sibi in collum imponit.*[1]

This is simple enough; yet it is not written in the simple style, which is a form, and not an easy form, of literary art. Quadrigarius is doing the best he can with a medium he has not yet mastered. He has a limited vocabulary, which drives him into dull repetitions. His simplicity is not that of the artist but of a man learning to write. He does not help us to understand Herodotus at all. Yet it is immensely important that Herodotus, or rather his art, should be understood. For whatever enchantment may have flown during the transmission of that art, he it was who taught the Greeks, and consequently

*Annales.

the rest of Europe, how to write prose. Where then did he find his art? For however much he may have refined it, he certainly did not invent it. It was the traditional way of telling the stories; therefore we must give some consideration to them, because it is the nature of the stories that determines the style in which they are told.

These traditional stories—myth, legend, *märchen*, folk tales, whatever may be the appropriate designation in a particular case—have certain invariable characteristics.* It will be enough to say here that they are so framed and expressed as to have the maximum of clearness, simplicity and vividness. These qualities will be observed in all the examples I have quoted and shall quote. A story which does not possess them is not likely to be heard with attention or remain in the popular memory. A story which does will not be odd or infantile or anile; it will be charged with a permanent interest, with the spirit of the ages. And this will be retained in the style in which the story is related. It will be simple but not simple-minded. That is why imitation (or translation) is so nearly impossible. A very simple style in English is almost certain to fall flat unless it is charged with irony, like the style of Swift or Voltaire, or tells a story so interesting in itself that it cannot be told too plainly. But simplicity in itself is not enough. Herodotus knows this very well, but what we find in his stories is not irony—though he has something of that too—but a spirit which modern civilizations have forgotten or pretend to have forgotten. It is the spirit which, in a somewhat less elementary form, permeates Greek tragedy, especially in its most typical representative, Sophocles. To us it appears strangely didactic, and it is important to take note of this. The traditional story is rarely told for its own sake, for its mere charm as a story. It inculcates a moral or at least a lesson. It is nearly always edifying, although it may not be, and very often is not, 'edifying' in the sense of the Christian moralist. There are indeed one or

*I have discussed them in my *Art of the Logos*, 1935.

two *fabliaux* which must be old, but not many: the typical story of the traditional kind is not, like the *fabliau*, told merely to amuse.

But is this so strange after all? Are we not apt to deceive ourselves on this point? We assume that the edifying story is no longer popular because educated readers will no longer put up with it. Yet it could be argued that no kind of story moves us more deeply, if it be told in such a way that the reader does not feel that he is being edified. When we read a traditional story we often get the impression that the narrator himself is hardly conscious of the moral his narrative conveys. It is something he heard as having been related in the days of old and he repeats it, allowing us to make of it what we please. That is an attitude which no one can resent. How could anyone resent this story in Herodotus? The Spartan king Leotychides came to Athens with a request that the Athenians should release certain hostages. When they refused he told this story.

We men of Sparta tell a tale that in the third generation before my time there was a man in Lacedaemon, Glaucus the son of Epicydes. This man we say was foremost in every kind of excellence, and in special he had a name for justice above all who dwelt in Lacedaemon in those days. But in due time there befell him this thing. A man of Miletus came to Sparta* and desired to enter into discourse with him, making this proposal. 'I am a Milesian and I have come out of a desire to profit, Glaucus, by thy uprightness. For because not only throughout Greece but also in the regions of Ionia there was much talk of thy justice, I considered with myself that Ionia is ever a perilous land, while Peloponnesus is safe and settled; and also that one never sees the same persons continuing in the possession of riches. As I pondered this and took counsel with myself, I resolved to turn the half of all my substance into money and trust it to thy charge, well knowing that it will be safe in thy keeping. Receive then, I pray thee, the money and take and keep these tallies; and whosoever shall ask it back again having the counter-tallies, to him repay it.' Thus spake the

* Lacedaemon is another name for Sparta.

stranger from Miletus, and Glaucus received what was entrusted to his keeping on these conditions. Much time went by, and the sons of the man who had entrusted the money came to Sparta and sought speech of Glaucus, and asked back the money, showing the counter-tallies. But he put them off, answering them in words like these: 'I cannot remember the matter nor does aught of what you say bring it back to my mind; yet I desire when remembrance comes to do what is just—if I had the money, to pay it back honestly; and if I did not have it at all, I will use the laws of Greece against you. Therefore I put off my final judgment in this matter until the fourth month from now.' The Milesians took these words to heart and departed as men who had been cheated of their money. But Glaucus journeyed to Delphi to consult the Oracle. And when he enquired of the Oracle whether he might make use of an oath to take the money for himself, the priestess rebuked him in these words:

'O Glaucus, son of Epicydes, for the moment indeed it is more
     profitable thus
To gain thy purpose by an oath and take the money for thyself.
Swear—seeing that Death awaits even the man that keeps his oath.
But Oath hath a son, nameless, nor are hands upon him
Nor feet; but swift he pursues until a man's whole
Race he has clutched and destroyed, and all his house.
But of the man that keeps his oath the race is ever blessed in after
     times.'

When Glaucus heard this he besought the god to pardon him for his question. But the priestess* declared that it was equal sin to tempt the god and to do the deed. So Glaucus sends for the Milesians and pays them back the money. And the reason why this tale was begun to be told you, O Athenians, shall be said. There is no descendant at all of Glaucus, nor any hearth accounted to be of Glaucus, and he has been utterly uprooted out of Sparta. Thus is it not well even to think of doing aught else with a thing entrusted except to give it back again.†

Most readers would probably agree that this is a beautiful, or at least a beautifully told, story; perhaps on reflection they

---

* Through whom the god spoke.   † I. 86.

would also agree that its beauty is largely dependent on the way in which its moral, as distinguished from its literary, beauty is made to shine through the words. But in fact nearly all these traditional stories appeal to the moral sense, by way of repulsion as much as by way of attraction. Whether it produces the one or the other makes no difference to the artist in this kind of story; he can make it beautiful in either case, like Herodotus in 'The Ring of Polycrates'.

In no long time the affairs of Polycrates prospered and were talked of throughout Ionia and Greece also, for wherever he set himself to march everything went luckily for him. A hundred fifty-oared ships he had and a thousand archers. And he plundered and despoiled all men without respect of persons: 'for', quoth he, 'I shall give more pleasure by restoring what I took than by not taking from him at all.' Many of the isles he conquered and many cities also of the mainland. Moreover, when the Lesbians came with all their forces to aid the Milesians he overcame them in a sea battle and took them alive; these were they who in their captivity digged the whole trench about the walls of Samos.

Yet did not Amasis fail to mark how Polycrates prospered, and the thing troubled him. And when his felicity became greater yet by far, he wrote upon a roll of papyrus this letter for Samos. *Amasis to Polycrates. A pleasant thing it is to hear of a friend that he is prosperous; but thy huge good fortunes are not to my liking, who know that the Holy One is jealous. Now I would that both I myself and whosoever are dear to me should have good hap in one matter and stumble in another, and live always in this alternation of fortunes, rather than be lucky in everything. For never yet have I heard it told of any man that he prospered in every matter and did not at the last come to an utterly evil end. Now therefore hearken to me and, to meet these happy strokes of fortune, bethink thee where thou shalt find that which is most precious in thy sight, and cast it away in such manner that it will not be seen in the world again. And if thereafter good and evil chances come not in due succession, get thee a remedy in the way counselled by me.* When Polycrates read this he thought that Amasis had advised him well; and he made search after that among his treasures for the loss of which he would be most sorely afflicted, and he found it. He had a seal ring that he wore, an emerald set in gold; Theodore of Samos, the son of Telecles, fashioned it. This ring then he concluded to throw away. Having embarked in a ship of fifty oars, he bade the crew with whom he had manned it to put out into the deep, and when he was a great way off the island he drew the ring from his finger and before the eyes of the whole company threw it into the waters. And when he had done this he sailed home, and entered into his house, and was very sorrowful.

But on the fifth or sixth day after a thing befell him which I shall tell. A fisherman caught a noble fish that seemed to him worthy to be given for a gift to Polycrates. So he carried it to the door and said that he wished to come into the presence of the king. When the king consented the fisher proffered him the fish, saying, 'O King, when I caught this one I did not think it right to carry him to market (though I live by the labour of my hands), but I deemed him fit for thee and thy state. To thee therefore have I brought him; here he is.' This speech pleased the king and he answered: 'Thou hast done exceeding well and I owe thee thanks twice over—once for thy words and once for thy gift; moreover we invite thee to dinner.' So the fisherman went into the house, accounting it a great honour. Then the servants cut open the fish, and lo in the belly of it the ring of Polycrates. As soon as they caught sight of it, they seized and carried it with joy to Polycrates and gave him the ring and told him how it was found. But when it was borne in upon him that the thing was of God he wrote in a roll all that he had done and what had befallen him in the consequence; and when he had written the letter he dispatched it to Egypt. But when Amasis read the letter which had come from Polycrates, he understood that it was not possible to fetch another clear of that which is fated to befall him, and that Polycrates would have no good end, since he prospered in all he did, even finding that which he had cast away. And he sent a herald to him in Samos severing their bond of friendship. For this reason he did it, that when some terrible great calamity came upon Polycrates he might not be sore at heart for him as a foreign friend.*

To be sure the terrible great calamity came. Polycrates fell into the power of an enemy and was put to death with abominable cruelties. This might have been considered (by political opponents) a just retribution for his crimes. But that is not the light in which the story views his fate; the story attributes it to a feeling on the part of the 'gods' that Polycrates was about as happy as themselves and therefore must be taught a lesson to show him that this could not be tolerated. And the method they employ—it is their favourite method—is to fill the cup of his felicity before dashing it from his lips. It is plainly impossible to justify them here to a modern reader. But Herodotus does not think of doing that. His sole concern is with the artistic problem, which he solves by using the moral (such as it is) to give dramatic unity and meaning to an otherwise inexplicable event. It is what the tragic dramatists do. The moral is there not so much because the story-teller as because the audience liked it and looked for it. We must count the desire to be instructed or edified as one of the springs of story-telling, which is in turn the source of prose. It was, however, understood that the instruction was to be conveyed delightfully. Greek art is a vehicle, not a form, of edification, and for the artist the problem lay in the creation or improvement of the vehicle. He would have accepted as true of prose also the saying of Dryden that 'Poesy only instructs as it delights'.

The simple style has naturally been found appropriate for the fable or parable, which is, or ought to be, a simple story with the moral emphasized. The fable differs from a narrative like that of Glaucus or Polycrates in this, that while they are at least professedly historical, it makes no such profession. It is not impossible, though less likely than was once believed, that the fable, and the parable too so far as it differs from the fable, had its origin far east of Hellas. But we know no earlier fables than those told among the Greeks, who came to attribute them to a more or less mythical Aesop. In their earliest, and best, form they were little stories generally told of animals but illustrating traits of human character. No collection of them survives in Greek of the classical age, but we sometimes hear about them from a classical author. Aristotle is one of these authors, and from him I now quote.

When Aesop was defending a demagogue who was being tried for his life at Samos he related a fable to the effect that once upon a time a vixen in crossing a stream got wedged into a cleft in the bank. She could not extricate herself and for long had a bad time of it, especially when a multitude of ticks fastened upon her. A hedgehog, who chanced to be strolling past, noticed her and sympathetically asked if he should rid her of the ticks. 'Not on your life!' 'Why not?' 'Because this lot are already gorged with my blood and can hardly suck another drop. But pick them off, and more will come with a fresh appetite and drink up all the rest.' *

That sounds like a good fable. But it is told in the words of Aristotle and not in its original form, which would have been in Ionic Greek, not unlike and perhaps not greatly inferior to that of Herodotus. The loss of the fables in their early form is much to be regretted, although most of them may never have been committed to writing at all. But if we cannot produce a classical Greek fable we can produce a classical Latin one. When in the early days of the Roman Republic the *plebs* left the city with the intention of founding a community free from what they regarded as the tyranny of the governing class, Menenius Agrippa was sent to reason with them. And this is how he did it.

The story goes that when he was admitted into the camp he addressed them in the rude and artless style of our fathers. He was content to tell them a story.—Once upon a time there was no agreement, as there is now, between the parts of a man's body, but each member had a separate power of thinking and speaking. A feeling of resentment against the belly arose among the other parts on the ground that, while everything was supplied to it by their labour and service, it did nothing but rest in the middle and enjoy the titbits with which it was supplied. So they took counsel together and

*Rhet. II. 20.

settled that the hands were not to convey food to the mouth, nor was the mouth to admit it if proffered, nor were the teeth to deal with what might be put between them. The result of this strike was that, wishing to starve the belly into submission, the members themselves and the whole body were reduced to a state of extreme emaciation. This convinced them that the belly too had no sinecure and that it furnished as well as received nourishment by supplying to every part of the frame this blood of ours that gives us life and energy after it has been concocted by the digestion of our food and distributed to the veins.

By this allegory, bringing out the resemblance of that mutiny of the bodily members to the revolt of the commons against the Senate, Menenius succeeded in making them change their minds.*

Nothing could show more clearly than this passage from Livy how essential it is for the fable that it should be told in the simple style. Here is one of the masters of Latin prose using a style which is not simple and failing to get the right effect. The Roman, like the English, Augustan Age tended to look on the prose of earlier centuries as incompetent—*prisco illo dicendi et horrido modo*, 'that antiquated and unpolished way of speaking' —and when they had to repeat an old story recast it in complex periods. Yet one can see how the fable of the Belly and the Members would have looked when simply told. Shakespeare, who knew it not from Livy but from North's translation of Plutarch, saw that, and his version, though written in his later manner, is nevertheless simpler and so more appropriate than Livy's.

> There was a time when all the body's members
> Rebell'd against the belly, thus accused it:
> That only like a gulf it did remain
> I' the midst o' the body, idle and unactive,
> Still cupboarding the viand, never bearing
> Like labour with the rest, where the other instruments
> Did see and hear, devise, instruct, walk, feel,

*Livy II. xxxii. 8–12.

And, mutually participate, did minister
Unto the appetite and affection common
Of the whole body. The belly answer'd . . .
'True is it, my incorporate friends,' quoth he,
'That I receive the general food at first,
Which you do live upon; and fit it is,
Because I am the store-house and the shop
Of the whole body: but, if you do remember,
I send it through the rivers of your blood,
Even to the court, the heart, to the seat o' the brain;
And, through the cranks and offices of man,
The strongest nerves and small inferior veins
From me receive that natural competency
Whereby they live . . .*

Fables have always been popular (except perhaps today) in both senses of the word, especially in the Middle Ages, when many collections were made, in verse as well as in prose, though it would seem that prose is the native medium of the fable—the simple colloquial prose of which we have been speaking. Professional authors have usually let the prose fable alone or have not been very successful when they tried it. A memorable fable is as hard to write as a good ballad and for the same reason. When it becomes too elaborate or ingenious it ceases to charm. It must seem to be born not made. The fables of Aesop give us that impression and so they are still the best. And though they may no longer influence our writers, they have influenced them in the past. For the student of mediaeval and Tudor-Elizabethan literature a knowledge of 'Aesop' is indispensable.

It is different with the prose allegory, which almost requires a professional author to write it and, probably for that reason, has been a somewhat favourite form with such authors. (Bunyan, if not exactly a professional author, was a practised writer.) As a kind of elaborated parable it may be touched on

*Coriolanus I. 1.

here in connexion with the fable, its elder sister. It has a longer history than is generally supposed. Traces of it have been detected in Hesiod and even in Homer; and if we rule these out from this chapter as being poets, we can pursue the history of allegory in prose at least as far back as Prodicus, who was a contemporary of Socrates. It was Prodicus who wrote a famous allegory *The Choice of Hercules*. The original has not survived, but we have a paraphrase or summary of it by Xenophon in what he modestly describes as a less impressive style. It is too long and (to be plain) too dull to be reproduced here. But the gist of it may be told. When Heracles reached the age of discretion he came to what we have learned from this story to call 'the parting of the ways'. One of these ways was the path of Virtue, the other was the path of Vice. As he sat wondering which to choose, two female figures approached, one looking modest in white, the other bedizened, bold-eyed and over-ripe. The young man listens to their arguments and prefers those of the lady in white, who is Virtue, to those of the more wanton dame, who—would you ever have guessed it? —is Vice. This cannot but strike us as excessively naïve, but the contemporaries of Prodicus admired it very much, and not only his contemporaries, for we find it imitated six hundred years later in Lucian's *Dream*. We can even say that it continued to be admired till at least the end of the eighteenth century, both Johnson and Goldsmith priding themselves on their skill in composing similar allegories. The student of literature has to take into consideration a fact so remarkable. Whatever may be the explanation, we seem to have lost the taste for allegory, unless it is a good deal subtler than *The Choice of Hercules* or even the *Vision of Mirza*. Among the works of Lucian there is a piece on Calumny, which describes an imaginary picture by the great painter Apelles—an allegorical picture in which Calumny was represented as overcome by Truth. This piece, at any rate after it had been translated into Latin, had a great popularity and influenced painting as well as literature, as we

see from Botticelli's picture.* I will not translate Lucian's
description but content myself with reporting that it is composed in a style which intends simplicity, that being the
appropriate style for the allegorical story. It will be enough to
note for the moment that allegory played a large and increasingly important part in ancient literature, where it tends to
become more complex in itself and to be expressed in less
simple language. When that happens, as we shall find it
happening, it approximates to the literature of philosophy, and
so passes beyond the strict limits of this chapter.

* We find the theme repeated in Mantegna, Raphael and, if that matters, in
Reynolds' portrait of Beattie.

B

CHAPTER TWO

THE MATURE NARRATIVE STYLE

A STYLE like that of Herodotus, however adequate for its own purposes, has of course its limitations. It is good for telling a story but not for arguing a case or stating a problem. Its simple structure cannot be bent to follow the involutions of a train of thought which calls for the balancing of various considerations. Thus it happened that in the incredibly rapid flowering of the Greek spirit in the fifth century before Christ the *Histories* of Herodotus, though heard with delight, was no sooner given to the world than it was out of date. This, if we may judge from some symptoms of distress felt by him at the scepticism of the age, was not unobserved by the author himself. But the real enemy was not scepticism, it was simply the law of growth. The complexity of affairs had become too great for a history of them to be written in the simple terms of Herodotean thought, which found its natural expression in the Herodotean style. There was a new spirit which required a new organ of expression. This it received, almost in the lifetime of Herodotus himself, in the work of Thucydides. The contrast between them is felt by every reader; on a first impression it seems almost absolute. But when we look deeper we find that this impression is not wholly justified; we have let the more striking and characteristic parts of Thucydides' book outweigh the more traditional qualities of the rest. The truth is that Thucydides has two styles: that of the speeches and more reflective passages, and that of the purely narrative sections of his History. That the speeches should be touched by the new rhetoric was to be expected. But for narrations the traditional manner was so firmly entrenched that it could still repel intruders. There is such an idiosyncrasy in everything that

Thucydides writes that we are carried from one style to the other without too painful a consciousness of the gulf between them. But the gulf is there. Of that however this is not the place to speak; nor of his rhetorical style; what concerns us at the present is his narrative. In comparison with that of his predecessor it is laconic and austere, but expresses a more intense imagination. Herodotus is in the highest degree picturesque; no other historian has such attractive charm. Thucydides has no charm, but when he describes an action it happens before your eyes. And while the intellectual power of Thucydides, his stern rejection of the mythical, his detachment, his controlled and sometimes unexpressed sympathies and indignation make him seem very different from the other, yet it is certain that his ordinary narrative manner, in which after all two-thirds of his book is written, is developed from the same oral style as that of Herodotus—developed a stage farther in the direction of complexity and logical refinement, but one stage only. It is not easy to show this by a brief quotation, but I may give here, in as faithful a rendering as I can, his account of a sortie made by the besieged Plataeans.

When everything was ready they watched for a night stormy with wind and rain, and at the same time moonless. Then they sallied forth led by the men who had actually suggested the enterprise. The first stage—crossing the trench which contained the city—successfully accomplished, they got up to the enemy's wall unobserved by the sentinels, who were prevented by the darkness from seeing a yard in front of them. The noise of their approach was drowned by the howling of the wind, while as they advanced each man kept clear of the next in case the clatter of arms clashing together should give the alarm. Their equipment was the lightest possible. To keep them from slipping in the mud they had only the left foot shod.

They began their attack on the battlements—which they knew to be undefended—in the space between towers. First came the party that was carrying the scaling-ladders, and these they put in position.

Then twelve men armed only with a short sword and a breastplate proceeded to climb the ladder, led by Ammeas the son of Coroebus, and he was the first to reach the top. The rest followed and then separated, six men to each of the towers, which they began to scale. Next came more light-armed infantrymen with spears but without their shields which, to make it easier for them to press on, were carried for them by others who followed, the plan being that these were to give them the shields when it came to fighting. Most of them had already got up when they were detected by the sentinels on the towers. One of the Plataeans, trying to get a grip, had dislodged a tile from the battlements, and the clatter of its fall immediately raised the alarm. The besiegers made a dash in the direction of their wall, although the blackness of the stormy night kept them from discovering where the point of danger was; at the same time the Plataeans who had been left behind in the town made a sortie and attacked the wall at a point in the opposite direction to that in which their comrades were getting over it, so as to create a diversion. This had the effect of making the enemy halt in confusion, not a man of them venturing to go to the support of his comrades because they could not understand what was happening. Yet three hundred of them, whose instructions were to give support wherever wanted, did advance beyond the wall in the direction of the sound. Also beacons were raised as a signal to Thebes. But the Plataeans in the city countered by raising on their walls a great many bale-fires, which had been got ready for the purpose of confusing the signals for the enemy, so that he would think the fact to be other than it was and so not come up in support until the men of Plataea who were making their way out should have made good their escape and caught hold of safety. And in the meantime these Plataeans—when the first of them had got up and secured the two towers after killing the guards—posted themselves in the passages connecting the walls and kept watch that nobody should come along to help. They then applied ladders from the wall to the towers and sent a number of men up the ladders. These kept off all succours by hurling missiles upon them from their loftier station, aided in this by those below. During the time so gained the main body, planting numerous ladders and at the same time wrenching away the battlements, kept crossing the space between the towers. As each man got across he took his stand on the edge of the trench, and from that position they shot arrows and threw spears against anyone who tried to come up along the walls and stop the crossing. Last of all, after everyone had got across, the men in the towers scrambled down and advanced to the trench.

At this point they were attacked by the three hundred.

These were carrying torches. So the Plataeans, standing in the dark at the edge of the trench, could see them and thanks to the torches were able to discharge spears and arrows into the exposed parts of their bodies, while they themselves were comparatively invisible. The result was that even the last of the Plataeans got across the trench before they could be stopped, although their crossing was attended by difficulty and involved violent exertions. For there was no more than a skin of ice, not strong enough to bear but half melting, as happens when the wind is in the east, while the snow, borne all that night upon the wings of such a wind, had left a great deal of water in the trench, which made it hard for them to get over it. It should be added however that the violence of the storm favoured their escape.*

This narrative Thucydides put together from the accounts of eyewitnesses who had escaped to Athens and were no doubt interviewed by him there. Such accounts are always confused, partial and contradictory, as Thucydides elsewhere complains. Yet what a story he has made of it, how clear and intelligible, and told with what vividness of imagination! The style is simple, but not with the naïve Herodotean simplicity. In reading Herodotus one forgets Herodotus, but the reader of Thucydides never becomes so unconscious of the narrator. In him the traditional style has become, so to speak, aware of itself and its own hidden potentialities. Thucydides accepts the tradition that the proper method of narration is that of the storyteller, but in his hands it loses its impersonality and becomes what I am disposed to call 'mature'. It is still the basis and even the model for a good narrative style in history.

He did not live to complete his work, which was carried on

* Hist. III. 22, 23.

by Xenophon in his *Hellenica* or 'History of Greece'. The *Hellenica* cannot be compared in any of the higher qualities of thought or style with that of which it was the sequel. But it had a great success, which was not undeserved. The style is lucid, natural and unexacting; and it is, as that of Thucydides is not, homogeneous. Xenophon was therefore an easier model for the imitation of later writers, and that makes him important as an influence. While he can hardly now be restored to the position he held so long, we must do him justice. He had the ultimate, the inexplicable gift of the born narrator. Since it is so short and so good an example of his skill, I need not be deterred from quoting one of the most familiar passages of ancient prose. It is in the *Anabasis,* the main theme of which is the retreat of the Ten Thousand to safety through a hostile land.

On the fifth day they reached the mountain named Theches. When the van got to the summit and caught sight of the sea, up went a mighty shout. Xenophon and the rearguard heard it and thought that the van was being attacked by a fresh body of the enemy. . . . But when the shouting got louder and nearer, and each body of men as it advanced started to run towards the shouting, which never stopped but grew louder and louder as more joined in, Xenophon came to the conclusion that something serious was on foot. So he mounted his charger and rode to the front, taking with him Lycius and the cavalry. Presently they could make out that the soldiers were shouting *The Sea, The Sea,* and passing the words along. Thereupon the rear also came running up in a body, the very baggage animals and cavalry horses galloping along with them. When they had all got to the top they flung their arms about each other, not excepting their corps- and company-commanders, and cried. Then at some-body's suggestion all at once the men began carrying stones and made a big cairn.*

Thucydides never expected, probably did not even wish, that his book should be widely read; it was written for men who were not completely immersed in the present but could

*Anab. IV. 7.

look before and after. Xenophon wrote for the general reader; he popularized history. He may not have done this of set purpose, but that was the effect of his easy and picturesque manner. He is the father of all those who have made history readable by the ordinary man. It is a distinction which ought not to be undervalued. It would be impossible to enumerate all the good, though perhaps never great, books which have carried on the tradition founded by Xenophon. The tradition is clear enough and can be traced deep into modern literature. Among the Greeks themselves it tended to outlast in popular estimation the work of more important historians; as late as the beginning of the second century we find Arrian taking Xenophon and not Thucydides or Polybius as his model in writing of the wars of Alexander. The great Greek historians called for more intense study than the average reader, more particularly the average reader of Latin, was prepared to give them, though he was prepared to read the kind of anecdotal history which we find in writers like Suetonius and Curtius Rufus, and which is a further simplification of Xenophon's easy manner of writing history. These Latin authors continued to be read all through the Middle Ages. As for Xenophon himself he was taken up again at the Renaissance, though less as a historian than as the author of the *Cyropaedia*. So far as style goes however there is no real difference, for we cannot say that the style of the *Hellenica* is distinguishable from that of the *Cyropaedia*, which in fact is fictitious history. All this contributed to form a taste which in modern times has found satisfaction in what has been called 'arm-chair' history. Goldsmith was excellent at it, though his Histories of Greece and Rome are not only outmoded but unread. Scott's *Tales of a Grandfather* still survives or ought to survive, for of its kind it is a masterpiece. It could be argued that 'school histories' are normally of the Xenophontine sort, and if this is true, it is evidence that Xenophon still, however remotely, impresses himself on the mind of the general reader.

It may be thought that, among the Romans, Caesar writes in the style discussed in this chapter. Here is the passage in which he describes the last fight of Curio, his lieutenant in Africa.

But the enemy's horse began to work round both flanks of our line and to ride down our men in the rear. When any of our companies broke formation and charged, the Numidian cavalry eluded attack, thanks to their speed, and escaped without loss; later, when the companies were falling back they rode round them and cut them off from the line. Thus it became evident that our men could neither safely keep their positions and ranks nor charge without suffering casualties. The forces of the enemy were steadily augmented by supports sent up by the king, while our men were becoming exhausted; at the same time the wounded could neither leave their rank nor be carried to a place of safety in the rear, because the whole line was hemmed in by the enemy's cavalry. Despairing of life, the wounded did as human beings do when they are at the last gasp—bemoaned their death or commended their parents to the kindness of any who might have the good fortune to escape with their lives out of that peril. It was a scene of anguish and of terror.

When it became obvious to Curio that in the alarm which had spread to all ranks no one listened to his words of encouragement or appeal, he came to the conclusion that their one chance of safety in their plight was to seize some nearby heights in a body, and he gave the order to retire upon them. But this move was anticipated by Saburra, who sent a mounted force to occupy these hills also. Thereupon our men gave themselves up for lost; some were cut down by the horsemen as they fled, others fell on their faces without a wound. Our cavalry commander Domitius came to Curio with a few mounted men as a bodyguard and urged him to save himself by flight, promising him that he would not leave him. But Curio said that he would never come into Caesar's presence again after losing the army which had been committed to his charge, and so fought on until he was killed. Only a handful of our men—those with horses—got safely out of the battle. On the other hand the cavalry detachment which, as I explained before, had stayed in the rear of the marching column to rest their horses, observing the rout of the whole in the distance, returned to the camp without loss. The infantry was annihilated.*

This is about as clear an account as could be given of so confused a business, and the restrained sympathy of the writer adds an almost Thucydidean quality. But the imaginative intensity of Thucydides will not be found in Caesar, nor has he much of that feeling for the magic of words which is the ultimate proof of literary genius. He expressed the opinion that the writer or speaker should avoid 'the unusual word' as a pilot avoids a rock. It is a good general rule, but to make it so important as Caesar appears to have done betrays the limitations of Caesar's art. Yet his clear, concise, undecorated style has its own virtue. Its simplicity is of course quite different from that of Herodotus and we must not think of him as reverting to that manner. It is the simplicity of the great executive putting his meaning into the fewest and plainest words at his disposal, yet with full consciousness of the difference between good and bad writing. It is therefore suited to the composition of reports and dispatches—the *Gallic War* and the *Civil War* are little more than front-line reports with a connecting link of explanatory, not always quite ingenuous, narrative—and has in this way become a model for the authors of military memoirs and the like in all the modern languages. Yet the style of Caesar has never been very successfully imitated in English prose. The reason may be that, while it seems to be severely impersonal—everyone knows that Caesar speaks of himself in the third person—it is not truly so. It is the expression of a unique personality. To write like Caesar one must be like Caesar.

*Bell. Civ. II. 41, 42.

CHAPTER THREE

RHETORICAL NARRATIVE

XENOPHON felt the influence of rhetoric, which by his time had acquired a formal grace and a facility never attained or perhaps desired by Thucydides. Xenophon's writings indeed are so full of speeches that it is evident he considered himself to possess a natural gift of oratory. If we were to characterize this we should have to say that he belonged to the school of Lysias, concerning whom it will be necessary to say something when we come to treat of oratory. That of Thucydides has an almost unequalled power and impressiveness but does not belong to any school and therefore does not fall within the province of one who is writing on the history of literary influences. For such a writer the important name is Isocrates. He was by no means the inventor but he was the chief master and propagandist of the rhetoric which was destined to invade almost every branch of ancient prose. In the writings of Isocrates every sentence is a 'period', perfectly formed to eye and ear. He may be called the founder of 'ornate' prose, although we must not let this description mislead us, for the ornateness of a classical writer is seen in the elaborate structure of his sentences rather than in a profusion of coloured imagery. He himself, though content to be regarded as an orator, was in fact a writer. He believed that the style he had perfected was the appropriate medium not only for oratory but for philosophy and history. The philosophers did not accept this view, but the historians did. There arose among them a very successful school who applied to their subject all the devices of the Isocratean rhetoric. The Greek evidence is mostly lost; but we happen to possess in Livy a belated follower of the Isocratean school of historians. It will then be no anachronism if the new kind of narrative is illustrated by a passage from the Latin author. I select that in which he describes the duel between Manlius and the Gaul already described by Claudius Quadrigarius, for Livy's account is obviously based on that of Quadrigarius, so that we can actually watch the later craftsman as he remodels the work of the earlier.

Dictator cum tumultus Gallici causa iustitium edixisset, omnes iuniores sacramento adegit ingentique exercitu ab urbe profectus in citeriore ripa Anienis castra posuit. pons in medio erat neutris eum rumpentibus, ne timoris indicium esset. proelia de occupando ponte crebra erant nec, qui poterentur, incertis viribus satis discerni poterat. tum eximia corporis magnitudine in vacuum pontem Gallus processit et, quantum maxima voce potuit, 'Quem nunc' inquit 'Roma virum fortissimum habet, procedat agedum ad pugnam, ut noster duorum eventus ostendat utra gens bello sit melior'. diu inter primores iuvenum Romanorum silentium fuit cum et abnuere certamen vererentur, et praecipuam sortem periculi petere nollent. tum T. Manlius L. filius, qui patrem a vexatione tribunicia vindicaverat, ex statione ad dictatorem pergit. 'Iniussu tuo,' inquit 'imperator, extra ordinem numquam pugnaverim, non si certam victoriam videam: si tu permittis, volo ego illi beluae ostendere, quando adeo ferox praesultat hostium signis, me ex ea familia ortum quae Gallorum agmen ex rupe Tarpeia deiecit'. tum dictator 'Macte virtute' inquit 'ac pietate in patrem patriamque, T. Manli, esto. perge et nomen Romanum invictum iuvantibus diis praesta'. armant inde iuvenem aequales: pedestre scutum capit, Hispano cingitur gladio ad propiorem habili pugnam; armatum adornatumque adversus Gallum stolide laetum et—quoniam id quoque memoria dignum antiquis visum est—linguam etiam ab inrisu exserentem producunt. recipiunt inde se ad stationem et duo in medio armati spectaculi magis more quam lege belli destituuntur, nequaquam visu ac specie aestimantibus pares. corpus alteri magnitudine eximium, versicolori veste pictisque et auro caelatis refulgens armis; media in altero militaris statura modicaque in armis habilibus magis quam decoris species. non cantus, non exultatio armorumque agitatio vana, sed pectus animorum iraeque tacitae plenum omnem ferociam in discrimen ipsum certaminis distulerat. ubi constitere inter duas acies tot circa mortalium animis spe metuque pendentibus Gallus velut moles superne imminens proiecto laeva scuto in advenientis arma hostis vanum caesim cum ingenti sonitu ensem deiecit: Romanus mucrone subrecto, cum scuto scutum imum perculisset totoque corpore interior periculo vulneris factus insinuasset se inter corpus armaque, uno alteroque subinde ictu ventrem atque inguina hausit et in spatium ingens ruentem porrexit hostem. iacentis inde corpus ab omni alia vexatione intactum uno torque spoliavit, quem respersum cruore collo circumdedit suo. defixerat pavor cum admiratione Gallos: Romani alacres ab statione obviam militi suo progressi gratulantes laudantesque ad dictatorem perducunt. inter carminum prope modum incondita quaedam militariter ioculantes Torquati cognomen auditum; celebratum deinde posteris etiam familiaeque honori fuit. dictator coronam auream addidit donum mirisque pro contione eam pugnam laudibus tulit.*2

Turn back to the account of Quadrigarius. You will see how greatly it has been elaborated by Livy. But while he has made it more picturesque, it can hardly be said that he has made it clearer. Clearness is not so important to Livy as effectiveness. So he labours to make as striking as possible the contrast between the huge and noisy Celt with his tartan dress, his target and claymore, and the soberly clad, silent, grimly efficient Roman. The working out of the contrast involves the use of balanced clauses and the careful arrangement of words, which Livy is fond of interlacing in a pattern. It is so important to understand this art that we may illustrate it by another passage.

*VII. 9,10.

The siege went on as before, food was both scarce and excessively dear, and Porsinna was confident that he would reduce the place by merely sitting still, when Gaius Mucius, a young man of good family, enraged to think that the Roman people had never, when it was enslaved under the kings, been besieged by any foe or beset by any hostilities; while now that it was free it was being blockaded by those very Etruscans whose armies it often routed—considering that what was needed to avenge the outrage was some great and daring action, resolved at first to make his way into the camp of the enemy upon his own responsibility, but then becoming apprehensive lest, if he should go without permission from the consuls and without anyone knowing his purpose, he might perhaps be arrested by the Roman sentries and dragged back as a deserter (the darkened fortunes of the city at that moment lending plausibility to the charge) presented himself before the senate. 'It is my desire, senators', he began, 'to cross the Tiber and, if I can, penetrate into the camp of the enemy, not seeking booty nor to take reprisals for the ravages they have inflicted; a deed of nobler note it is in my mind to do, if the gods assist me.' The senators give their assent. Hiding a sword under his dress, he sets forth. When he reached the place where the throng was greatest near the royal judgment-seat, he went no farther. There while, as it chanced, the soldiers were being given their pay, and a clerk, sitting beside the king and almost as splendidly attired, was taking an active part in the proceedings as the soldiers kept going up to him—fearing to ask which of the two was Porsinna, lest by his not knowing the king he should betray his identity—he followed the lead which chance had given to his enterprise and cut down the clerk instead of the king. As he stalked off along the lane which he had made for himself by his bloody sword through the startled crowd there was a rush in the direction of the shouting and he was seized and hauled back by the king's attendants. Then, more dreadful than dreading amid such threats of fortune, 'I am', said he, 'a Roman citizen; they call me Gaius Mucius. I intended to kill the enemy of my country, and I am just as ready to be killed as to kill; doing and suffering bravely is the way of the Romans. Nor am I alone in bearing this enmity towards you; behind me is a long line of candidates for the same distinction. Therefore, if it please you, prepare yourself to meet this danger of struggling for your life hour after hour, of having an armed foe in the vestibule of your palace. Such is the war that we, the young men of Rome, declare against you; have no fear of any battle line, of any engagement of armies; for you it will always be one against one.' When the king, at once inflamed by anger and terrified by the danger in which he stood, commanded burning braziers to be set about him, threatening him with these if he did not instantly divulge the meaning of the dark things he was uttering of designs against him, 'There now', said Mucius, 'that you may see how cheap a price they set upon their bodies who have glory before their eyes—' and thrust his right hand into a brazier that had been kindled for a sacrifice. While he let it burn as if he had lost all feeling, the king sprang from his seat thunderstruck by the marvel, and ordered the young man to be removed from the altar. 'Go your ways', said he, 'you who have dared to be a worse enemy to yourself than to me. I should praise you for your courage, if it was put to the account of my country. As it is, I let you go, out of danger of the laws of war, unhurt and unharmed.' Then said Mucius, as if he were rewarding a meritorious action, 'Since you respect merit, accept at my hands, what you could not extort from me by force, this information. There are three hundred of us, leaders of the Roman youth, who have jointly sworn an oath to attack you in this way. The lot fell on me first; the others will arrive each in his turn, beginning with the first on whom the lot next falls, as long as fortune provides us with a chance of attacking you'.*

Here is a story related not in the direct simple fashion of the old Story Tellers—for even the short sentences in Livy's narrative are introduced, like the short sentences in Burke, for a rhetorical reason, namely to relieve the monotony (felt for example in Isocrates or Doctor Johnson) of the unbroken roll of successive periods—but in a style which is more appropriate, we should now think, to oratory than to narration. At least nobody repeating such an anecdote as this of Mucius Scaevola merely for its interest as a story would involve it in these complicated clauses—look at that first sentence coiling and uncoiling itself like a serpent! Livy's anecdote is worked up as an orator might work it up with a view to arousing an audience. It is done with admirable skill, but Livy is fostering—he did not introduce—a dangerous element in the writing of history. Yet if he did not seek the truth diligently enough he had no intention of distorting it. And he remains a master of prose style, elaborate and yet sufficiently clear, with a fine pictorial quality. As this can hardly be displayed in a legendary anecdote, I add a passage with a better claim to be regarded as based on fact.

Bucar, an officer of the king's bodyguard, a man of a bold and enterprising spirit, was chosen for that duty. He had four thousand footsoldiers and two thousand mounted men assigned to him. He was led to expect golden rewards if he succeeded in bringing back the head of Masinissa or—what would give unbounded delight—in making him prisoner. Masinissa's men were roving about and taking no precautions when they were suddenly attacked by Bucar, who cut off from their armed protectors an immense number of men and cattle, and drove Masinissa himself, accompanied by a few horsemen, to the summit of a mountain range. Then, regarding the war as practically over, he not merely sent the booty of men and cattle, which he had taken, to the king but also sent back the bulk of his forces as unnecessarily large for the task of bringing hostilities to an end. Taking no more than five hundred infantrymen and two hundred horsemen he pressed the pursuit of Masinissa, who had come down from the heights, and succeeded in shutting him up in a narrow valley of which he blocked the exits. There the Maesulians*￼ were mown down. Masinissa however escaped with no more than fifty horsemen, who followed winding tracks in the mountains which were unknown to their pursuers. Still Bucar hung at his heels and, having come up with him in open country near the town of Clupea, reduced him to such straits that Masinissa's followers were wiped out with the exception of four riders and the wounded Masinissa himself, who in the confusion managed to give his enemy the slip. The fugitives were plainly seen; a whole wing of cavalry,

* Masinissa's tribe.

spread out upon a broad plain (some making a detour to get in front of their quarry) were in pursuit of five enemies. These plunged into a great river, sending in their horses without hesitation, since worse was at their heels, and there they were caught by the current and swept down in a diagonal direction. Two were drowned before the eyes of their foes in the fierce rush of the water, in which it was believed that Masinissa himself had perished. However with the two surviving horsemen he contrived to crawl out into the brushwood which clothed the opposite bank. That proved the end of Bucar's pursuit, for he did not venture into the river, besides which he had convinced himself that he no longer had an enemy to pursue. So he returned to the king, falsely claiming to have caused the death of Masinissa, while messengers were despatched to announce the glorious news at Carthage; and all Africa was filled with the report of Masinissa's end. It excited very different emotions.

For several days, during which he treated his wound with simples, Masinissa lived in a secret cavern upon what his two horsemen could steal. As soon as the new skin closed over his scar and he thought he could stand the jolting, he had the daring to set about the reconquest of his kingdom. On the road he collected not more than forty horsemen and entered the Maesulian country, now openly proclaiming who he was. His old popularity and the unlooked-for joy of seeing safe and sound the man whom they had believed to be dead created such a stir that within a day or two six thousand footmen under arms and four thousand horsemen joined him, and he was now not only master of his paternal domains but began to plunder the tribes which had an alliance with the Carthaginians and the territory of those Maesulians over whom Syphax reigned.*

This stately, elaborate way of telling a story can be very effective and is not ineffective here. Livy uses a larger canvas than Herodotus or Xenophon, works out a more intricate design and employs a wider range of colours. He may be called the founder—so far as our knowledge goes—of the *picturesque* style in history. The structure of the Latin language is so different from that of English that it is unprofitable to look

*XXIX. 32.

in our own literature for direct imitation of Livy. But it is certain that his narrative manner made a deep impression on our first modern historians, Hume and Robertson, especially Robertson, from whom I quote the following passage about Columbus.

It was about the middle of April that Columbus arrived at Barcelona, where every preparation had been made to give him a solemn and magnificent reception. The beauty and serenity of the weather in that genial season and favoured climate contributed to give splendour to this memorable ceremony. As he drew near the place, many of the more youthful courtiers and hidalgos of gallant bearing came forth to meet and welcome him. His entrance into this noble city has been compared to one of those triumphs which the Romans were accustomed to decree to conquerors. First were paraded the Indians painted according to their savage fashion, and decorated with tropical feathers, and with their national ornaments of gold; after them were borne various kinds of live parrots, together with stuffed birds and animals of unknown species, and rare plants, supposed to be of precious qualities: while great care was taken to make a conspicuous display of Indian coronets, bracelets, and other decorations of gold, which might give an idea of the wealth of the newly discovered regions. After these followed Columbus on horseback, surrounded by a brilliant cavalcade of Spanish chivalry. The streets were almost impassable from the countless multitude: the windows and balconies were crowded with the fair; the very roofs were covered with spectators. It seemed as if the public eye could not be sated with gazing on these trophies of an unknown world, or on the remarkable man by whom it had been discovered.*

That is picturesque history in the Livian manner made possible by the new (and very Latin) prose which Johnson had taught to his successors. The manner seems out of fashion with professional historians, but it was not so in the eighteenth and nineteenth centuries. Hume is sometimes picturesque, Gibbon

History of America.

often. Carlyle, professing to despise the picturesque, has the eye of a hawk for it in his own writing, while no one has ever denied picturesqueness to the pages of Macaulay or Froude or Green. We cannot suppose that any one of these historians set himself deliberately to imitate Livy. Nor can it be maintained that Livy alone among the ancients is pictorial in his writing; some of them have a more vivid touch than himself. But in their case such touches are occasional; Livy is pictorial or nothing. This stamps his literary character and entitles us to regard him as the founder, or at least the principal exponent, of this tradition.

It has been necessary to transgress chronological order a little so as to illustrate at once from its most typical master the rhetorical way of composing history. We may now go back to Sallust who, a generation before Livy, composed it in a manner of his own. He helped to make history as well as write it, but here we have nothing to do with his actions or even with his political views or prejudices; all we have to consider is his way of writing. It was at once more old-fashioned and more 'modern' than Livy's—affecting the antique and at the same time introducing novel turns of expression. His great, not his only, model is Thucydides. This choice, he felt, entailed the use of a style opposed at almost every point to that of his enemy Cicero, which was the admiration of his contemporaries. Instead of the Ciceronian periods he practises an abrupt, concise, gnomic manner of writing. The style is just as much a work of art as that of Cicero or Livy; it is just another kind of rhetoric and just as carefully contrived. With all its defects, and they are serious, it has striking qualities. Above all the writer had the seeing eye, more than Cicero, more than Livy, more than any other Latin historian until we come to Tacitus. Look at what he makes of the conspirator Catiline.

In a city so large and so corrupt it was not difficult for Catiline to form as it were a body of supporters for himself from all the villainous and evil characters. Whatever profligate, whatever adulterer, whatever gamester had wasted his patrimony in gambling and gluttony, whoever had contracted heavy debts to pay for his sin or shame, also all murderers and enemies of religion, all who had been already convicted in courts of law or were in fear of judgement for their crimes, those moreover whose tongue maintained them by perjury or hand by shedding the blood of their fellow citizens, finally all who were goaded by sin and destitution and a sense of guilt, were the close friends of Catiline. Even an innocent man, if he fell into friendly relations with him, was by daily association and allurements quickly made in degree and kind like the rest. Catiline made a point of ingratiating himself with the young, whose yet soft and pliable minds were easily ensnared. He studied the particular bent of each youthful passion, supplying one with a mistress, buying dogs and horses for another, sparing neither expense nor his own modesty provided he could make them his devotees.

To begin my story: even as a lad Catiline had committed fearful offences against chastity, with the daughter of a noble house, with a priestess of Vesta; not to mention other similar breaches of law, human and divine. At last he was seized by a passion for Aurelia Orestilla, whose beauty was the only thing about her praised by decent men; and because she hesitated to marry him from fear of her stepson, who was no longer a boy, he murdered the son—so it is firmly believed—and by a criminal marriage made a childless home. It was this action which in my opinion was the chief motive for hurrying on the plot. For that debauched spirit in its hatred of God and man could find no rest either waking or asleep; such were the ravages of conscious guilt in his hunted soul. Therefore was his face of a deathly white, his eyes bloodshot, his gait now hurried, now slow; to be sure insanity could be read in every lineament.*

That image of Catiline has stalked through the imaginations of men ever since. Nobody could deny the vividness of the writing; applied to a subject steeped in horror like that strange conspiracy, it is no wonder that readers were powerfully affected by it. If Livy is the founder of the *picturesque*, Sallust

Catilina 14, 15.

is the founder of the *sensational*, school of historians, where 'sensational' is used in no derogatory sense. It is not unnatural for an artist to dwell on the most striking, which are often the most harrowing, parts of his subject, and if he does it with sufficient art he deserves all the credit he can get. Of the classical historians it was Sallust who was the favourite throughout the Middle Ages and perhaps the Renaissance as well. He was translated over and over again, whereas Livy had to wait till 1600 for a complete English translation. The influence of Sallust—that is to say of the *Catilina*, for his *War with Jugurtha* was not found so interesting—on Tudor and Elizabethan writers is unmistakable. More's *Richard the Third*, for example, is distinctly Sallustian, and Richard a very Sallustian villain. The fact is that the *Catilina* was the classical model for the historical treatment of a villain, and More knew it as such.

Although we must call Sallust a historian, his surviving works happen to be historical brochures rather than full-dress histories. This also has set a precedent. To select a sensational episode and write it up in a highly coloured style with a dash of psycho-analysis—consider that analysis of the mind of Catiline—while at the same time maintaining an attitude of scientific detachment, is not so modern a technique as some may think.

But the greatest of the Roman historians is Tacitus, whose influence has been more lasting and pervasive than that of Sallust or Livy. He is actually a better historian, but he is also a greater writer. He is a better historian because he took more trouble to ascertain the facts, and a greater writer because he presents them with more power and persuasiveness. He may be called the founder of the *tragic* school of history. There was nothing new in the conception of history as a record of the human tragedy; even Herodotus has that conception. But in him it is not much more than the instinctive feeling that happiness cannot last and that great men and great houses are apt to be attended by what looks like an evil genius. Thucydides and Sallust take a less naïve view, but they also see man as a tragic figure on the stage of time, though they do not insist on what seems to them so obvious. But Tacitus never lets us forget it. When we read him it appears to us that the very fabric of his thought is dyed in the hues of tragedy.

Here is his description of Galba's end.

The body of Galba lay long uncared for, under the cover of darkness, exposed to many insults. Then Argius, a slave who had formerly kept his household accounts, gave it a mean interment in the grounds of his private residence. The head, which had been stuck on a spear and mutilated by sutlers and camp-followers, was discovered, but not till next day, in front of the tomb of Metrobius, one of Nero's freedmen, who had been executed by Galba. It was then joined to the trunk, which had already been cremated.

Such was the end of Servius Galba. Seventy three years old, he had lived through the reigns of five emperors with uninterrupted good fortune, happier under others' rule than his own. His family was old and distinguished, his means were ample. Not personally a man of eminent ability, he without possessing great qualities was comparatively free from bad. He did not seek publicity but was not ill pleased to have it. Without avarice he yet was sparing of his own and niggardly with public money. He put up with a great deal from his freedmen and personal friends when he had the good fortune to find them honest; when they were not, he was inexcusable in the way he shut his eyes to the facts. But the splendour of his lineage and the dangerous character of the times threw a veil over his conduct so that what was culpable weakness got the name of worldly wisdom. During the best years of his life he served with credit in the armies of Germany. As proconsul he had governed Africa, in later life Hither Spain; with the same probity in both commands. While a subject he had seemed above his station, and to the world he appeared fit to be emperor—had he not been emperor.*

That is a pungent example of the tragic irony which Tacitus employs with such mastery. His instrument is a style so

*Hist. I. 49.

personal that no description can give a fair idea of it. It is so far rhetorical that he uses every resource of expression, straining idiom to the breaking point, in order to attract and hold the reader's interest. Everything is sacrificed to vividness of presentation. In this Tacitus resembles Carlyle, although the resemblance comes by nature not imitation. Macaulay was thoroughly versed in Tacitus and was evidently influenced by his method of historical portraiture, his 'characters'. Yet neither Macaulay nor Carlyle writes in anything like the style of Tacitus. To Gibbon, as to the Roman, history was a record of 'the crimes, follies and misfortunes of mankind',* and he often refers to Tacitus with admiration. But Gibbon's style is his own and in its equable flow very different from the broken and tormented stream of the *Annales*.

All critics have observed that Tacitus carried the art of historical portraiture farther than any of his predecessors. (The method of Plutarch is different.) The passage about Galba is a typical example of his skill. Tacitus may not always have understood individuals, but he understood human nature, and that is the rarer quality. Its possession is more valuable to the historian than the power of accumulating and arranging materials, and for this reason no amount of research can superannuate Tacitus. Like most ancient authors he is too much inclined to regard events as brought about by persons rather than by currents of opinion or economic forces. But we must view him here as a writer and consider his point of view only as it affects the quality of his writing. When we do that we must admit that his interest in men rather than movements gives to his style an added pungency. I may add, not as a peculiarly brilliant but as a typical specimen of his psychological handling of history, his comments on the death of Augustus.

The funeral gave occasion for the expression of many views about Augustus himself. The common sort were struck by coincidences

---

* Gibbon got this from Voltaire: tel a été, tel est, et tel sera toujours le genre humain . . . je n'y vu que des folies, des malheurs et des crimes. *Dialogues d'Évhémére I.*

—that the last day of his life had been the anniversary of that on which he assumed the purple; that he had died in the same house and room at Nola as his father. Their talk also was of the number of his consulships, in which he had equalled Valerius Corvus and Gaius Marius taken together, of the thirty seven years in which he had held without a break the tribunician authority, of the twenty-one occasions on which he had been saluted as *imperator*, of the honours which had been enlarged or invented for him.

Intelligent criticism was sharply divided. Some argued that his duty to the memory of his adopted father* and the desperate state of the country at a time when there was no constitutional government had forced him into civil war, which can never be justified either in its inception or prosecution. Many of his actions were concessions to Antony and Lepidus to enable him to punish the assassins of his father. After Lepidus had become enfeebled by sloth and Antony had ruined himself by lust, nothing could save the land from party strife except government by one man. Yet the new constitution was not a monarchy or a dictatorship; it was a republic under a so-called *princeps*. The frontiers of the empire had been fixed on the Ocean or distant rivers; the army, the provinces, the fleet were completely organised; the Roman citizen could count on the protection of the laws, the allied states on a just administration. Rome itself had been rebuilt on a magnificent scale; the few examples of severity had for their object the peace of the community. —The arguments on the other side took the form of suggesting that filial piety and the condition of public affairs had been convenient excuses; the real motive was an ambition which revealed itself in stirring up the enthusiasm of time-expired soldiers by lavishing money among them, in the raising by a young man of a private army, in corrupting the legions of a consul, in pretending to favour the Pompeian faction. Later, when a decree of the senate had possessed him with the insignia and authority of a praetor—when Hirtius and Pansa had been killed, whether by the enemy or, in the case of Pansa, by poison applied to his wound, and, in the case of Hirtius, by his own men in a plot contrived by Caesar—he had seized the command of the forces of both consuls; Roman citizens (they went on) had been proscribed, land made over to soldiers in a

* Julius Caesar.

manner disliked even by those who profited by it. Brutus and
Cassius no doubt might be regarded as sacrifices to his father's
vengeful ghost, though one might reasonably expect that private
feuds should give way to public interest; but Pompey had been
deceived by an unreal peace, Lepidus by a pretence of friendship;
later Antony had been induced to swallow the baits of the treaty of
Tarentum, the treaty of Brundisium, and marriage to Octavia; and
had then paid in blood the penalty of that insincere alliance.*

It is worth while to trace the artistic design of this passage.
Instead of giving his own judgment of that inscrutable character
Tacitus gives in highly condensed form the conflicting views
held about Augustus by his contemporaries. That is the method
of the dramatist, and the truth is that the dramatic instinct is
almost as strong in Tacitus as the historical. What interests
him most is how people felt in moments of the kind which
try men's hearts. A brief example of his power to extract its
emotional value from an incident of little or no historical
importance will be worth giving. It describes the feelings of a
Roman army when it entered the scene of a dreadful defeat
when a force under Varus had been cut to pieces by German
tribes under Arminius.

For this reason Germanicus conceived a strong desire to pay the
last rites to the fallen soldiers and their general; indeed the whole
army there assembled was deeply moved by the tragedy of their
kinsmen and friends, in fine of the calamities of war and human
destiny. Caecina was pushed forward to see that the glens and passes
were clear and to build causeways of solid earth over the treacherous
ground of the bogs. Then the main body enters upon the mournful
scene, which presented a grim spectacle to their eyes and in their
recollections. They first come to the camp of Varus, the wide extent
of which and the dimensions of its headquarters showed it to have
been the work of three legions. Next a half-levelled rampart and
shallow fosse indicated where the few survivors had rested; the
intervening space was covered with whitening bones, scattered

*Annal. I. 9, 10.

where the Romans had fled, in heaps where they had made a stand. Beside them lay broken weapons and the skeletons of horses, while skulls could be seen fastened to the trunks of trees. In the nearby woods they came upon the cruel altars, where tribunes and high-ranking centurions had been sacrificed. Then survivors of that defeat who had escaped from the field or been ransomed from captivity repeated the story how 'here fell the legates, there the eagles were carried off'. They told where Varus had received his first wound and where he found death by a blow from his own ill-fated hand, where the platform was from which Arminius harangued the tribes, how many gibbets were erected for the prisoners, what graves dug, how insolently he gloated over the Roman standards and eagles. There-fore the Roman army then present in the sixth year after the year of of that defeat proceeded to inter the bones of three legions, though no man could tell whether the relics he was burying were those of friend or foe; in sorrow and anger they buried them all as united to them by ties of blood or comradeship feeling in their hearts a rising tide of rage against the enemy.*

Everyone who can read Latin at all must be sensible how the Dantean brevity and concentration of the phrasing in the passage I have thus weakly translated adds to its effect. That is a matter of style. But it is not only the style that is remarkable. We have here an imaginative treatment of history which reminds us of the great historical novelists. If the author of *Waverley* or the author of *Salammbô* or the author of *War and Peace* had described that scene in the German forest, they would have used different words but they would have given it much the same imaginative quality. Carlyle and Macaulay owe much to the Waverley Novels, which revealed a new way of treating the past. Yet, as the passage I have quoted shows, it was not altogether new. It is not altogether new even in Tacitus.

It may be asked what the effect of ancient on modern historical literature amounts to after all. It must be said that direct imitation is rare enough; English historians have

Annal. I. 61.

pursued their own path in their own way. But it is equally true to say that they were directed to this path by classical example. Anyone who should now write history in a wholly different fashion from that of Thucydides or Tacitus would run some risk of being thought not to be a man of letters at all. He might be more learned and more accurate, more impartial, better qualified to assess the value of his authorities, in a word he might be more scientific. But none of this would of itself make him a writer, and it is literature that is our subject. The truth appears to be that no modern has so far discovered a better way of turning historical knowledge into literature than the way that was gradually opened up by the ancients. It can be and has been greatly extended and in many respects no doubt 'improved', but essentially it is still the same. History as a work of art is a Greek invention. Without the classical precedent history as Hume and Robertson understood it would never have come into existence, for such models as were available to them in Italian and French were themselves modelled chiefly upon the Latin historians. Gibbon could hope that the *Decline and Fall* might serve as a continuation of Tacitus' *Annals*, and no one has better understood the continuity not only of history but of historical writing.

Whether the work I now take in hand of writing the history of the Roman people from the foundation of their city will be found of value, I do not well know nor, if I did know, would I venture to affirm, seeing that the subject is neither new nor unhackneyed, there being a ceaseless stream of authors who have persuaded themselves either that they can add to the sum of human knowledge or can defeat the baldness of the ancient record by the accomplishment of their style. Be that as it may, it will be a gratifying reflection that I too have done what in me lay to recount the achievements of the foremost people of the world; and if amid such a crowd of historians my own reputation never emerges into the light, I can console myself with the distinction and eminence of those whose fame shall cast mine into the shade. Add that the labour involved is incalculable, the story of Rome going back more than seven hundred years, and the city which arose from slight beginnings having grown to such an extent that it now staggers under the burden of its immensity; while most of my readers, I cannot doubt, will, in their eagerness to reach the present day when the strength of a long predominant people is beginning to prey upon itself, receive less pleasure from its origins and early history, though I myself shall be glad of this recompense for my labours that I can avert my eyes from the long train of evils which this age has witnessed, while at least I recall what happened in days of yore, free from all that anxiety which, while it cannot turn the historian's mind from the truth, is able for all that to trouble it.

That is the beginning of Livy's *Preface* to his history. With little modification it might be the preface to *The Decline and Fall of the Roman Empire*.

CHAPTER FOUR

THE ANECDOTE

IT IS a fair, if incomplete, description of history to call it a true narrative. But a narrative need not be true, it may be what we now call fiction. The most elementary form of narrative is the anecdote, and it may be either true or false. When it first appears in literature, which is at the very beginning of prose, it is often impossible to say how much of it is true and how much fiction. Indeed it may be neither one nor the other, for that is how we must describe most of the first recorded anecdotes. The reason is that they are almost invariably traditional, which means that whatever the original fact may have been it has gradually and insensibly come to be encrusted with the deposits which the popular imagination never fails to leave upon a traditional tale. The anecdotes in Herodotus are nearly all of this nature. Some are clearly mythical; of others it can only be said that there is probably some truth at the core of them, if one could discover it. As here.

There befell this Syloson a piece of luck such as I shall tell. He got a flame-coloured cloak, and put in on, and paraded in the market place at Memphis. And when Darius, who was of the bodyguard of Cambyses and not as yet of great account, cast eyes on him he coveted the cloak, and went up to him and would have bought it. Now when Syloson perceived that Darius had set his heart on getting the cloak, he was inspired to say: 'This cloak I am not selling for anything, but to you I give it freely, if you must by all means have it.' 'Good!' said Darius and took the garment. Now Syloson felt sure that it was lost to him through his simplicity. But when in course of time Cambyses died, and the Seven rose against Magus, and of the Seven Darius obtained the kingship, it was told to Syloson that the kingship had come round to the man to whom once in Egypt he had given the garment when he asked it. And he went up to Susa, and sat in the doorway of the King's house, and said that he was a benefactor of Darius. When the porter heard this he told it to the King, and the King marvelled and said to him: 'But who is there among Greeks my benefactor to whom I am beholden, that am but newly set in authority? Few or none of them has come up to our palace as yet, and I owe almost nothing to any Greek. Nevertheless bring him in, that I may know what he means by this.' The porter brought Syloson in, and as he stood among them the interpreter asked him who he was and what he had done that he should say he was a benefactor of the King. Then Syloson told the whole tale of the cloak and said that he was the giver. To this Darius makes answer: 'Most generous of men, thou art he who, when as yet I had no power, gavest me a gift small indeed yet one for which I feel such gratitude as if I were now to get from somewhere a great favour. For this I give thee gold and silver without measure, that it may never repent thee of having performed a kindness to Darius the son of Hystaspes.' To this Syloson answers: 'Unto me, O King, give neither gold nor silver, but rescue my native land of Samos, which since the death of my brother Polycrates at the hands of Oroites is held in thrall by a slave of our household; grant me this without slaying or selling into slavery.' When Darius heard this he despatched an army under the command of Otanes, one of the Seven, with orders, whatever Syloson desired, to perform it for him utterly.*

It is not impossible that there is some truth somewhere in this anecdote. But where? It is beyond discovery now because the storyteller deals with the historical and the unhistorical in exactly the same way. His art is to make everything it touches seem true and equally true. It is used by Herodotus with beautiful skill. One admires the felicitous choice of details, the verbal economy. Not a significant word is wasted, yet the story is completely told. Here was a lesson for future narrators. There are a great many anecdotes in Herodotus, and all are perfectly told. His way of telling them is naturally old-

* III. 139, 140.

fashioned, yet a better has still to be invented. His only rival here is the Old Testament, which however cannot be said to have the variety of Herodotus, who is no better at the grave story than the gay.

Even in days of old the Alcmaeonids were notable in Athens, but after Alcmaeon, and Megacles who succeeded him, they became very notable indeed. For Alcmaeon the son of Megacles shared in their business and zealously aided the Lydians who came from Croesus in Sardis to the oracle at Delphi. Therefore Croesus, having heard from the Lydians who were visiting the oracles that Alcmaeon was doing him good service, sent for him to Sardis and when he had come offered him as much gold as he could carry away upon him at one time. With such a gift before his eyes Alcmaeon contrived and put in execution this device. Putting on an ample tunic and leaving in it a deep fold, also putting on the widest boots he could find, he went into the treasure chamber to which they led him. And flinging himself upon the pile, he first crammed with gold all the space between his legs and boots, and then filling all his bosom and powdering his hair with the precious dust, he issued from the treasury lugging along the boots and looking like anything rather than a man—his mouth was stuffed, and he bulged out in all directions. When Croesus saw him he fell to laughing and not only gave him all that but presented him with as much again.*

That is a gay story; now for a more serious one.

When it was told Darius the King that Sardis had been taken and set on fire by the Athenians and Ionians, and that the man who first caused them to join in this plot was Aristagoras of Miletus— as soon as he heard these things, they say, he made no account of the Ionians, knowing well that they at any rate would not escape the punishment due for their revolt, but asked who were the Athenians. When he was told who they were he asked for his bow and took it and put an arrow on the string and shot the arrow up to the sky, and as he shot it into the air he said, 'O God, let it fall to me to take

*VI. 125.

vengeance on the Athenians.' And thereafter he gave orders to one of his servants that, whenever dinner was set before him, he should say thrice over 'Master, remember the Athenians!'*

After Herodotus the traditional anecdote tends to disappear. We still get anecdotes, but they are now for the most part told to illustrate an argument or simply to amuse, and the style is as modern as the story, which however need not be absolutely new. We get in fact what we now generally understand by an anecdote. But the art (as distinguished from the style) of the anecdote remains what it was in the hands of Herodotus, so that the link with him is not broken. It is impossible to find room for more than one or two examples. The following is about Socrates when he was serving in the Athenian army before Potidaea in Thrace, and it is told by Plato.

A problem having presented itself to his mind, he stopped in his tracks, thinking. This was early in the morning. When the answer did not occur to him he did not give up, but stood there trying to find it. By this time it was actually midday, and people began to take notice, one saying in a surprised way to another 'Socrates has been standing stock still since daybreak, pondering something'. At last some men of the Ionian contingent, when it was evening and they had eaten their supper, carried their palliasses outside—I should have said it was summer—and lay down, partly to be in the cool, partly keeping an eye on Socrates to see if he would positively stand there all night. He did stand till dawn came and the sun had risen. Then he offered up a prayer to the sun and went upon his way.†

This anecdote exemplifies a quality very necessary to that form—a kind of tact in the telling. Plato resists, as an inferior artist would not, the temptation to hold up Socrates for the amusement of the reader. (That great artist, Boswell, has the same virtue in dealing with Doctor Johnson.) He contents himself with that single touch of the Ionian soldiers, which has the

*V. 105.　　　　†*Symposium* 222c–f.

effect of dramatizing the situation. The reader may smile or not as he pleases. Not but what Plato can be deliberately funny when he likes, even funny in a rather obvious way.

This Stesileos fellow—the one we saw together in that big crowd giving a 'demonstration' and making those large professions—was once seen by myself in another place making a real demonstration, though an involuntary one. It happened when he was serving in the marines. When his ship rammed a merchant vessel he did his fighting with a 'spearhook', a weapon as unique as himself. Personally he is not of the smallest importance, but the story of how his invention of a reaping hook lashed to a spear worked out makes a good yarn. As he fought it got stuck somewhere in the rigging of the merchantman, while he gripped his end of it. So you had Stesileos tugging away in his eagerness to get the thing free, but unable to do so. Meanwhile his vessel was passing the other. For a time indeed he ran along his ship hanging on to the shaft, but when his ship was getting clear of the other, the other began to pull him to itself as he clung to the shaft. So he let it run through his hand until all he had hold of was the butt. There was laughter and cheers from the crew of the merchant vessel at the figure he was cutting; and when somebody threw a stone at him which landed on the deck at his feet and he let go the shaft, then even the men on the warship could no longer keep from laughing when they saw the famous 'spearhook' dangling from the merchantman.*

But the great storehouse of anecdotes in ancient literature is the Works of Plutarch, consisting of the *Parallel Lives* and the *Moralia* or 'Moral Essays'. Many of these stories have long been public property, Plutarch having been, in the period between the Renaissance and the nineteenth century, almost or altogether the most popular writer of antiquity. This and the circumstance that he is not a great literary artist capable of teaching others how to construct a story makes it unnecessary to quote from him at length. On the other hand one has to remember that both in France and in England he had the

Laches 183c–184a.

happiness to find translators who were admirable stylists, and it was Amyot and North and Philemon Holland who were read, not the Greek Plutarch; so that for us the stories rather gained in their new setting. I content myself with one.

The father of the orator Aemilianus, whom some of you have actually heard speaking, was Epitherses, a fellow-citizen of mine, by profession an elementary schoolmaster. He told me this story. Once on a voyage to Italy he embarked on a ship carrying articles of commerce together with a number of passengers. Off the Echinades the light began to fade and the wind dropped. The ship ran on until they were off Paxi. Most of the passengers, he said, had not gone to their bunks and many were lingering over their wine after dinner. Suddenly a voice was heard from the island of Paxi calling loudly for 'Thamous'. Everybody who heard it was surprised. Now Thamous was our helmsman, an Egyptian, whom few of those on board knew by name. Twice he was called and twice he said nothing; but the third time he answered the summoner, who thereupon raised his voice to its full pitch and said, 'When you come opposite Palodes announce that the Great Pan is dead'. Everybody, said Epitherses, was astounded on hearing this and they discussed among themselves whether it was best to do what they were told or not to bother and let the matter pass. What Thamous decided to do was this. If there should be a wind, they would sail quietly past, but if there should be a windless calm in that part, he would announce the news as he had been told. Well, when they came opposite Palodes there was neither wind nor swell. So Thamous, looking from the prow towards the land, repeated the words he had heard—'the Great Pan is dead'. Hardly were the words out of his mouth when there arose a mighty groan, not of one but of many, mingled with a sound of wondering.*

Plutarch cannot use words like Plato or Herodotus, but he writes without affectation and, as may be seen from this story, not without art. Though it is a beautiful story in itself, it could only too easily have been spoiled in the telling.

D. Defect. Orac. 419a–e.

We may now pass to the Latin writers, and first to Cicero. Cicero has no doubt been extravagantly praised at certain periods of history. But perhaps he has never been sufficiently praised for his skill in anecdotes, his admirers probably considering that he had loftier claims to admiration. That may be true, but it should not lead us to overlook his excellence as a raconteur. In this character no other Latin author surpasses or perhaps quite equals him.

I am sure, gentlemen, you will not think me egotistic if I tell you a story about myself. It relates to my quaestorship. Although I made a success of that, I take it that my subsequent administration of the most important offices was such that there isn't very much glory to be got now from the credit I won for my quaestorship. At the same time I am confident that no one will venture to say that any man's tenure of that office in Sicily was more famous or popular than mine. One thing I may say with perfect sincerity—I was quite sure at the time that my quaestorship was the sole topic of people's conversation. When corn was at famine prices I had sent a very large consignment to Rome. I had been polite to big business, fair to the middlemen, generous to the contractors, not oppressive to our allies, in all men's opinion a model administrator in every branch of my department. The Sicilians actually invented new distinctions to confer upon me. Consequently when I demitted office I expected that the Roman people would come forward with no end of offers to me. But happening on my way home from the province to come to Puteoli, where my itinerary chanced to take me for a day or two in the middle of the season, you could have knocked me down with a feather, gentlemen, when a man asked me on what day I had left Rome and if I had any fresh news. When I replied that I was on my way home from my province, 'Of course!' he said. 'Africa, I believe?' In a huff I said, 'No. Sicily'. Then one of those know-alls interposed. 'What?' said he. 'Don't you know our friend here has been quaestor at Syracuse?' Shall I go on? I swallowed my chagrin and merged myself in the society that had come to the spa.*

*Pro Plancio XXVI. 64f.

It is a virtue of the anecdote that it should strike the right note, that is the note suited to the particular anecdote. Very often this involves a certain amount of preparation; a certain atmosphere must be created. Cicero understands this very well. If the first two of the sentences I have quoted expose the vanity of the speaker, that only adds to the effect of what follows. Indeed nothing could be happier than the humorously rueful tone of the conclusion. It shows, what may surprise some people, that Cicero could tell a story against himself. This gives his anecdote an appearance of modernity, since it is a modern, perhaps a specially English and American, characteristic to tell a story against oneself. However, Cicero is always more than willing to tell a story to his own credit. Here is one which he recalls with justifiable pride. It is his account of how he discovered the tomb of Archimedes at Syracuse.

I was the person who discovered the tomb of Archimedes—it was when I was a quaestor in Sicily—though the Syracusans knew nothing about it and even denied its very existence, and you could not get at it for the brambles and undergrowth which clothed it. For I remembered some verses, inscribed, as I had been told, on his tomb, which stated that a sphere combined with a cylinder had been placed on the top of his gravestone. Well, as I looked carefully all round—the whole place, which is close to the Agrigentine Gate, is crowded with the memorials of the dead—I spied a slender column with only the top of it visible above the undergrowth, and on this was the figure of a sphere and cylinder. At once I told the Syracusans —their principal officials had accompanied me—that I believed that was the very thing I was looking for. A gang of labourers were put on the job, and they removed the obstructions with sickles and opened the place up. When a path had been cleared for us we went up to the pedestal, and there was the inscription plain to every eye, although about half the verses had been obliterated at the end. So one of the most famous of Greek cities, and at one time one of the best educated, would not have known where to find the tomb of their

greatest genius, if it had not been told where to look for it by somebody from Arpinum.*

The common belief that Cicero is verbose comes from reading his speeches, which undoubtedly in some degree justify
the criticism, although we ought not to forget that ancient
audiences judged a speech by its sound as well as its sense and
expected an orator to fill its ears with the harmony of rolling
periods, for which the modern Englishman cares nothing. But
when Cicero has a story to tell he employs quite a different
style—concise, pointed and rather colloquial; as we have seen.

An instructive, as well as amusing, example of his anecdotic
style may be found in his 'Offices'.

There was a Roman knight, by no means devoid of brains or
education, who came to Syracuse not on business (so he insisted) but
to have a quiet time. He was often heard to remark that he would
like to buy a little place to which he could invite friends and enjoy
himself away from snoopers. When this became public knowledge
one Pythius, a private banker in Syracuse, mentioned to him that he
had a country house, *not* for sale, which he would be glad to put
at the disposal of Canius; at the same time he invited him to dinner
there next day. Canius accepted the invitation, whereupon Pythius,
who as a banker could pull strings in every rank of society, sent for
some fishermen and asked them to fish next day in view of his
country house, explaining what he wanted them to do. Canius
arrived in good time and was sumptuously entertained by Pythius.
Before their eyes was a fleet of boats. Whenever a fisher 'caught'
anything he brought it in his own hands and tossed it down at the
feet of Pythius. 'Tell me, Pythius,' said the guest, 'what is the
meaning of this? What a lot of fish!' 'Nothing wonderful about that,'
said his host. 'All the fish in Syracuse are to be found here in my
water; those fishermen are dependent on this house.' The cupidity of
Canius was aroused. He begged and prayed Pythius to sell. The
latter was most reluctant, at first. But—not to make a long story of
it—the Roman carried his point; the rich greedy fellow bought the

*Tusc. Disp. V. xxiii. 64–66.

estate, lock, stock and barrel, at Pythius' price. The transaction is
duly recorded in Pythius' books and the sale completed. Next day
Canius invites his friends and turns up early himself. Not even a
rowlock was to be seen. He enquires of his nearest neighbour if it is a
fishermen's holiday. 'Not so far as I know,' said the other. 'But
people are not in the habit of fishing here. That is why I wondered
yesterday what had happened.' An angry man was Canius; but what
could he do?*

The devices employed by Cicero in relating this story are
now familiar to every competent writer. But it is just this
which makes his employment of them historically important.
Here we find the adroit alternation of narrative and conversation. Here is the artifice, by which the reader's interest is held
in suspense—'he told them what to do'. Here is the conclusion
beyond which there is nothing more to be said. Observe too
that a good deal—much more than would be found in Herodotus—is left to the imagination and intelligence of the reader.
No author who had deeply studied his Cicero, as men of letters
did at the Renaissance and long after, could blame anyone but
himself if he bungled the telling of an anecdote. Erasmus, for
instance, who is excellent at anecdotes, obviously learned the
art from his favourite Cicero, or more from him than from
anyone else. Erasmus in turn was certainly one of the channels
through which it passed to English authors.

One more anecdote may be given—a ghost story. It would
hardly frighten a child today, but it is important for the student
just because it is so conventional. We see that a ghost like that
of Marley in *A Christmas Carol* or that of the Antiquary's
progenitor in Scott's novel has a classical ancestry. The story
is told by the Younger Pliny in one of his letters.

There was at Athens a house, large and roomy but unhealthy and
with a sinister reputation. In the silence of the night a metallic sound
could be heard, which, if you listened more attentively, resolved

De Officiis III. xiv.

itself into a clanking of fetters, starting at a distance and coming nearer until it sounded quite close. Presently appeared the phantasm of an old man in a state of extreme squalor and emaciation, with long beard and unkempt hair, his legs fettered and his hands bound with chains, which he rattled. As a result the inmates could not sleep for terror in the haunted darkness; want of sleep brought on illness and (as their fears increased) actual death. For even in daylight, though the phantom had gone, they kept imagining they saw it, their alarm outlasting the causes of their alarm. The consequence was that the building was deserted and abandoned altogether to that uncanny being in the solitude to which it was now condemned. It was nevertheless advertised for sale on the chance that somebody who did not know of the curse upon it might want to buy or rent it.

At this moment the philosopher Athenodorus came to Athens. He read the advertisement and was told the price, which was so low that his suspicions were aroused. Making enquiries he learned the whole story. This instead of being a deterrent to him was an inducement, and he hired the house. As soon as it grew dark he gave orders that a couch should be got ready for him in the front part of the house and asked for a writing tablet, a pen and a light. He then sent all his attendants into the inner quarters of the house and concentrated his attention on his writing, which employed his hand and eyes, in case his mind, not being occupied, should fancy it heard things and create empty alarms for itself. At first, here as elsewhere, there reigned the silence of the night. Then came a clanking of iron, a shaking of chains. The philosopher did not once raise his eyes or stop writing but steeled his nerves and listened with all his ears. Now the noise grew louder, came nearer, was at last, to judge by the sound, at the threshold, then over it. Looking behind him Athenodorus recognises the ghost from the description given to him. It stood and beckoned with its finger as if summoning him. Athenodorus on his part made a gesture bidding it wait a little and once more applied himself to his waxed tablet and his stilus. The spectre rattled its chains over his head as he wrote. He looked round and saw it repeating the signal, so without more ado he took his lamp and followed it. It moved at a slow pace as if it felt the weight of its chains. Then it turned into a courtyard belonging to the house, where it suddenly vanished leaving its companion, who plucked some leaves and blades of grass to mark the spot. Next day he called on the magistrates and suggested that they should order the spot he had marked to be dug up. They found bones wreathed in chains. The body had rotted from time and the action of the soil, and had left the fleshless and corroded bones in their fetters. The bones were collected and buried at the public expense, and after that the house was rid of the ghost, which had been duly laid.*

The Anecdote is not so important a branch of literature that it need detain us longer. But it has its own art or technique, better known to Cicero than to Pliny, whose touch is not light enough. And it is instructive to observe that something which might appear to be entirely a matter of improvisation has its own rules, and that these were discovered and handed down from the ancient to the modern world.

*Ep. VII. 27.

CHAPTER FIVE

THE SHORT STORY

THE short story carries us a stage beyond the anecdote. It should develop a theme and have some kind of plot. It does not seem to matter whether it is history, myth or fiction; often in the earliest examples it is all three inextricably commingled. Since Herodotus is as good at the short story as at the anecdote, we ought no doubt to begin with him.

This king (Rhampsinitus) acquired great wealth, which none of the kings who were bred after him could surpass or come near to equal. Desiring to treasure up his riches in safety, he built him a chamber of stone, of which one wall was set against the outer wall of the palace. But the builder contrived a knavish device, preparing one of the stones so that it might be drawn with ease from the outward wall by two men or by one. When the chamber was finished the king stored his riches in it. But in process of time when the builder was near the end of his life he summoned his sons (for he had two) and told them how, with forethought for them that they might have the means of life abundantly, he had contrived in building the king's treasury; and when he had plainly set forth to them all that concerned the taking out of the stone, he gave them the measurements of it, saying that, if they kept these, they would be the dispensers of the king's wealth. So he died, and immediately his sons went to work. Going to the palace by night they found the stone in the wall of the building and easily handling it, they drew out much treasure.

When the king opened the chamber he wondered to see the vessels without their treasure, but there was none on whom he could cast the blame, the seals being unbroken and the chamber shut. But when he had opened the chamber for the second and third time, and still found the treasure less (for the thieves did not cease from their plundering) he did this. He commanded gins to be made and set by the vessels in which his wealth was stored. Now when the robbers came as before and one of them passed in, when he approached the vessel he was straightway held in the gin; and when he perceived his evil case he immediately called his brother and showed him his plight and bade him pass hastily within and hew off his head, that he might not be seen and known and so be the death of his brother also; who considering that his words were good did what he was bidden and, when he had fitted the stone again in its place, went away home, carrying his brother's head. Now when day had come the king entered the chamber and saw with amazement the body of the robber headless in the gin, but yet was the chamber whole and no way out or in. And in his perplexity he did this. He hung the dead body of the robber over the city wall and set men to guard it, commanding them that, if they should see any man break out into compassion or weeping, they were to sieze him and hale him into his presence.

Now when the dead body was hung up the mother was sorely distressed and, speaking to the son that was left to her, she bade him contrive somehow or other to loosen his brother's body and bring it off, threatening that, if he should have no care to do this, she would go to the king and inform him that he had the treasure. As the mother dealt hardly with this son, and he could not by his much speaking bring her to his opinion, he devised this plan. He saddled him asses, and filled some skins with wine, and set them on the asses, and so drove them. And when he had come by where the men were guarding the corpse that was hung he tugged at two or three of the bottles and loosened their fastenings; and as the wine ran he beat himself on the head with loud cries, as not knowing to which of the asses he should address himself first. And when the guards saw the wine pouring out abundantly they ran together into the street carrying vessels and collected the wine that was spilt, counting it their profit. And the man railed against them all, making a pretence to be angry; but when the guards sought to comfort him, in time he feigned to abate and slacken the fierceness of his anger, and at last drove the asses out of the way and refashioned their furniture. And as they fell deeper in discourse, and one even made a jest and drew him to laughter, he bestowed on them another bottle; and they lay down where they were and purposed to drink, and made him one of themselves and bade him stay and drink with them; and he was persuaded and stayed. And as they entertained him heartily in their drink he gave them yet another bottle, and the guards having partaken abundantly of the liquor became exceedingly drunk, and overcome by sleep they lay down in the very place of their drinking. Then the man, when the night was far spent, took down the body of his brother, and after shaving in mockery the right cheek of each of the guards he put the dead man upon the asses and drove them home, fulfilling the commands of his mother.

Now when it was told the king that the thief's body had been privily removed he was sore displeased, and wishing that it should by all means be discovered who it was that wrought so cunningly he did, as they say—but I will not believe it—this thing. He put his own daughter in the stews, bidding her entertain all men alike, but before she had to do with any to make him tell her what he had done in his life that was of greatest cunning and naughtiness; and whosoever should tell the story of the robber, him she must seize and not suffer to go forth. When the princess did what her father had bidden her, the robber hearing for what reason it was done, and wishing to surpass the king in craftiness, did thus. He cut off an arm at the shoulder from a newly slain corpse, and went with it under his cloak, and entered in to the king's daughter, and when he was questioned like the rest he told her that the naughtiest deed he had done was when he cut off his brother's head in the king's treasury when he was caught by the gin, and his most cunning deed was that he had made the guards drunk and had taken down his brother's body where it was hanged. Now when she heard this she sought to lay hold of him; but in the darkness the robber held out to her the arm of the dead man, which she grasped and held, believing it to be the arm of the thief himself. But he, yielding it to her, escaped through the door and was gone.

When this also was reported to the king he was astonished at the subtlety and boldness of the man, and at last he sent messengers abroad to every city and made proclamation offering to pardon him and promising great rewards, if he would come before the face of the king. Trusting to this, the robber came before him, and Rhampsinitus had great marvel of him, and married him to that daughter as the wisest of men; for as the Egyptians excelled all mankind, so he excelled all other Egyptians.*

This, it may be said, is rather a *fabliau* than a short story in the modern sense. I might agree if I could discover what a short story in the modern sense actually is, or in what essential way it differs from a story like this of Rhampsinitus. But our argument will be served if it is allowed that this narrative, or that of King Candaules in the first book of Herodotus, which was actually worked up into a *nouvelle* by Théophile Gautier, would naturally lead to stories like those of Maupassant or Kipling. This in fact is what happened. The Rhampsinitus story is written in an old-fashioned, even an archaic, fashion, but it is not self-evident in what ways Maupassant himself could have told it more cunningly or succinctly than Herodotus. The notion that the short story is something quite new or modern is a piece of self-deception on the part of those whose reading does not go much beyond the present century. To prove this, though it should not need proof, is not possible here, for even a 'Short' story is not short enough for quotation. Yet one, which happens to be unusually brief, may be given. It is the tale of the Matron of Ephesus.

There was a matron of Ephesus so much celebrated for her chastity that she attracted even the women of neighbouring countries to the sight of her. Well, after burying her husband she was not content to mourn for him in the usual manner by loosening her hair, or to bare her breast in the public view and beat it; she followed the dead to the very funeral chamber and there began to keep watch over the body, which had been laid according to the Greek custom in an underground vault, and to weep all day and all night. Thus mortifying her body and starving herself to death, she could not be drawn away either by her parents or her kin; at last the very magistrates went away rebuffed; all cried despairingly that never was woman so faithful; it was the fourth day in which she had not

*II. 121.

touched food. The poor lady was attended by a devoted maid, who shed sympathetic tears along with the mourner, and fed the lamp in the tomb as often as the oil gave out. So this was the one topic of conversation all over the town, and people in every station of life agreed that never had there shone so genuine an example of love and chastity.

Just then the governor of the province ordered some bandits to be crucified close to the little building in which the matron was lamenting for the newly dead. This had a sequel the very next night. The soldier who was guarding the crosses to prevent anyone from taking down a body for burial noticed a light shining brightly among the tombs and heard the groan of a mourner. With natural curiosity he conceived the desire to find out who it was and what they were doing. So he went down into the vault and, seeing there an exceedingly beautiful woman, he stopped dead as if he had seen a spirit or phantom from another world. Then catching sight of the body on the ground, and drawing his inferences from the lady's tears and nail-marked face, he arrived at what was of course the true conclusion, that she was overcome by grief for her husband. He brought his supper into the tomb and began to urge the mourner not to persist in superfluous sorrow or break her heart with unavailing sighs, saying that all must come to the same end and the same home, and uttering all the other consolations which draw wounded hearts back to their healing. These words from a stranger pierced her like a sword, and their effect was to make her beat her breast more violently and tear her hair and lay it on the bosom of the corpse. For all that the soldier did not retire but went on urging the little lady to take some of the food he offered her, until the maid, seduced by the nectarous perfume of the wine, first made her own surrender to the kindness of the offer. Then, refreshed by what she had drunk and eaten, she began to assault the obstinacy of her mistress. 'What good will it do you', says she, 'if you bury yourself alive, if you breathe your last before the fates pass their doom and demand your life?

Think'st thou the buried ashes crave this care?

Do you wish the dead to come to life again in fate's despite? Do you wish to scatter the mist of female error and enjoy the good things of life as long as you may? The very body lying here should exhort you to live.' Everybody likes to be told that they must eat and live. So the lady, who felt shrivelled up by her fast of several days, suffered her obstinacy to be overcome and stuffed herself with food as greedily as the maid, who had been first to give in. But you know what sensations usually attack people after a good meal. The soldier laid siege to the lady with the same enticing words with which he had won her consent to live. In her chaste thoughts he began to appear neither bad-looking nor ineloquent, while the maid pleaded in his favour, quoting the lines:

> Still, still wilt thou with love approv'd contend,
> Nor think wherein thy wanderings have an end?

Need I dwell on this? Charmed by madam's beauty and his secret, the soldier used to buy whatever delicacy he could afford and bring it into the tomb as soon as it grew dark. So the parents of one of the crucified robbers, seeing their guard relaxed, took him down by night from his cross and paid him the last rites. But when the soldier, who had been thus outwitted while he was neglecting his duty, saw next day one cross without a corpse, he was afraid of the punishment of death which he would suffer and explained to the lady what had happened, declaring that he would not wait for sentence but would make his sword the judge of his neglect of duty; all he asked was that she should give him that place to die in and make it the common death-vault of her husband and her friend. The lady, whose pitiful-ness equalled her modesty, exclaimed, 'Heaven forbid that I should look at the same time on the deaths of the two men dearest to me; I would rather make use of the dead than be the death of the living.' In fulfilment of this speech she orders the body of her husband to be taken out of its coffin and fastened upon the empty cross. The soldier profited by the ingenuity of the intelligent woman, and next day the populace wondered how the devil a dead man had climbed up the cross.*

This is an even more cynical story than that of Rhamp-sinitus, though neither is cynical in the sense of being mis-anthropic; the reader is invited to laugh in a not unkindly way.

*Petronius, Sat. III.

There is however a literary difference between them. The Rhampsinitus story has genuinely the character of a *fabliau*, being a folk tale put in the simplest words. The *Matron*, though it is probably worked up from a *fabliau*, is the product of a man of letters who is master of all the devices of Roman rhetoric, that is to say practised literary skill. It is the kind of thing Voltaire, and indeed a great many French authors, could do so well; it is perhaps particularly in the manner of Anatole France. In England it was not perhaps till the eighteenth century—for we must not compare the Herodotean art of the mediaeval storytellers with this sophisticated art of Petronius— that a narrative like the *Matron of Ephesus* could have been told with the accomplished ease of the original.

I said I would not quote another short story, but after all, to obviate an impression that the two I have quoted reflect the normal mood of the short story in antiquity, I will add one still more famous than they—the story of Androcles (who ought rather to be called Androclus) and the Lion. It is found in the *Attic Nights* of Aulus Gellius, a literateur who wrote when the Roman Empire in the West was beginning to decline. The tale is not his own but is quoted from the book of a certain Greek-writing Appion, who lived much earlier, chiefly in Alexandria.

'A show', he says, 'involving a "hunt" of wild beasts on a very great scale was presented to the public in the Circus Maximus. As I happened to be in Rome, I was an eye-witness of the incident. There were many ravening beasts there, enormous monsters, all of them either rarely seen or exceptionally ferocious. Among all these the wild lions were particularly admired, one of them especially, who attracted everybody's attention by his size and charge and the terrifying sound of his roar. Among many others brought into the arena who were condemned to fight with the beasts was the slave of a man of consular rank; the name of the slave was Androclus. When the lion caught sight of him from a distance he suddenly checked himself as if in amazement, then slowly and gently came up to the man as though he recognised him, then wagging his tail in a friendly and ingratiating way came into contact with him and quietly licked his legs and hands. The man Androclus almost died of fear, but during the caresses of the monster he recovered his spirits and by degrees ventured to look at the lion more closely. What you might call a mutual recognition took place and you might have seen man and lion overjoyed and on the friendliest terms.' He goes on to say that this wonderful incident aroused the wildest enthusiasm among the spectators, and that the emperor sent for Androclus and asked him why he alone had been spared by the fiercest of the lions. Thereupon Androclus told him a wonderful story. *When my master*, he said, *was governing the province of Africa with proconsular authority his unjust and daily punishments forced me to run away. That my hiding place might be safer from him, I withdrew to the lonely expanse of the level sands with the resolve that, if food failed me, I should seek death in some way. Then at noon in the scorching heat of the sun I found a distant, well-concealed cave suitable for hiding in, and I made my way into the recesses of it. Not long after there comes into the same cave this lion here with one foot lame and bleeding, growling all the time and loudly voicing his rage at the cruel pain of his wound.* Androclus said that when he first saw the lion coming he was terrified out of his wits. *But after the lion had entered what was obviously his own den and saw me trying to hide in a far corner, he came quietly up to me and lifted his paw, apparently for me to see, and held it out as if imploring my assistance.* Then, said he, *I pulled out a great thorn which was sticking in his pad, squeezed out the matter which had gathered inside the wound and, without much fear now, carefully dried it in a thorough manner, wiping away the blood. Then after he had been relieved by these attentions of mine he placed his paw in my hands, lay down and went to sleep; and from that day forth for three whole years the lion and I lived in the same cave and on the same food.**

Gellius gives the story for what it is worth, though clearly he would like to believe it. If Appion (or Apion) really said that he was an eyewitness of that scene in the Circus, he was not telling the truth. The story is a moral apologue or fable invented to show the noble and generous nature of the king of

*Attic. Noctes VI. 14.

beasts and to illustrate the virtue of gratitude. Gellius was an amiably gossiping pedant with very false ideas of what constitutes good writing. He has a penchant for archaisms and frequentatives and doublets, and in his hunt for them he blurs the lines of his tale, an unforgivable fault in a 'short story'. For what he has to tell is a story, not merely an anecdote, as was proved when Balzac wrote *Une Passion dans le Desert*, which was evidently suggested by *Androcles*. It is not worth while to criticize the narrative of Gellius, though it may be noted that he employs, not skilfully, the device of alternating direct with indirect speech which is now part of the novelist's technique. The true importance of the story, apart from its immense celebrity, lies in its date. Gellius was a contemporary of Lucian and Apuleius, yet he might, almost, pass for an author of the Middle Ages. We may at least call him a precursor of the Middle Ages. It is not surprising to find his story, or a variant of it, in the *Gesta Romanorum*. He therefore marks a stage—a stage, we must call it, of temporary deterioration—in the history of the story-telling art in Latin.

CHAPTER SIX

THE ROMANCE

THE title of this chapter will seem anachronistic only to one who takes too absolute a view of the difference between the 'classical' and the 'romantic'. The difference exists and is important, but it is not always clearly marked. There are romantic elements in the *Odyssey*, though what is characteristic of Homer is a tendency to reduce their importance in comparison with its classical qualities, Homer being indeed the founder of the classical tradition. Nevertheless even in the most 'classical' age of Greek literature there began a movement in the opposite direction, a movement towards something hardly if at all distinguishable from what we generally mean by 'romance'. The romance differs from the short story in having a more complex plot and a wider range; for it can be very long. We may therefore regard it as an amplification of the short story without denying that this amplification may modify or alter its artistic quality. As for its contents, it is nearly always a tale of true love in peril among strange circumstances. From the novel it differs chiefly in being less concerned with individual psychology and the details of ordinary life.

The first (surviving) romance in European literature is the story of Abradatas and Panthea embedded in Xenophon's *Cyropaedia*. Its influence has been quite extraordinary. It suggested the kind of subject and set the tone not only for most of the Greek romances of the Roman Empire but for those sixteenth-century *romans* from which the modern novel has been largely derived. It is too long to be quoted at length; what will be given here is a synopsis of the plot and a typical passage from those dialogues of which the story is so largely composed.

When Cyrus the Persian defeated the Assyrians, among the spoils of their camp was found a woman of singular beauty, Panthea, whose husband Abradatas, king of the Susians, had gone on an embassy to Bactria upon business of his overlord, the Assyrian king. Cyrus committed her to the charge of Araspas, a young Mede of noble birth. (All four are young.) Despite the warnings of Cyrus and his own protestations Araspas falls madly in love with Panthea, whose virtue however is equal to her beauty. When this comes to the knowledge of Cyrus he sends for Araspas, whose conscience is so touched by the king's grave homily that he begs to be despatched on a mission which took him away from the camp altogether. Then out of gratitude to Cyrus Panthea undertakes the winning of her husband to the Persian service. Cyrus approves, and there is a touching reunion of Panthea and Abradatas. Not to be outdone in generosity, Abradatas puts himself and his forces at the disposal of Cyrus. Soon after, but not before he has performed prodigies of valour in a battle against the Egyptians, he is found dead under heaps of the slain. When the body is carried to Panthea she feels that she cannot survive so true a consort and kills herself beside him.

The story, it must be confessed, is feeble enough, being (by our standards) naïve and conventional. But beginnings are apt to present this appearance, and undoubtedly *Abradatas and Panthea* was a beginning. It is a prophecy of all that later fiction was to do with the tragic love-story. My summary does not do the *Abradatas* justice, because the really significant thing—I mean for the future—is not what happens to the lovers but how the characters talk. They talk almost like characters of La Calprenède or Scudéry; that is to say they discourse of love and the psychology of lovers in terms such as these.

The young man (Araspas) burst out laughing and said, 'Do you imagine, Cyrus, that human beauty can make a man do what is against his best interests, unless he wishes to do it? Why, if that were its true nature, it would make everybody behave like that! Look at fire—it burns everybody without exception, for that is the nature of it. But in the case of beautiful *persons* some are loved and some not—

this person is loved by one man and that by another. It is a voluntary thing, each loving whom he chooses. A man does not love his sister, though another man does; nor a father his daughter; fear and the law are strong enough to keep love in check. Suppose a law were passed that those who refrain from eating are not to feel hunger, and those who refrain from drinking are not to feel thirst, and that people are not to feel cold in winter or hot in summer—nobody would succeed in getting us to obey these injunctions, for it is human nature to be subject to such feelings. No, one loves of one's own free will. At all events everybody loves what he associates with himself, like his shoes and his clothes.'

'Why is it then', said Cyrus, 'if falling in love is a voluntary action, that a man does not fall *out* of it when he pleases? You know, I have actually seen people weeping aloud from the pain they felt from love, yes and making slaves of themselves to the objects of their affection—though, before they were in love, they thought slavery a dreadful condition—and giving far more than they could afford, and praying to be rid of their trouble, as if it were some contagious disease, and yet unable to rid themselves of it, but bound in a stronger duress than if they were in chains of iron. At least they surrender themselves to the service of those they love in many reckless ways. Yet for all their sufferings they do not seek to escape but even keep close watch on those they love in case *they* should run away somewhere.'*

As a serious contribution to the philosophy of love nothing could be feebler. Understandably it made no impression on Xenophon's contemporaries, one of whom was Plato. But a generation or two later, when the conquests of Alexander the Great spread a superficial knowledge of the Greek language and culture over many alien peoples, a public came into existence which liked stories of the romantic cast of *Abradatas and Panthea*. 'The literature of escape' was just as popular among citizens of Alexandria and Antioch as it is said to be now in our urban populations. Not that life was ever very safe in Alexandria or Antioch, but it is not unpleasant to read of

*V. I. 7.

dangerous adventures such as we ourselves may not impossibly encounter, when all comes to a happy end, as it invariably does in these later stories. As for *Abradatas and Panthea*, let us remember two things. First, it was a love-story; secondly, it was pure fiction, not a traditional tale. These two characteristics persist through all the romances (or 'novels', as they are sometimes called) of the later Greek literature. They are fictions, and they treat of love.

The two which have had the greatest influence on European literature are the *Aethiopica* of Heliodorus and the *Daphnis and Chloe* of Longus. In many ways they differ extremely one from the other. The *Aethiopica* is full of bustle and incident, the movement of *Daphnis and Chloe* is generally slow and leisurely; the *Aethiopica* is sensational, *Daphnis* is domestic; the *Aethiopica* is long, the other short; the *Aethiopica* is written without distinction of style, the author of *Daphnis* is an accomplished man of letters. But their resemblances are more profound. Both are the love-histories of beautiful young persons which end happily, and what little incident happens in *Daphnis* is the same kind of incident as happens over and over again in Heliodorus. Neither he nor Longus is able to create individual character; their persons are types. Their hero is an ideally beautiful and ingenuous boy, their heroine an ideally beautiful and charming girl—a tradition which lasted long enough to have some influence on the *Waverley Novels* and persists in the novelette to this day. The characters in both stories can talk of practically nothing but love—love in the abstract and love in their particular cases; and this too has remained in the novelette and the melodrama.

The *Aethiopica* has a fine, mysterious opening in the full-blooded romantic manner.

Day had just begun to smile and the sun to gild the mountain peaks when men armed in brigand fashion crested the range of hills which overlooks that outfall of the Nile called the Heracleotic

Mouth. Halting for a moment they scanned the sea that lay before them, letting their gaze wander across the deep. Not a vessel was in sight which held out the prospect of a prize. Then they turned their eyes to the beach at their feet, and this was what they saw. Riding at anchor, laden with a cargo but with no one on board, lay a ship. Even at a distance they were able to deduce that she was laden, for the water was pressing on the hull as high as the third load-line. But the fore-shore! It was littered with the bodies of men who had fallen in a recent battle, some of them not long dead, others writhing in the death agony—proof that the fighting was not long over. But there were indications of more than just fighting. Scattered about were the pitiful remainders of a fatal feast—tables still covered with viands, others lying on the ground still grasped in the hands of the fallen, who in some cases had used them as weapons in the course of the struggle, which had been engaged in with the first objects that came to hand. By others some of the tables had been made use of as a means of sheltering and—as they fancied—concealing themselves. Bowls lay overturned or slipping from the grasp of those who had held them either in the act of drinking or of throwing them like stones, for the suddenness of the disaster had suggested novel methods of fighting and taught them the use of drinking-cups as missiles. There they were, one man wounded by an axe, another hit by a pebble furnished on the spot by the beach, a third with his bones cracked by a billet of wood, a fourth scorched by a flaming brand, others killed in other ways but most by spears and archery. Over a little space of ground death in a thousand varied forms had been scattered by the hand of Destiny, which defiled wine with blood and added fighting to feasting, which conjoined slaughter and potations, truce and tragedy. Such was the grim spectacle revealed to the Egyptian banditti who, seating themselves on the hills as spectators of the scene, were unable to understand it, having the conquered party before them but nowhere able to descry the conquerors—clear victory and the spoils of victory untouched. Also they beheld the solitary ship abandoned by its crew but showing no signs of having been plundered, looking rather as if it were protected by many men and rocking peacefully on the water. But though they could not make out what had happened, that did not prevent them from thinking of booty and the main chance. So they acted as if *they* had won the battle and dashed forward. Their movement had brought them close to the vessel and the slain when a sight met their eyes still stranger than any they had so far seen. A damsel was seated on a rock, incredibly beautiful, beautiful enough to make one think her a goddess. . . .

Who would not wish to read further in a story which has excited the imagination so cunningly? Yet, it must be admitted, the rest of the book does not live up to this promise. It is as closely packed with sensations as the scenario of a certain type of motion picture; indeed the *Aethiopica* might have been written with an eye to Hollywood. Unluckily the author has not succeeded in making his episodes, or at least the characters involved in them, at all credible. Conventional pirates carry off paragons of female beauty and virtue, and the reader, unable to believe in them, quickly tires of the whole business. In addition to that, the characters of Heliodorus never say anything at all memorable or revealing. One thing however he did achieve. He made wild and strange things happen, and in a romance things ought to happen and they ought to be wild and strange. Heliodorus was on the right track, though his method of pursuing it was mechanical and uninspired. It is certain that his rediscovery at the Renaissance gave a new impulse to the development of fiction. If he had possessed genius he would have been a great writer. As it is, we may at least call him an important one.

Daphnis and Chloe on the other hand is the work of a man of some genius and can still be read with pleasure. It is a minor classic. It has been called a prose pastoral, and this describes it fairly enough. It was (so far as we know) the first romance to put a love-story in a pastoral setting—and keep it there—instead of driving the lovers over remote lands and waters. It should be remembered however that the country was almost as strange to the urban populations who were likely to read the story as Thule or Ethiopia, so that the romance did not lose this essential element of strangeness in the hands of Longus.

The scene is the island of Lesbos, the home of Sappho, a land famous in Greek history and literature, but in the age of Longus fallen from its ancient glory, so that he may have thought of it much as Doctor Johnson thought of the Hebrides. *Daphnis and Chloe* must have had its readers in antiquity, otherwise it would not have been preserved, but its immense celebrity is modern. Even from so influential a book however a brief citation must serve to indicate its character. I give it in the words of the seventeenth-century translator Thornley because, although his version is by no means the best or the most faithful, it belongs to the century for which *Daphnis and Chloe* had a special attraction.

There was a spring, one that Daphnis first discovered, and that served rarely to this purpose of watering the flowers, and in favour to him, it was always called Daphnis his Fountain. But Lamo besides commanded Daphnis to use his best skill to have his Goats as fat as might be; for their Lord would be sure to see them too, who now would come into the Countrey after he had bin so long away. And Daphnis had a good mind to it, because he thought he should be lookt upon, and praised for them. For he had doubled the number he had received of Lamo, nor had the Wolf raven'd away so much as one, and they were all more twadding fat than the very sheep. And because he would win upon the Lord to be more forward to approve and confirm the match, he did his businese with great diligence and great alacrity; he drove out his Goats betimes in the mornings; and late in the evening brought them home; twice a day he water'd them, and culled out for them the best pasture ground; he took care too to have the dairy vessels new, good store of milking pales and piggins, and fairer Crates, or presses for the Cheese. He was so far from being negligent in any thing, that he tryed to make their horns to shine with vernich, and comb'd their very shag to make them sleek. Insomuch, as, if you had seen this, you had said it was Pan's own sacred flock. Chloe herself too would take her share in this labour for the Goats; and Daphnis thought 'twas Chloe's hand and Chloe's eyes that made his flock appear so fair.*

*IV.

This prettification of country life made an extraordinary impression on Western Europe. The Greek was translated into French by Amyot in 1559, and that translation gave extreme pleasure to its readers. *Daphnis and Chloe* was, with Virgil's *Eclogues*, the main source of that idealised pastoralism which for nearly a century threatened to submerge great areas of French literature. It cannot be said to have produced so great an effect on English literature or in England as it did in France and Italy and Spain, perhaps because it is so 'Latin' a book. But at second hand, as it were—chiefly as it came from France—the cult of pastoralism invaded England too. Shakespeare, who must have known what life on the Cotswolds was like, is inclined to satirise the new enthusiasm, but it is felt by Spenser and Lodge and Fletcher and a good many others of that time. As a rule the English preferred it in verse. The so-called Elizabethan novel was but little touched; the most one can say is that it would not have taken the form it did in every respect but for the Greek romances. For these influenced the authors who directly influenced the English. Sidney's *Arcadia* could have been written under the sole inspiration of Montemayor and Sannazaro, but *they* wrote under the direct inspiration of the ancient romances. In the same way Lyly and Greene and Lodge can hardly be said to have gone to the Greek originals; they went to convenient intermediaries.

We must look elsewhere—to France—if we are to understand why the Greek romances have been so important. They, in combination with what survived of the mediaeval tradition of courtly love, produced those romances which begin with the *Astrée* (1610–12) of D'Urfé and proceed through the *Grand Cyrus* of Madeleine de Scudéry and similar works to the *Princesse de Clèves* of Madame de La Fayette, in which we arrive at something that in the opinion of many critics can be regarded as the first true novel. After Madame de La Fayette we have Marivaux (1688–1763), and, after Marivaux, Richardson; and the English novel is born. The lineage is clear. Not only is the title of *Le Grand Cyrus* reminiscent of the *Cyropaedia* but the French book has the multiplicity of violent incidents and the preoccupation with the casuistry of love— though much of that is mediaeval—together with the interest in types rather than individuals which we find in the Greek romances. The somewhat sentimentalized pastoralism of Longus also intrudes. But gradually attention is centred on individual character, acutely analysed by Marivaux and then, in extraordinary detail, by Richardson.

We turn now to Latin—to the one great romance which has survived from Latin antiquity, the *Metamorphoses* of Apuleius. It must have been written about the middle of the second century, which makes it earlier than the *Aethiopica* or perhaps *Daphnis and Chloe*. At any rate it owes nothing to them and, except in so far as it too must be called a romance, is extremely different. It may however be less original than it seems. Certainly the plot of the story—the adventures of a young man transformed by magic into an ass—was not invented by Apuleius. It had already been treated in a Greek *nouvelle* which bears the title of *Lucius or the Ass*. This cynical story is brilliantly written with such sharpness of observation that it calls for mention in any history of fiction. It is however quite short, whereas the *Metamorphoses* is long, written in a very different style and conceived in a different spirit, romantic and rarely, except in imitation of its prototype, cynical.

The world of romance is never the world as it is but a place in which anything may happen. It is always more or less enchanted. The problem of the artist is to present it in such a way that the reader accepts it, while he reads, as real. There have always been writers whose genius has lain in their power to make us accept the truth of their dreams by the magic of their descriptions. Such are in English prose Bunyan and Borrow and Emily Brontë. Apuleius belongs to this class. The plot of the *Metamorphoses* is pure fantasy but it is told with such vivid richness of detail that the Middle Ages believed every

word of it, took the hero of the story to be Apuleius himself
and regarded him—even Augustine regarded him—as a
magician.

Apuleius, like Flaubert, is master of two kinds of detail, the
exquisite and the ordinary, by which is meant not the commonplace but that kind of detail which used to be called
'naturalistic'. I shall first give an example of his exquisite,
though too precious, detail.

Psyche in a place of tender herbage softly recumbent on a very
couch of dewy grass, after that strong perturbation of her mind had
been allayed, fell into a sweet sleep. Then when she had been refreshed by a sufficiency of peaceful slumber, her spirits rose again.
She beholds a grove planted with tall slender trees, she beholds a
spring of crystal water pellucid in the heart's heart of the grove. By
the lapsing water is a palace built not of human hands but by divine
artistry: at the very entrance you will know that what you are looking upon is the glorious and delicious lodge of some divinity. For
the panelling of the roof, curiously sunk in citrus wood and ivory, is
supported by columns of gold, every wall is covered with chased
silver, on which are carven beasts and cattle confronting those that
enter. Marvellous surely the man, nay a demigod or god at least, who
with such subtlety of art embruted the silver; yea the very floors
are picked out in mosaic with precious marbles cut into little pieces.
Verily twice and thrice blessed are those who tread on gems and
jewellery! Furthermore all the other parts of the far-stretching house
are rich beyond valuation, and the walls, all plated with solid gold,
flash with their own splendour to such a degree that the palace
makes its own daylight, though the sun refuse to shine; so flash
the chambers, the colonnades, the very doors. And no less elsewhere does the richness of the house answer to its majesty, so that
it seems to be verily a celestial palace builded for Jove, wherein he
may hold converse with men.*

This (which comes from the fairy-tale of Cupid and Psyche
incorporated in the story) is undeniably pretty, but the strength

*V. I.

of Apuleius does not lie here. The details are drawn not from observation but from the author's reading, especially his reading of the poets. And the style is affected to meretricious-ness—the muse of Apuleius is a demi-mondaine. For most English readers this has been obscured by the existence of two translations, one by Adlington, the other by Pater, whose English is better than the Latin of Apuleius, who nevertheless supplies the essential thing, the lovely story. It has been com-plained that the style of Apuleius (in this fable) is peculiarly inappropriate to the narrator, a bibulous crone, who probably could not read. But this is a mistaken criticism. Apuleius was not aiming here at that kind of truth, for the old woman was telling a fairy-tale, which may suitably be told by anyone and even by an animal. Again his fantastically jewelled style may be so far defended, that Apuleius wished to distinguish her kind of story from the ordinary course of his narrative. Though even in that he has an African love of finery.

The charm of the *Metamorphoses* is concentrated in the Cupid and Psyche story, but the power and main significance of it, as I have noted, lie elsewhere. For when Apuleius brings his hero into contact with everyday existence he is as sure in his touch as Defoe or the author of *Gulliver's Travels*. In the following passage Lucius, having been transformed into an ass, has fallen into the hands of robbers.

And now, bowed down under so heavy a burden, worn out by the mountain's steep ascent and the long, long march, I nothing differed from one that is dead. But there came to me—late indeed but charged with meaning—the thought of having recourse to the subject's defence, an appeal to the worshipped name of Caesar to set me free from the multitude of my afflictions. So when at last in full daylight we were passing through a populous village, where it was market day with plenty of people about, in the thick of the throng I began to invoke the august name of Caesar in pure Greek. 'O' I cried, loud and clear, but the rest of Caesar's name I could not pronounce. Disregarding my tuneless bray, the robbers thwacked my wretched hide on this side and on that until they had left it in such a state that it would not have been of much use even as a sieve. But at last Jove offered me an unhoped-for means of escape, for as we passed many small country houses and large cottages I spied a pretty little garden, in which besides every other pleasant growth there were virgin roses blowing fresh from the morning dew. Gaping after these, glad and inspirited by the hope of my salvation, I went up to them and was already touching them with a watering mouth, when a thought struck me which tended much more to my salvation, to wit that, if I were to put off the ass and become Lucius again, certain death would be my portion at the hands of the robbers, who would either suspect me of art magic or fear that I would bring an action against them in a court of law. At that time therefore I refrained, and that perforce, from eating the roses and kept munching my hay in my asinine shape, submitting to my present evil fortune.*

Lucius, the youthful hero of the story—which like Gulliver and Robinson Crusoe he relates in his own person—is desperately anxious to find rose leaves, because eating them is the specific to change him back from asinine to human form. His search is constantly baffled—this became a fruitful motif in later romance—until at last he succeeds through favour of the goddess Cybele. This quest for roses leads him into strange situations and stranger experiences. It gives Apuleius the fullest opportunity to exercise his genius for observation—for it is in observation not in style that his genius is found—upon many and varied subjects. Here is a passage which, though touched with compassion, is as good an example of 'pitiless realism' as may easily be found in any modern novelist. It is a description of the slaves and gin-horses at a mill. It is exaggerated? Perhaps a little, for artistic purposes. But it is obviously based on things that Apuleius had seen and known.

Since Apuleius is a difficult author, full of archaisms and neologisms, I give the version of Adlington, which is inaccurate

*III. 29.

and incomplete, but produces a more natural impression than any modern translation could do of a style better suited to Elizabethan than contemporary taste.

O good Lord what a sort of poore slaves were there; some had their skin blacke and blew, some had their backes striped with lashes, some were covered with rugged sackes, some had their membres only hidden; some wore such ragged clouts, that you might perceive all their naked bodies, some were marked and burned in their heads with hot yrons, some had their haire halfe clipped, some had lockes on their legges, some very ugly and evill favoured, that they could scarce see, their eyes and face were so blacke and dimme with smoake, like those that fight in the sands, and know not where they strike by reason of dust: And some had their faces all mealy. But how should I speake of the horses my companions, how they being old and weake, thrust their heads into the manger: they had their neckes all wounded and worne away: they rated their nosethrilles with a continuall cough, their sides were bare with their harnesse and great travell, their ribs were broken with beating, their hooves were battered broad with incessant labour, and their skinne rugged by reason of their lancknesse.*

The weakness of all these ancient romances is that there is no development of character in them. That is one point in which they differ from the novel. The romance is primarily a tale of adventures, and it is therefore more appropriate to call the *Metamorphoses* a romance than a novel. It has in fact been called the parent of all subsequent romances. That is an exaggeration; Apuleius' book is only one out of several distinct sources of the modern romance. Yet his influence has been very great. He was much read in the Middle Ages, perhaps with more wonder at his marvels than understanding of his technique. Looking (as they always did) for a moral or an allegory, they suspected something beyond humanity in the 'Golden Ass', the hero of the tale. Boccaccio, without troubling about a possible symbolism, worked matter from the *Metamorphoses* into his *Decamerone*.

*IX. 12, 13.

Cervantes also found Apuleius 'good to steal from', and so did many another celebrated writer of the Renaissance. The picaresque novel which, beginning in Spain, spread, with new characteristics derived from the countries which received it, to nearly all civilized Europe, clearly owed much to Apuleius. It influenced the work of Nashe, Defoe, Smollett, Borrow and others. Before the earliest of these John Barclay, whose Latin romances, *Euphormionis Satyricon* and *Argenis*, were very widely read and admired both in England and abroad, was an open imitator of the *Metamorphoses*. If it cannot be called the only spring of the modern prose romance it may fairly be called the source of the prose romance of adventure when that is spiced with humour or even satire. From this point of view even *Don Quixote*, essentially one of the most original of books, is in true succession to the *Metamorphoses*, although the element of humour or irony is no doubt stronger in the Spanish book.

But the importance and significance of Apuleius as a literary influence consists perhaps mainly in this, that he first showed on a large canvas the application of a realistic art to a fantastic or dreamlike subject. The great 'realists' have all known how to create like this; it is not in them that one finds the photographic reproduction of everyday life. In this art Apuleius is a pioneer. He showed the way and others, sometimes with greater genius and a purer sense of style, followed him in it.

CHAPTER SEVEN

THE NOVEL

THE romance is essentially a story, and the characters must adapt themselves to that. They are such persons as could have undertaken or undergone the adventures described, and it is not necessary for the purposes of art that they should be more. The characterization, it hardly needs saying, should be true so far as it goes, but it need not go far. Those who criticize the psychology of the Waverley Novels for not going deep enough forget this, for of course they are not novels but romances. To concentrate the interest of *Ivanhoe* more on the characters than the incidents would have been to defeat its artistic purpose. (One must distinguish too the *sense* of character, which Scott possessed in the highest degree, from the propensity to analyse it.) But it is different with the novel. In the novel the characters in a sense make the story. The incidents are just so many opportunities for them to reveal their qualities; consequently the incidents need not be hazardous or strange or striking. They are not so, for instance, in Jane Austen, the typical novelist. But the characters must be interesting, that is treated in an interesting way. This can hardly be done if they are but lightly sketched in, or if they are types rather than individuals. The romancer may draw them so, but not the novelist, whose task it is to portray the uniqueness of his persons.

Now the psychology of the ancients, particularly of the Greeks, is almost always the analysis of types. When they have to depict some individual character their instinct is to do this by classifying him. Thucydides, having to discuss the character of Cleon, can only describe him as 'the most violent of the citizens'. And yet Thucydides has a good, even a profound, knowledge of human nature. This weakness or artlessness in characterization was largely due to the fact that psychology was not yet a science, as it now is or believes itself to be, with a terminology which enables it to discriminate between the finest shades of character. Even Plutarch, versed as he was in all the subtleties of Greek philosophy, falls into mere *clichés* and generalizations when he comes to distinguish the qualities of the great men whose lives he was writing. In this matter however it is important to keep in mind the profound and essential difference between creative and analytic psychology. When it comes to creating an imaginary character the Greek dramatists, and not the dramatists only, are as good as the modern. But if they had been asked to analyse such a character into its components they could not have done it. However what I am here discussing is creative psychology, of which there are two kinds: that which is content with broad outlines, and that which goes into particulars. The Greeks pursued the former, the novelist pursues the latter. The novel as now practised is a modern thing.

A form of such importance is not likely to be one person's invention; otherwise we should have no doubt who invented it. This however is a point which has never been and never will be settled, the truth of the matter quite obviously being that the novel is the result of a long process of evolution. Whereupon the question arises, when did that process begin.

Though the detailed presentment of character, which forms the essence of the novel, is not a specially Greek thing, it is not absent from Greek literature. We find it for example in Plato, above all in his delineation of Socrates. I suppose every reader would admit that the Platonic Socrates is a triumph of characterization. If it be objected that he is a historical figure, we may answer that the Socrates of Plato, like the Johnson of Boswell, is none the less a work of art, perhaps even greater as a work of art than if Socrates were an imaginary character. The Platonic Socrates *could* be a character in a novel—a historical novel; in the *Symposium* he very nearly is so. It is true that we cannot call the *Symposium* a novel of any kind, for it is a great deal more than that. But it is also true to say that it possesses, among other qualities, some qualities of a novel, including its special quality of character-drawing. To show this one extract must serve. By way of introducing it let me remind the reader that Alcibiades, flushed and garlanded, has just burst in upon a party where Socrates is a guest, and that it is Alcibiades who now speaks.

'If I am to praise Socrates it shall be by similes. He will think of course that I am making fun of him; but I am not; my simile is an attempt to express the truth about him. Well then, what I say is that he is very like those statuettes of Silenus in the carvers' shops which are carved with pipes or flutes in their hands; you know they are constructed in such a way that when you open them up you find images of the gods inside. Or again he is like the satyr Marsyas. I am sure that so far as outside appearances go you yourself, Socrates, won't dispute the fact; but listen now and I will tell you the other points in which you resemble them. You are a ravisher, what? Admit it or I shall produce my evidence! And are you not a flute-player like Marsyas? Yes, and a far more wonderful player. For he needed his instruments to charm men . . . whereas you produce the same effect by words unaccompanied by any music. At least when we hear anyone else speak, even if he be a fine speaker, we don't care twopence; but when we hear you, or some one else repeating your words—let him be as poor a reporter as you like, masculine or feminine, old or young—we are beside ourselves. Speaking for myself, gentlemen, if it were not that I am afraid you would think me drunk, I would tell you—and swear to the truth of my statement—what an influence his words have always had on me. When I listen to him my heart beats more wildly than a Corybant's and the tears gush out of my eyes to hear him. And I notice that many others are affected in the same way. I have heard Pericles and other great orators, and I used to admire their eloquence, but they did not move me in the way Socrates does; my soul was not troubled and disturbed to think of my degradation; but that was the feeling which was often produced

in me by this Marsyas here—if I had to go on living as I was, I felt
I could not bear it. You know, Socrates, that this is true. Besides I
am quite sure in my own mind that, if I could be induced to listen to
him now, I would succumb to the same emotions. He compels me
to admit that, while I busy myself with public affairs, I neglect myself, though there is still great room for improvement in me. So I
put my hands over my ears and tear myself away from him in a great
hurry, to prevent myself from sitting beside him till I become an old
man. You would think I was incapable of feeling abashed, but
Socrates, if no one else, makes me feel like that. I am well aware that
I cannot meet his arguments; I know I ought to do what he bids me.
But when I have gone out of his company the love of public admiration is, I know, too much for me. So I avoid him as if I were a
runaway slave and, when I see him, I remember what I confessed
to him and am ashamed. Many a time I would be glad to see him
dead and gone, although, if that were to happen, I know well that
my grief would be far greater; so I can do nothing with him.'*

Does this passage throw more light on the character of
Alcibiades than of Socrates? Perhaps, but this would only
enforce the point that Plato has discovered the art, the proper
art, of the novelist as of the dramatist, whereby a speaker is made
to reveal his nature in what he says. As for Socrates, his portrait is given full-length in Plato's *Dialogues* and must be
studied there and not in a quotation which leaves out some of
his most striking characteristics—his irony, his proud humility,
his physical and moral courage. Plato's method is both descriptive and dramatic, but it is the dramatic method that is the more
significant and effective. A Socratic dialogue is not merely an
exchange of ideas, it is a revelation of character, of individual
character; for Socrates is not a type, he is an individual. He is
as much an individual as any character in a novel. For that
reason he is of endless significance in the history of literature.
No intelligent reader of the *Gorgias* or the *Protagoras*, not to
mention the *Symposium*, can fail to see that Plato has at least

*Sympos. 215–216.

the makings of a very great novelist. To be a novelist however was not his ambition, and subsequent philosophers, even when they wrote in the dialogue form, neglected or were unable to develop the seeds of the novel latent there. Yet the seeds did not die. The Platonic *Dialogues* were always read and always admired, and the skill in characterization so wonderfully exhibited in them continued to be a stimulus and a model.

There is another possibility, worth mentioning, although it can never go beyond a possibility. The Greek romances which have survived entire are all late, and none, with the exception of *Daphnis and Chloe*, of distinguished merit as literature. Yet it is not very unlikely that the books which have been preserved because they were best-sellers in Alexandria or Constantinople are inferior to earlier works of the kind which have perished because they were not so popular. This must remain conjecture, since all we have of the earlier romances are a few scraps rescued from the sands of Egypt. But it may be worth while to translate one of these fragments, because it is the earliest thing—it seems to have been written in the second century before Christ—that might be said to foreshadow the novel.

The girl could not speak to Thambe with the freedom needed for the true expression of her feelings. It was not proper for a maid, brought up as she was in the women's quarter, to speak for herself. Asking for an opportunity to speak, she burst into tears; wishing to say something, she stopped before she had uttered a word. Then indicating an immediate intention of speaking, she parted her lips and looked up, as if she were going to make a remark, but in the end said nothing. Tears burst from her eyes; her cheeks first grew red with shame at the idea of speaking and then pale from fear as she suddenly tried once more to say something. She hovered between longing and a maidenly modesty. So as her feelings were excited to the point of audacity while her courage failed her, she was in a condition of extreme and noisy emotion. Thambe, wiping away the girl's tears, bade

her take heart and say whatever she wanted. ' Your silence', she said,
'tells me more than any words. Don't blame my son; he has not been
guilty of any rudeness and he has not come back to us flushed with
his successes and trophies, and behaved brutally to you like one of
the soldiery; no doubt if that had happened you would not have held
your tongue about it. But perhaps the law moves slowly for those
who are already ripe for marriage? Perhaps my son is getting impatient? Is that not the reason why you are lamenting that you have
been so dreadfully pressed?' She put her arms round the girl, at the
same time smiling, and hugged her. Even then the shamefaced girl
had not the pluck to say anything, but laying her throbbing heart
against the other's bosom and kissing her warmly because of her
former tears and her present joy, she all but decided to blurt out
what she wanted.

This is the opposite of good writing; the author would be
intolerable if he went on—and no doubt he did—in this
pedantic style, all repetition and false antithesis. But his
attempt to analyse the feelings of the girl, however lacking in
subtlety and precision, is the sort of thing a novelist tries to do.
It is a very long way from this author to Samuel Richardson,
but he has got his feet upon it.

Again, it is possible that the *Milesia Fabula* or 'Milesian Story'
may have had something of the novel about it. It got its name
from Miletus, a Greek town on the Aegean coast of Asia
Minor, and the earliest examples of the style were written in
Greek. They were very numerous but are now all lost, and
their character has to be deduced from external evidence. This
suggests that the *Ephesian Matron* is a sort of Milesian story,
though told perhaps with greater conciseness and even with
greater decorum than the common run of such narratives,
which were evidently in most cases frankly pornographical.
We are not to suppose that any of the Greek authors of Milesian
Stories (who would be hacks writing for a special market) had
anything like the genius of Petronius. What Petronius did was
to show the possibilities of the genre.

The *Ephesian Matron* however is only a short story within the framework of his complete work, much as *Wandering Willie's Tale* is set in the larger framework of *Redgauntlet*. The complete *Satyricon* (as Petronius' book came to be called) cannot itself be regarded as a Milesian Story. It would seem to be more akin to another genre, of which also we do not know as much as we should like. This was Menippean Satire, so called from its inventor, the Cynic Menippus. It was a kind of prose satire, dramatic in character and interspersed with verses, and that is not a bad general description of the *Satyricon*. For our knowledge of Menippean satire we are indebted mainly to Lucian, who wrote several brilliant pieces in that manner. But Lucian was not genuinely interested in giving a faithful presentation of the world he lived in or even of the ideas he attacked. In any case he wrote more than a century after Petronius. On the other hand Petronius is sure to have read the *Apocolocyntosis* of Seneca, which is a Menippean satire, though there is no certain trace of its influence on what is left of the *Satyricon*. All we can say is that the book of Petronius was probably indebted to more than one, now lost, original.

But for us in our ignorance of such models as it may have had that book is unique. It is impossible to call it a novel *sans phrase*; like *Don Quixote* or *Pantagruel* or *Tristram Shandy* it is at once something more and something less. We should be in a better position to describe it if we had more of it; but of the very long book only a portion remains. What plot it had, or whether it had a plot at all, we can no longer determine. It has been guessed that the whole may have been a kind of satiric *Odyssey* in prose—which would indicate some resemblance to *Joseph Andrews* and *Humphrey Clinker*, more perhaps to the *Ulysses* of James Joyce. But that is mere surmise. From what is left we can see how varied the contents of the whole must have been. The fragment which has been most completely preserved is the account of a grand dinner given by an excessively rich parvenu. The description of dinners was almost a branch of ancient literature, and this of Petronius stands easily first in point of vividness and vulgarity. Even the banquet in the *Peau de Chagrin* cannot stand the comparison, for Balzac, it is to be feared, did not see how vulgar his banquet was. In other fragments we find literary criticism, a brilliant parody— for it seems to be that—of Roman epic versification, social satire, other things.

But let us hear Petronius himself.—The guests arrive at the house of Trimalchio, their millionaire host.

We were by this time as full as we could hold of wonderment and followed Agamemnon to the door, on a post of which a notice had been stuck up with these words written upon it: ANY SERVANT GOING OUT WITHOUT THE PERMISSION OF HIS MASTER WILL RECEIVE 100 STROKES WITH THE BIRCH. At the entrance itself stood the porter in a green livery with a cherry-coloured sash; he was shelling peas into a silver platter. Over the threshold hung a golden cage containing a black-and-white magpie, which said 'How do you do?' to everybody who came in. As I was gaping at all this I nearly fell backwards and broke my legs; for on the left as we entered, not far from the porter's box, an enormous dog had been painted on the wall with an inscription over it in tall block letters: BEWARE OF THE DOG. While my companions had a laugh at my expense I recovered breath and spirits and went on to examine every part of the wall. There was the picture of a slave market with short descriptions of each slave, and a picture of Trimalchio himself with his hair long and holding the wand of Mercury, while Minerva conducted him on his progress and entry into Rome. Then how he had learned to do sums and at last had become cashier—it had all been depicted with scrupulous care, and with the aid of a descriptive note, by the artist. At the far end of the porch you could see Mercury lifting him by the chin and hoisting him on to a lofty platform. Close by was a figure of Fortune, cornucopia and all; also the three Fates spinning the threads (which were of gold) of their apportionments. I noticed too a corps of running footmen in the porch being put through their paces by their trainer. Oh yes, and in a corner I noticed a big cabinet containing a miniature shrine in which silver *lares* had been placed, a

marble statuette of Venus and a gold pyx—of no mean proportions
—in which they told me the great man's first beard had been
deposited.*

The writing could hardly be more vivid and exact. It is what
makes Petronius seem so modern. The surviving portions of
his work generally exhibit his method applied to the more
scabrous aspects of life. This was evidently what he could do
best, and an artist is perhaps bound to practise what he can
do best. It is impossible now to discover if Petronius had any
other motive for writing than just the conviction that he could
write; if he had, it was evidently satirical. We might say this
about Fielding, who has many affinities with Petronius, whose
book he knew very well. In other ways Smollett is more akin,
especially in the matters he chooses to write about, and his
following of Petronius is often open and even elaborate. Then in
some respects the Elizabethan novel, when it deals with low
life, is rather close to Petronius and probably to some extent
influenced by him, Petronius being a favourite author with
young men who had Latin enough to read him.

Trimalchio, who gives the dinner, had been a slave and had
gradually worked himself up to his present grandeur. He is,
though irritable, a soft-hearted lump, ridiculously vain and
incurably vulgar. He has tried to get some 'culture', but his
ignorance and stupidity are boundless. He cannot even speak
correct Latin, only an illiterate slang. This makes translation
nearly impossible, but I will attempt a specimen of his conversation.

He flung a good-natured glance at us. 'If you don't fancy the wine
you're drinking, I'll change it—it must be something to your taste.
Thank God, I don't have to buy none; there ain't a drop of the right
stuff but what comes now from that estate of mine near town—I
can't say I know it, but I'm told it marches with my Terracina and
Tarentum properties. I've a good mind to tack on Sicily to my bits

*Cena Trim. 28. 6–29. 9.

of land, then I can travel over nothing but my own domains all the way to Africa, when I take it into my head to go there.—But tell me, Agamemnon, what was the question debated in your speech today? Me, I don't go in for stating cases in public, but for home use I'm a bit of a scholard. And if you think I turn up my nose at study, let me tell you I've got *three* libraries—one Greek and the other Latin. So do tell me the subject of your debate.' Agamemnon replied 'Poor *versus* rich'. 'Poor?' said Trimalchio. 'What's that?' 'Capital!' said Agamemnon and proceeded to explain the question discussed in some debate. Trimalchio came back at him: 'If it's a fact, there's no question about it; if it ain't a fact, it don't exist.' We rapturously applauded. Then he says, 'Tell me, Agamemnon old boy, do you remember them twelve jobs of Hercules, or a yarn about Ulysses, how the Cyclops put his thumb out with a thingummy? Used to read about it in Homer when I was a kid. Why, with my own eyes I saw the Sibyl at Cumae. Hanging in a bottle she was, and every time the boys said *Sibylle, que veux-tu?* she would answer *Je veux mourir.**

The persons in the *Satyricon* are clearly distinguished, and they speak and act in character. Petronius is not much interested in the analysis of their thoughts and feelings in the way that Richardson or Henry James or Conrad would be. He is content to record what they do and say; he is as objective as the newest novelist. Nor is it a dream world that he displays, though it may sometimes affect us like a bad dream. He writes of what he knows. And each of his characters has at least the elements of a personality. It seems therefore quite fair to call his book a novel, at least more of a novel than anything else. To deal objectively with bourgeois notions of culture and with sexually abnormal types, as Petronius so vividly does—is this so different from the practice, here and there, of contemporary novelists? There is this difference, that the authors of these contemporary novels for the most part pursue their method with becoming seriousness, whereas Petronius, it is to be

*Cena 48. Greek words in a Latin context I translate into French.

feared, is just cynically amused. But he was a courageous and witty person, and a very remarkable writer.

This chapter ought perhaps not to end with Petronius. The novel is indebted to other ancient sources as well as his *Satyricon*. But some of these are in verse, as Latin Comedy, while those which are in prose—Theophrastian character-drawing, Lucianic satire—will be noticed in later chapters.

CHAPTER EIGHT

BIOGRAPHY AND AUTOBIOGRAPHY

BIOGRAPHY is the history of individuals and, though there was a tendency in antiquity to claim biography for philosophy, biography and history are clearly best treated together. The first biography (apart from more or less mythical 'Lives' of Homer, Aesop and the like) seems to be the *Agesilaus* of Xenophon. It is written in exactly the same style as the *Hellenica*, of which it might be an inset or appendix with a larger element of personal detail than was thought compatible with the dignity of history. Xenophon knew Sparta well and had special opportunities of learning the facts about the Spartan king. This gives a value to his biography which is not destroyed by its tone of hero-worship, for his praise of Agesilaus is not intemperate. It must be said, however, that unfavourable comment is excluded.

The same may be said of Tacitus' *Agricola*. It is rather an obituary notice (of the old-fashioned type) than a biography of the modern sort. If we read it as such we cannot fail to be touched by its eloquence.

If there is a place for the spirits of good men; if, as philosophers hold, great souls do not perish with the body—rest thou in peace and summon us thy household from weak regrets and womanish wailing to the contemplation of thy virtues, which should not be mourned, either in silence or aloud. Rather let us cherish thee in our admiring thoughts and lasting praises and (if our powers are adequate for that) in becoming like to thee: that is the true way to honour thee, that is genuine love from all thy nearest and dearest. To thy daughter and thy wife my further advice would be that they should revere the memory of the father and the husband by pondering in their hearts all that he did and said, and in imagination embrace the form and figure of his mind rather than of his body, not because I think we should forbid images of marble or bronze, but because just as the features of a man have the weakness of mortality, so have their representations in art, whereas the form of the soul abides, and this you may grasp and reproduce in your own way of living, but not through art working in an alien material. All we laud in Agricola, all we admired in him, abides and is destined to abide in the thoughts of men from age to age, preserved by the fame of his achievements. For whereas the veil of oblivion is taking from many of our ancient worthies the renown and even the knowledge of them, Agricola will survive for a posterity which has the story of his exploits handed down to them.*

The *Agricola*, like Carlyle's *Life of Sterling*, is open, as biography if not as literature, to the criticism that we are more interested in the biographer than his subject. It is not Agricola (who never comes alive in the book) that we care about, it is Roman Britain and the feelings of Tacitus about the emperor Domitian. This is not to deny that the *Agricola* is of its kind a masterpiece. But the kind is now out of favour; readers do not want an idealized portrait, however beautifully done. Yet the historian has to record that English biography—Roper's account of Sir Thomas More, Cavendish's Life of Wolsey, Izaak Walton's *Lives* will serve as examples—was of the Tacitean kind until we come to Boswell's *Johnson*, or at least Johnson's own *Life of Savage*, which to a considerable extent showed the way to Boswell.

The creator of what we regard as true biography was Plutarch, a contemporary of Tacitus, but a Greek, who wrote in Greek. Though he had so clear a vocation, he may have taken some time to discover it. He was a student of philosophy, chiefly moral philosophy, and this led him to the study of human nature. His reading was guided by that bias, being directed mainly, though by no means entirely, to histories, memoirs and the like. For all that he did not think he could be

Agricola 46.

a historian; the most he could do, he felt, was to paint historical portraits in words. As he says himself, the portrait painter selects characteristic traits in the sitter, leaving out whatever is less revealing, and the biographer should pursue a similar method.

The matter of this book is the Life of Alexander the king and the Life of Caesar, by whom Pompey was overthrown. The multiplicity of the actions which form my subject is so great that I must begin by craving the indulgence of the reader if I do not give an exact and circumstantial account of every famous event but deal with most things concisely, though without misrepresentation. It is not history I am engaged in writing but biography. It is not always in a man's most brilliant achievements that his good or bad qualities come out most vividly. Often a trifling action—a phrase—a pleasantry stamps a man's character more distinctly than bloody battles, and vast forces arranged against one another, and the siege of cities. The biographer is a sort of portrait painter. The painter catches in the features of the sitter their characteristic traits, especially the expression of the eyes, which best reveals a man's character, and does not trouble much about the limbs in general. So the biographer must set himself to penetrate whatever betrays the mind rather than the body and so be enabled to portray the life of the individual, leaving to others the important happenings and contentions.*

The truth, the insight and, it should be added, the originality of this passage explain and illustrate the genius of the man who wrote it. He is the true creator, in some respects the greatest exponent, of the art of biography. Others have excelled him in penetration and accuracy; others have written with a better grace. None has his range and general fairness, and none can rob him of his priority. By modern standards no doubt he interprets the duties of a biographer with insufficient strictness. He repeats too many anecdotes of dubious authenticity; even the authentic evidence is not too carefully reported. Plutarch

*Plutarch, *V. Alex. ad init.*

more or less pleads guilty to this charge but evidently does not—as of course he should—think it very important. The question he really asks about each of his subjects is, 'What impression did this man make on his contemporaries?' Now the stories popularly believed about a man do, even if they have been invented, help us to answer that question. Accordingly the biographer is entitled to use this evidence as an aid to understanding the man he is presenting to the reader. Napoleon was the sort of man who could create the Napoleonic legend; therefore the legend in turn sheds light upon the character of Napoleon. Boswell shows that many of the stories current about Doctor Johnson had no basis in fact. But the stories are in character. There is obviously some truth in this. Yet it puts a dangerous weapon into the hands of a sentimental or unscrupulous biographer. Plutarch cannot with justice be called sentimental, and he was the opposite of unscrupulous; so we are reasonably safe in his hands. But his supreme service to biography lay in another direction. He saw that, if the portrait of a man was to be faithful, his characteristic defects must be brought out as clearly as his virtues. This is what Plutarch always tries to do, and it is this which entitles him to be regarded as the creator of true biography.

As a stylist he is not remarkable, but there is artistry in the conception and construction of each biography. Plutarch has a 'tragic' view of life—tragic, that is, in the Greek sense of the word. Death ends all, and 'the bad things are more in number than the good' in human existence. What then? We are here to make the most of life such as it is. We can win a victory of the spirit by the way we meet disaster. The spectators in the Athenian theatre would have felt there was something wrong with a tragedy which did not send them home exalted by what they had seen of the hero's fight with fate. The great man shows his greatness in the spirit with which he fronts his destiny. The lives of Plutarch are instinct with this idea. It is the tragedy of Julius Caesar, the tragedy of Antony, the tragedy of Coriolanus that he writes. This gives a dramatic quality to his work which Shakespeare for one instantly felt and developed in his own way. That is why the tragedies of Shakespeare are conceived in the Greek rather than the Christian spirit.

There can be no occasion to quote Plutarch; indeed if one has read *Julius Caesar* or *Antony and Cleopatra* or *Coriolanus* one has read Plutarch. But, since his influence on style has been negligible, it is easy to underestimate the force of his impact on European literature. His value to Shakespeare would be enough to glorify him, but our business is with prose. His direct influence on certain writers, such as Montaigne, is, of course, unmistakable; it is his indirect influence that escapes notice. It is not too much to say that the picture of the ancient world in the minds of cultivated persons everywhere in modern Europe was, until about a century ago, in the main the picture drawn and coloured by Plutarch. This was not without practical consequences. The founders of the American republic, the founders of the French republic, had their heads full of his democratic idealism. His heroes supplied names for their children. The humane and liberal sentiment which characterizes so much (not all) of the nineteenth and part of the eighteenth century was nourished, if not inspired, by Plutarch more than by any other single writer of antiquity. And that sentiment of course runs through a great deal of English literature, not merely when it is Victorian.

About a generation after Plutarch certain *Lives of the Caesars* were written by a Roman civil servant, Suetonius, who had access to information preserved in government archives. It has always, until comparatively recent times, been a very popular book, so that a number of the anecdotes he tells are among the best known in the world. It was indeed largely for these anecdotes that he was read. The value of his work is unequal. When he is using his special sources of information he appears to be careful and accurate, and historians feel that they can rely upon him. But he was not writing only for historians; he was also appealing to a wider public. No doubt he had to, if his book was to sell at all. It is very easy for us today to understand the poor man's dilemma. He tried to solve it by adding to his authentic material a quantity of scandalous anecdotes, some of which may even be true but all of which are more interesting to the amateur psychologist than the historian. If Suetonius was the first to write this kind of book—and probably he was not—he was certainly not the last. But, leaving that on one side, we can say that Suetonius had a genuine contribution to make to our knowledge of the Caesars even after the work of Tacitus, who covers a good deal of the same ground, though Tacitus never permits his writing to become a *chronique scandaleuse*, nor is Suetonius comparable as a literary artist. The *Lives of the Caesars* is shapeless in form and has no claim to what people called 'rhetoric' then and now call 'style'. That may be no loss to us, because literary Latin in the age of Suetonius had become a studied and somewhat artificial medium, too much resembling 'Latin prose composition'. Tacitus got out of this difficulty by inventing his own kind of prose, original and inimitable. Suetonius gets out of it by not attempting any style at all. He is content to use the current Latin of his time, and this if rather ugly is at least alive. We may go farther and maintain that, as Suetonius writes it, it has some of the qualities we expect in good journalism. Certainly his account of Nero's end is good journalism.

In the meantime the news came through that the other armies too had revolted. He was eating lunch when the dispatch was delivered. He tore it up and kicked over the table; a pair of goblets which he used to call 'my Homeric cups' because they were engraved with scenes from the Homeric Poems were dashed on the floor by him, although he had been very fond of using them; then taking a poison, which he had got from Locusta and had put in a gold box, he changed his quarters to the Servilian Gardens, where, after sending the faithfullest of his freedmen in advance of himself to Ostia to get the fleet there ready for him, he tested the willingness of the officers of the imperial guard to accompany him on his flight. But when of these some would neither say yes nor no, while others flatly refused, one of them even quoting aloud

Is it so hard to die?,

he turned over in his mind various conflicting schemes. One was to go to Parthia, another to approach Galba as a suppliant, another to dress in black, appear in public and beg pardon for past offences in a speech from the tribunal delivered with all the pathos at his command; if this failed to melt his audience, could he not ask that at least the administration of Egypt be entrusted to him? There was found afterwards in his desk a carefully composed harangue on this topic. But it is supposed that he was frightened to proceed with this plan in case he should be torn to pieces before he got as far as the forum. So saying to himself that he would think about it tomorrow, he went to bed, but awoke in the middle of the night, only to find that the guard had been withdrawn. He sprang out of bed and sent round among his friends. When he could get no answer, he went himself with a companion or two from door to door. But when he found every one barred against him and nobody to answer his knock he went back to his room. There he found that even the grooms of the chamber had run away after stripping it of all its tapestries and even carrying off the box of poison. His immediate impulse was to call for the gladiator Spiculus or any other killer. When none could be found, 'What,' he cried, 'have I neither friend nor foe?', and made a rush for the door as if to throw himself into the Tiber. Then he checked himself and said he would like a more secluded place where he could collect his thoughts. His freedman Phaon offered his sub-urban house, less than four miles away, between the Via Salaria and the Via Nomentana. Thereupon, bare-footed as he was and in his tunic, he flung a faded cloak about him, then covering his head and holding a handkerchief before his face he mounted a horse and rode off, accompanied by four persons only, one of whom was Sporus. Almost immediately there was an earthquake shock and a flash of lightning in his face. Startled, he heard the soldiers shouting in the nearby camp, crying that it was a good omen for Galba and a bad one for himself. Again, when they passed some travellers on the road he heard one of them saying 'These fellows are after Nero'. Another wayfarer asked 'Any news in Rome about Nero?' Again, his horse shied at the smell of a corpse which had been left lying on the road. The result was that his face was uncovered, and he was recognised and saluted by an old soldier of the Guards. They came to a road house, where they let their horses loose and got into a brambly thicket, where a track led through a maze of reeds. By putting a cloth under his feet he managed after a struggle to get to the wall in front of the villa. There Phaon made a new suggestion. He urged him to withdraw for the time being into a cave which had been excavated in the sandy soil. But Nero said no, he would not pass underground while he was still alive. There was a short delay until a secret entrance into the villa could be dug out. During this time he scooped up some water from a puddle at his feet with the intention of drinking it. 'This', said he, 'is Nero's special.' Then observing that his cloak had been torn by the brambles he picked out the thorns which had pierced it. And so crawling on his hands and knees he got through the narrow passage which had been dug underground for him and into the nearest room, the only furniture of which was a smallish pillow and an old blanket. He now began to feel the pangs of hunger and thirst. He refused some coarse bread which was offered him but drank a little half-warm water. Then, as everybody kept pressing him to lose no more time in saving himself from the insults which threatened him so closely, he ordered a grave to be dug in his presence, measuring it out in the proportions of his own body. At the same time he ordered that any bits of marble that could be found should be symmetrically arranged, and water and faggots collected, for the due disposal of the body after-wards, shedding tears as he gave each order and saying over and over again, 'What an artist is being lost in me!' In the middle of these delays a note was delivered to Phaon by his courier. Nero snatched it first and read it. It said that Nero had been adjudged by the Senate an enemy of the Roman people and that he was being sought in order that he might be punished *according to the method of our ancestors*. Nero asked what sort of punishment that was, and was told that the criminal was stripped naked, had his head fixed between the branches of a 'fork', and was then flogged to death. In an access of terror he seized two stilettos which he had brought with him, and then after

feeling the edge of both sheathed them again, explaining that the
fated hour had not yet come. After that he was to be heard at one
time urging Sporus to begin the funeral mourning and beating of
the breast, at another begging someone else to help him by setting the example of killing oneself, sometimes upbraiding his own
cowardliness in expressions like these. 'It is a shame and disgrace for
me to go on living like this. *Ce n'est pas comme il faut, Neron, ce n'est
pas comme il faut; il faut de la sagesse en telles circonstances; courage,
rassurez-vous.* Presently nearer and nearer rode the men who had
orders to bring him alive. Nero heard them and stammered out the
words of Homer:

> *A sound of swift-foot horses smites mine ears,*

and drove a dagger into his throat, his efforts being seconded by his
secretary Epaphroditus. He was still alive when a centurion burst
in and put his soldier's cloak to the wound, pretending that he had
come to help him. To the centurion Nero made only this answer, *Too
late* and *Is this your loyalty?* With these words he expired, his eyes
protruding in a fixed glare that froze the blood of the survivors.*

What a pleasure after reading masses of Latin rhetoric to
come upon an author who lets the facts speak for themselves!
Even Plutarch did not quite do that, for he likes to comment,
though in a pleasant, unobtrusive way, on what he records.
Suetonius refrains from comment, and so passed on the lesson
of his practice to future biographers, who were, however,
remarkably slow to learn it. Why was this? Partly no doubt
because authors, being mortal, find it hard to sink their in-
dividuality; but chiefly perhaps because mere reportage is dull
unless the facts are interesting in themselves. The author must
select the most interesting of the facts and set them in such
an order that they illuminate one another. Suetonius could
do this; at least he does it in his account of the last hours of
Nero, which, besides being good journalism, is a notable piece
of literature.

.   .   .   .   .

Vit. Ner. ad finem.

If an autobiography is the complete Life of a person as related by himself, we cannot point to anything in ancient literature which altogether comes under this definition. But if there is no full-dress autobiography there is abundance of autobiographical matter. Latin literature is full of it. Greek authors are much more reticent; only sometimes an orator or even a philosopher may be driven by an accusation into making an *apologia pro vita sua*. The most famous utterance of this kind is no doubt the *Apology of Socrates*, which, however, was not composed by Socrates himself, and in any case is hardly a 'Life'. It is perhaps too famous to be quoted here; enough that it has made a deep impression on the minds of men, though no subsequent writer has found it imitable. More strictly autobiographical is a passage in Plato's *Phaedo*, which is not too long to quote. Socrates speaks.

'One day I heard a man reading aloud from a book which he said was by Anaxagoras. The argument of Anaxagoras was that it was Mind, if you please, that is the cause of everything and introduces order into everything. I was delighted. I thought that the explanation that Mind is the cause of all things has some truth in it, and I considered that in such a case the Mind which sets all things in order must also set every single thing in the best possible order. Reasoning as I did in this way, I rejoiced to think that I had found in Anaxagoras a teacher to my mind who would explain to me why things are as they are and tell me, first, whether the earth is flat or spherical and then go on to expound the cause and necessity of its being so, arguing not only that that is the better account of the facts but that it is better that it should be so and not otherwise; or, if he should aver that the earth is in the centre of the universe, then go on to explain that it is better that it should be in the centre. If he should make all this clear to me I was prepared to stop longing for any other sort of cause. In like manner I was ready to question him about the sun, the moon and the other stars, their relative velocities, their turnings, and the other phenomena attendant upon them, in what way it is better that each should do what it does and have done to it what it has done to it. For when he positively declared that those things had been put in order by Mind, it would never have occurred to me to suppose that he would assign them any other cause than that it was best that they should be as they are. I assumed then that to each separately and to all collectively he assigned as cause what was best for each and all and then went on to show wherein that excellence lay. I would not have sold for a thousand pounds the hopes he had raised, but would most eagerly have got hold of his book as soon as I could and read it to find out as speedily as possible what was best and what was not so good.   Well, my friend, the anchor of this grand hope slipped and I was swept down the current away from it. For as I read on I saw a man who was making no use of Mind at all but giving as causes of the order in which we find things airs and atmospheres and waters and many other irrelevant matters.'*

That is part of the autobiography of a philosopher. It would be possible to quote similar passages from the writings of Xenophon and Plutarch. The frankness of Plutarch, it can hardly be doubted, encouraged the even greater frankness of Montaigne, who is for ever quoting the Greek biographer. Montaigne in turn has encouraged other essayists to lay open their hearts to readers, so that if Plutarch really started this movement it adds considerably to his otherwise enormous importance in the history of literature. But in fact Plutarch was not the sole impulse here.

Latin authors are so much more expansive that the impersonality of Greek art is the exception among them rather than the rule, and this is just as true of their prose-writers as of their poets. The exceptions no doubt are very eminent—Virgil is one among the poets, Tacitus another among the prose-writers—but we have to consider the larger tendencies. The contrast between Greek and Latin literature in this respect would certainly be less striking (though it would not be less real) if we possessed anything like the same number of private letters from Greek authors that we have from Latin. But the letters of Cicero and Pliny exist because their egotism craved

*Phaedo 97b-98c.

this form of expression. It would be possible to construct the autobiography of Cicero—and it would not be a short one—from the mass of his correspondence, speeches and treatises, for his own experiences and opinions are his favourite topics. In the same way one could extract a more slender, but still fairly comprehensive, autobiography of Pliny from his letters. It did not occur to either to write his own Life in a separate book. The matter, however, is largely one of terminology. And we are in a position to say that two of the most intimate records of a human experience come out of antiquity: the so-called *Meditations* of Marcus Aurelius and the so-called *Confessions* of Augustine.

The form of the *Meditations* is singular, for it is written by the emperor to himself. He had a habit of jotting down, when he had a moment to spare from the labours which wore him to death, reflections of a nature to console, encourage or reproach himself. They are not in themselves particularly original or profound, but they are often expressed in a peculiarly touching and penetrating way. What Walt Whitman said about *Leaves of Grass*, 'Who touches this book touches a man', might be said of the *Meditations*. But Marcus would never have said anything like that himself. He was too modest, and, besides, what he wrote was not meant for any eyes but his own. The last of his reflections will serve as an example of the rest.

You have played your part, O man, in this great city.* What does it matter to you if for five years or three? All lawful service ranks the same with God. Why then should you think it unfair if you are sent away from the city? The Sender is not a tyrant or an unjust judge but Nature, who brought you into it. It is as if you were an actor whom the manager had put on and now took off the stage. 'It was not five acts I had in mind but three.' True, but three acts compose the whole drama of life. The last scene is settled by Him who is responsible for the dénouement as He was for the construction of the plot. You

* Marcus means the City of the World, the Cosmos, and the 'man' is himself.

are respo nsible for neither. Depart then in gentle mood, for He is gentle who s ets you free.

It may be said of Marcus that he wrote, so far as we know, the first *jo urnal intime*, and this gives his book the special interest o f an origin. So personal a record could hardly be imitate d but it could, and did, influence the character and even the form of many later books. One of them surely was the *Pensées* of P ascal. Indeed the *journal intime* has been and continues to be a favo urite literary form with French authors. If the influence of M arcus upon English writers is not so obvious, that may sim ply be due to the fact that the English are not so good at, o r so prone to, that way of writing. It is certain that his charm has been deeply felt by persons so different as Matthew Arnold and Walter Pater. That it has been felt by others would seem to be proved by the numerous translations of his little volume.

Still it could never be maintained that the diary of Marcus affected the mind and conscience of European readers as they were affected by the *Confessions* of Augustine. The reasons are clear enough. Marcus wrote in difficult Greek, Augustine in a Latin which, though not exactly easy, was at least far more readily understood in times when Latin was commonly possessed by educated men, while Greek was known only to a few. Moreover the emperor's style is highly condensed and makes no concession to the literary graces, whereas the style of the saint expands in a flood of emotional eloquence. That makes his book more exciting to read and, as his subject is largely his own conversion to Christianity, it has a much wider appeal than the quiet self-communings of a Stoic philosopher like Marcus.

Here is a famous passage from the *Confessiones*.

I was saying this and weeping in most bitter contrition of my heart when lo! from a neighbouring house I hear the voice of some-one, I know not whether boy or girl, saying in a refrain and repeating over and over again *Take up and read, Take up and read.* And immediately with changed countenance I began to think most intently whether children were in the habit of chanting such a burden in any sort of game, and I could not recall having heard it anywhere at all. Controlling my inclination to weep I rose up, giving no other meaning to the words than a divinely sent command that I should open the volume and read the first chapter I should light upon. For I had heard a story about St. Antony, that he had been enlightened by a sentence in the Gospel on which he had come by accident, taking what was read as spoken to himself, *Go, sell all thou hast, give it to the poor, and thou shalt have a treasure in Heaven: and come follow Me;* and by that oracle straightway was turned to Thee. Therefore deeply moved I went back to the place where Alypius was sitting; for I had set down the roll of the Apostle there when I had risen to my feet. I seized it, I opened and read in silence the chapter on which my eyes first fell: *Not in riotings and in drunkennesses, not in chambering and wantonness, not in strife and envying, but put ye on the* LORD JESUS CHRIST, *and make not provision for the flesh to fulfil the lusts thereof.* No more desired I to read, nor was there need. For with the conclusion of this sentence, as if the light of assurance had been poured into my heart, immediately all the darkness of doubt vanished away.*

Since Augustine 'confessions'—not always under that title —have been numerous, increasingly numerous. It would, however, be wrong to say that they are all the progeny of the *Confessiones.* Bunyan was not thinking of that model when he wrote *Grace Abounding,* though his subject is much the same and he has the same flowing emotionality; he was only following a practice common in the religious denomination to which he belonged. Newman was, of course, familiar with the Latin book, but his *Apologia* was not suggested by that but arose out of a controversy. Rousseau no doubt had some acquaintance with the *Confessiones,* from which he may have borrowed the title of his own *Confessions.* But what impelled Rousseau was the need for self-expression. What we can truly say is that

Conf. VIII. 12.

Augustine brought into literature a note which had scarcely been heard before and which preluded such books as Rousseau's and all those volumes in which later (and often quite minor) authors have laid bare their souls to the world. Richard Jefferies wrote a book which he called *The Story of My Heart*. Augustine was the first to tell that so often repeated story.

RHETORICAL PROSE

'RHETORIC' means 'the art of the public speaker', whom the Greeks called a *rhetor*. But he is a special kind of public speaker—the kind that argues a case, not the kind that tells a story. Therefore a special way of speaking is appropriate or necessary to him. Aristotle has described rhetoric as the art of persuasion, and this to an English reader may look like the definition of a philosopher who imagines that audiences are influenced by logic. Aristotle, however, knows very well that it is necessary to stir the feelings of audiences; his point is that they must be moved in such a way that they are convinced of the reasonableness of what the speaker urges. This is good psychology. Even the most shameless demagogue tries to prove that the course he is recommending is the reasonable course. We must also remember that the emotions have a logic of their own, for which the formula is 'I feel sure that this is so'. The orator does not prove his case by logical demonstration; his art is directed to making the audience 'feel sure' that he is right.

When we first read the masterpieces of Greek eloquence we are apt to feel unsatisfied or even disappointed; we cannot see why they produced the impression which it is known they did produce. The explanation involves a paradox. It is much more difficult to arouse a typical British audience than the sort of audience which was addressed by Pericles or Demosthenes. Consequently the British orator has recourse to every device of verbal stimulation. To do this constantly was, according to Greek feeling, to be 'frigid'—that is to produce in the listener a cold shiver of distaste. The insistent repetition of highly coloured and highly flavoured expressions was felt by the classical Greek to be an assault upon his sensibilities, and he did not like it; he suffered enough from his sensibilities as it was. But the common run of English readers have been so long dieted on highly seasoned language that they have almost lost the taste for any other. English prose, except in the hands of good writers, has for long now been overloaded with emphasis and with trite or even meaningless metaphors. In the state of mind produced by this abuse of words, bludgeoned into an apathetic receptiveness, we approach Demosthenes and find him dull.

The great critic who wrote the treatise *On the Sublime* quotes with admiration this sentence from Demosthenes:* 'That decree of the people caused the danger which hung over the city to pass by like a cloud.' It is not very likely that a modern orator would use such a phrase; it would sound old-fashioned. The modern critic would say, justly enough, that the metaphor was now trite. But the audience to whom Demosthenes was speaking had perhaps not heard it before, at least they had not heard it in the circumstances which gave it so extraordinary an aptness and significance. They were seated in a place from which they could view the range of high mountains which guarded their country on the landward side. To that range they were in the habit of looking to note changes in the weather. A storm-cloud up there—and it is that kind of cloud which is meant by the word Demosthenes uses—was apt to burst in torrential rains or big hailstones which could ruin vineyards and fruit-blossom in an hour. This frequently happened, and the small fruit-farmers, who composed a large part of the Athenian population, lived in constant dread of its recurrence. So did the seamen of the Piraeus, who formed another large section of the orator's audience. But these hills contained more than the menace of storm. Through them ran the pass by which an invader would come from the north. At the time of which Demosthenes was speaking such an invader was hourly expected—Philip of Macedon. So when the orator began 'The danger that hung over us', would not the eyes of all be lifted to the mountain barrier, to which in his dramatic way he no

* *De Corona* 188.

doubt pointed? 'But then', he continued, 'you acted; you acted and the danger passed away.' Then he added 'like a cloud'. They *saw* that cloud. That was how Demosthenes used figurative language. Like a sword, not like a cosmetic.

So much for the spirit of the best ancient rhetoric; we may now look at its technique. The unit is the complete sentence. In mature classical prose this was normally the 'period'. The period might be constructed in a good many ways but it was always, in practised writers, constructed according to rule. It cannot be denied that it often gives the English reader an impression of artificiality. He may even wonder how the attention of an audience could have been held. But in fact nothing holds the attention like a period, if it is framed in the right way. It is so framed when it does not give up its meaning until it has come to an end. The inexpert speaker begins with a statement of what principally occupies his mind, and then adds conditions and qualifications. That is fatal to interest. The audience, once it has grasped your main point, becomes first impatient and then inattentive as you proceed to qualify and modify it. The art is to make them hang on your words until you have uttered the last of them. Natural orators seem to possess this art by instinct. Thus John Bright can say:

I tell the noble lord, that if he be ready honestly and frankly to endeavour, by the negotiations to be opened at Vienna, to put an end to this war, no word of mine, no vote of mine will be given to shake his power for one single moment, or to change his position in this House. . . . By adopting that course he would have the satisfaction of reflecting that, having obtained the object of his laudable ambition—having become the foremost subject of the Crown, the director of, it may be, the destinies of his country, and the presiding genius in her councils—he had achieved a still higher and nobler ambition: that he had restored the sword to the scabbard—that at his word torrents of blood had ceased to flow—that he had restored tranquillity to Europe, and saved his country from the indescribable calamities of war.

These are periods in the classical style, which Bright had learned to make not from any ancient orator—for he did not read Latin or Greek and was rather scornful of both—but because he found himself in the tradition of English oratory established by men like Burke and Fox and Canning, who had studied the ancients and the rationale of classical rhetoric. It will be observed that Bright's audience had to wait for his meaning till the end of each sentence. Contrast now a short passage from Grote, the historian of Greece, who ought to have known better.

The subjects of Xerxes conducted themselves generally with great bravery. Their signal defeat was not owing to any want of courage; but, first, to the narrow space which rendered their superior number a hindrance rather than a benefit; next, to their want of orderly line and discipline as compared with the Greeks; thirdly, to the fact that when once fortune seemed to turn against them. . . .

Obviously no audience could go on listening to more of this; its attention would flag before the middle of the second sentence, the first having told them all they cared to know. Grote is writing, not speaking, and his problem is not the same as the orator's. But it is so far the same that a writer must hold the attention of his readers as much as an orator that of his audience. Now see how Livy does it in the passage I now proceed to quote. (A proposal had been made to abolish the sumptuary law, *Lex Oppia*, which applied to women. The proposal was violently resisted—it would be—by Cato (M. Porcius Cato) who was consul at the time.* In what follows the tribune Lucius Valerius seeks to meet his arguments.)

Si privati tantum modo ad suadendum dissuadendumque id quod ab nobis rogatur processissent, ego quoque, cum satis dictum pro utraque parte existimarem, tacitus suffragia vestra exspectassem. nunc cum vir gravissimus, consul M. Porcius, non auctoritate solum, quae tacita satis momenti habuisset, sed

* 195 B.C.

oratione etiam longa et accurata insectatus sit rogationem
nostram, necesse est paucis respondere. qui tamen plura verba
in castigandis matronis quam in rogatione dissuadenda con-
sumpsit, et quidem ut in dubio poneret utrum id quod repre-
henderet matronae sua sponte an nobis auctoribus fecissent.
rem defendam, non nos, in quos iecit magis hoc consul verbo
quam ut re insimularet. coetum et seditionem et interdum
secessionem muliebrem appellavit quod matronae in publico
vos rogassent ut legem in se latam per bellum temporibus duris
in pace et florenti ac beata re publica abrogaretis. verba magna
quae rei augendae causa conquirantur et haec et alia esse scio, et
M. Catonem oratorem non solum gravem sed interdum etiam
trucem esse scimus omnes, cum ingenio sit mitis.*3

The longer one examines this passage (which is typical of
endless others) the better one will see how wonderful is its
construction. Observe how in every sentence the subordinate
clauses balance one another to sustain the whole, the effect
being enhanced by internal correspondence and assonance—
suadendum, dissuadendum; per bellum temporibus duris, in
pace et florenti ac beata re publica; non solum gravem, sed
etiam trucem, and the like. All is designed to hold the reader's
attention while the elaborate structure unfolds itself from
beginning to end. It is hardly possible to attain all these effects
in English, where the order of words is fixed. But most
of them are attainable and have been attained by English
masters of prose who have taken as much care with their
sentences as Livy.

'We charge this offender with no crimes that have not arisen from
passions which it is criminal to harbour; with no offences that have
not their root in avarice, rapacity, pride, insolence, or ferocity,
treachery, cruelty, malignity of temper; in short in nothing that does
not argue a total extinction of all moral principle; that does not
manifest an inveterate blackness of heart dyed in grain with malice,
vitiated, corrupted, gangrened to the very core. If we do not plant

*XXXIV. 5.

his crimes in those vices which the breast of man is made to abhor, and the spirit of all laws human and divine to interdict, we desire no longer to be heard on this occasion. Let everything that can be pleaded upon the ground of surprise or error, upon those grounds be pleaded with success; we give up the whole of those predicaments. We urge no crimes, that were not crimes of forethought. We charge him with nothing that he did not commit upon deliberation; that he did not commit against advice, supplication and re-monstrance; that he did not commit against the direct command of lawful authority; that he did not commit after reproof and reprimand of those who are authorized by the laws to reprove and reprimand him. The crimes of Mr. Hastings are crimes not only in themselves, but aggravated by being crimes of contumacy. They were crimes, not against forms; but against those eternal laws of justice, which are our rule and our birthright.'

Thus Burke, denouncing Warren Hastings. The passage I have quoted—and it is typical—what is it but the application of Roman rhetoric to English prose? And you will find the same thing in 'Junius', in Canning, even in the speeches of Macaulay and Gladstone.

CHAPTER NINE

THE PLAIN STYLE

WE CAN follow the development of rhetoric in the litera-ture of Athens. When it came there—it is said from Sicily—it made its effects too obviously and too cheaply. Attic taste gradually refined it, pursuing a more natural elegance. The composition of the audience would make a difference. A jury has to make up its mind on the facts of a case. So what it likes to hear is a clear and plain exposition of these, although it may be gratified no doubt by an appeal to its feelings as well. The main thing is, it must not be puzzled. It was, we may assume, the necessity of addressing juries which led to the gradual evolution of what was called the plain style in oratory. Its most accomplished exponent was the advocate Lysias, who was most effective about the beginning of the fourth century before Christ. But while the style may be said to have been perfected by Lysias, it can hardly be said that he invented it. An older and more interesting man, the Athenian statesman and advocate Antiphon, had discovered that juries prefer a clear statement to a brilliant one. His style, compared with that of Lysias, is a little stiff and old-fashioned and much less uniform; but when he has a story to tell he tells it as clearly as his successor. Is this simply the old narrative style of Herodotus? Not really, because the object now is to convince, not to charm, or to charm only as a means of producing conviction. In other words the simplicity of Antiphon is not artistically inevitable, as it is in Herodotus, but is a part of his 'rhetoric', his art of persuasion. It is therefore proper to distinguish between the 'simple' narrative style and the 'plain' style of the orators. In the passage I am about to quote the style could not be plainer. To under-stand it we must bear in mind that the defendant in an Athenian court of law spoke in his own defence, but what he spoke had generally been written out for him by a professional pleader whom he had feed for the purpose. This was not thought dishonourable then and need not be thought so now. In the present case then, while the voice is the voice of the accused, the words are the words of Antiphon.

'I made the voyage from Mytilene in the same ship as this Herodes, who they say was murdered by me. We were sailing to Aenos, I to my father, who was there at the time, Herodes to restore some slaves to certain Thracians on receipt of a ransom. The slaves were travelling with him and so were the Thracians who were to pay the ransom. We ran into a storm which forced us to land at a port in the territory of Methymna, and there we found anchored the ship to which, they say, Herodes changed before meeting his death. Now in the first place you must see that this was pure accident and not the result of any plot. For quite evidently I did not induce him to sail with me; he went of his own volition and on business of his own. In the second place it is proved that I had a perfectly good reason for sailing to Aenos. Neither did we land at this place in fulfilment of some previous arrangement but because we had no choice in the matter; nor again, after we had anchored, was it any plot or deception which induced us to change ships, but, once more, necessity. For the ship in which we were sailing was undecked, while that into which we transferred had a deck—we had to make the change on account of the rain.

After we had transferred into the other vessel we had a drink. And then? The evidence proves that Herodes left the ship. He never came back. For my own part I stayed on board all that night. Next day—no sign of Herodes. Search was made for him, by no one more thoroughly than by me, and I was as much concerned as anybody. It was I who urged that a messenger should be sent to Mytilene, and this suggestion was adopted. When no one else on board even among Herodes' fellow-travellers would go, I offered to send my personal attendant—and it was hardly likely, was it, that I should be deliberately sending one who might inform against me? But when the object of our search could not be found in Mytilene or anywhere else, we resumed our voyage; all the other ships put to sea, and I sailed with them. . . .

The prosecution says that Herodes was killed on land and that I threw a stone at his head—I who never left the ship. They know this quite well but they can give no plausible explanation of the man's disappearance. In all likelihood it happened near the harbour. For in the first place the man was not sober and secondly it was dark when he went ashore. Probably he could not walk straight, and his abductor could have had no reason for taking him far in the darkness. The search went on for two days, but nobody was found who had seen him nor was blood or any other clue discovered. Not content with that, I countered the charge of my accusers by producing witnesses that I never left the ship. Even if I had it would still be most unlikely that Herodes could have vanished without trace unless he had gone quite a long way from the sea. "But", say they, "his body was flung into the sea." On what ship? Obviously it must have been outside the harbour itself. How then was it that he could not be found? Surely if the man had been killed and thrown overboard, there would have been some sign of that in the ship. As it is they profess that they have found signs in the ship in which he drank and which he left, although they admit that this was not the ship in which he met his death. As for the ship from which they allege that he was thrown overboard, they have found neither that ship itself nor any clue.'*

Was this then the perfect murder? It may amuse some readers to think out how it was done. At any rate we have the perfect statement of a murderer's case, if we assume that the defendant was guilty. I think myself that he was, because if the facts were as he states them he would not have been prosecuted for murder at all. He must therefore be suppressing some of the evidence. But on any assumption with what skill does Antiphon plead his client's case! He does not profess to explain the mystery —it was for the prosecution to do that—but to describe it, and this he does with a simple plainness and lucidity which must have prepossessed the jury in favour of the speaker. Plainness

*De Caede Herodis 20–28.

E

of this kind is a product of laborious art rather than of natural facility, and it was used for his own purposes by this ambitious, daring and immensely able man, to whom it may never have occurred that he was founding a style. Yet this, consciously or unconsciously, is what he did.

Lysias was the man who took it up and perfected it. Although he came, largely by accident, to be involved in Athenian politics, he was not in the full sense an Athenian citizen and had therefore to content himself with writing speeches for the law-courts; and this explains much in the character of his eloquence. It is a little difficult for us now to understand why it was so much admired by the ancients, for he has seldom anything of permanent interest to say, and what he does say is said with little colour or passion. But what was admired in Lysias was the exquisite purity of his Attic diction, of which the final judgment must lie with the Greeks themselves. It cannot be reproduced in English, but a straightforward translation of the opening words of one of his most celebrated speeches will show the simplicity if not the exquisiteness of his language.

'I perceive a difficulty, gentlemen of the jury, not in opening my speech for the prosecution, but in bringing it to an end. So many and so shocking are the crimes which have been committed that a man could not invent charges worse than the facts nor with the best will in the world make mention of them all; either the prosecutor must sink exhausted or his time be up. This would appear to be a novel situation. Formerly the prosecution had to prove that it was animated by hatred of the accused; today it is from the accused that we must learn what hatred they felt for their country to make them attempt such wickedness against her. Not that I am without personal grounds for enmity and grief as I address you; but we all have more than adequate reasons for indignation on public as well as on private grounds. For my own part, gentleman, I have now been compelled by events to bring a charge against the man in the dock, with the result that, inexperienced as I am in affairs both public and private, I have more than once felt a good deal of despondency in case my lack of practice leads me to plead the cause of my brother and myself against the accused in an inadequate and ineffective manner.'*

In reading this one is tempted to exclaim, 'There is nothing in it; anybody might begin a speech like that.' But this is exactly what Lysias wished the jury to think. It was his art to conceal his art. Conversational ease in combination with perfect lucidity is the fruit of a long and hard apprenticeship to the craft of letters, as Addison and Swift would have confessed. Yet a reader of Lysias may be left with the impression that a style like his could never rise to a very lofty eloquence. Perhaps on the lips of Lysias it could not. But with others it did. Here is the conclusion of the speech in which Socrates addressed his judges after condemnation had been passed by the majority upon him.

'You too, my judges, should be of good hope in the face of death, sure of the truth of one thing, that no evil can befall a good man either in this life or the next, and that the gods are not regardless of what happens to him. Even the situation in which I now stand is not an accident; I am sure that it has become best for me to be dead and out of it all. That is why the warning Voice nowhere stopped me, and I have no very hard feelings towards my accusers and those of you who voted for my condemnation. Still they did accuse me and you did so vote with the intention of inflicting hurt upon me, and so far I am justified in blaming them. I have however one request to make of them. It concerns my sons. When they grow up and vex you, as I used to vex you, punish them if it seems to you that they have more regard to money or anything else than to goodness; and if they seem to you to be worthless persons upbraid them, as I upbraid you, for neglecting what they ought to pursue and thinking themselves to be men of some merit when they are of none. If you do this, I shall have had justice done to me—I and my sons. But now the hour has come when we must go upon our different ways—I to die and you to live; though which is going to the better fate is hidden from all but God.'†

*De Caede Eratosthenis ad init.   †Apol. ad fin.

Is this not eloquence? Lysias had not the moral and artistic genius to write like Plato and his style is somewhat tighter and more formal than the style in the passage I have quoted. (Plato is the real author of the speech, though no doubt Socrates may have said something like it.) But Lysias must not be denied the credit due to him. He had a far sounder notion of what the plain style could do than some of his followers and imitators, who loved to form every sentence on a schematic pattern, one antithetic clause exactly balancing another. There was a revival of his manner (in this more rigid and desiccated form) in the first century before Christ, especially in Rome, where it was practised by Brutus and, up to a point, by Caesar. I have remarked elsewhere that the speech composed by Shakespeare for Brutus in *Julius Caesar* is so exactly in the style of the historical Brutus that it might be a translation. It is short enough to be quoted.

'Romans, countrymen, and lovers! hear me for my cause, and be silent, that you may hear: believe me for mine honour, and have respect to mine honour, that you may believe: censure me in your wisdom, and awake your senses, that you may the better judge. If there be any in this assembly, any dear friend of Caesar's, to him I say that Brutus' love to Caesar was no less than his. If then that friend demand why Brutus rose against Caesar, this is my answer: not that I loved Caesar less, but that I loved Rome more. Had you rather Caesar were living, and die all slaves, than that Caesar were dead, to live all free men? As Caesar loved me, I weep for him; as he was fortunate, I rejoice at it; as he was valiant, I honour him; but as he was ambitious, I slew him. There is tears for his love, joy for his fortune; honour for his valour; and death for his ambition. Who is here so base that would be a bondman? If any, speak; for him have I offended. Who is here so rude that would not be a Roman? If any, speak; for him have I offended. Who is here so vile that will not love his country? If any, speak; for him have I offended. I pause for a reply.'*

Julius Caesar III. 2.

The oratory of Caesar, though not excessively formal like that of Brutus, who was not free from pedantry, also followed on the whole the manner of Lysias. Unfortunately his speeches have not been preserved, for that given in Sallust's *Catiline* is the work of Sallust and not of Caesar. Yet it is not impossible to get a notion of what they were like. In his *Gallic War* and *Civil War* we find a number of speeches reported in condensed form and in what grammarians called *oratio obliqua*; and it is a simple process, guided by fixed rules, to reconstruct the direct speech from the indirect. Besides this there is at least one speech directly reported, that of a certain Critognatus, the language and style of which are Caesar's own.

I do not propose to discuss the proposal for 'capitulation', which comes from men who give that appellation to a very dishonourable thing, slavery. Such people in my opinion ought not to be treated as our fellow-countrymen or summoned to our councils at all. I address my remarks entirely to those who favour a sortie. This is a plan you all approve, for it makes you think that the old Gallic spirit is not dead! Yet it is a form of weakness not of strength of character, if we cannot face a short period of famine. You will more easily find men to volunteer to confront death than to suffer pain with fortitude. And yet I would be in favour of their proposal (such is my regard for them) if it seemed to me that nothing more was involved than the loss of our own lives. But we have summoned the whole of Gaul to come to our aid, and in forming our plans we are bound to take that into consideration. What courage do you think the slaughter of eighty thousand men of us on a single battle-field will inspire in our kinsmen, if they are compelled to fight it out while almost tripping over the corpses? Do not make it impossible for us to help those who have neglected their own safety in order to rescue us. Do not be so rash and foolish and irresolute as to ruin all Gaul and subject her to perpetual servitude. Is it because they have not come on the agreed day that you question their good faith and steadfastness? Well now do you suppose that the Romans are being kept at it day in and day out working on those outer fortifications of theirs for fun? If no messenger from our friends can get through the closed lines of the enemy, that should prove to you that they cannot be far off, and it is just this that has scared him into toiling day and night at these outworks. What then is my advice? To do what our fathers did in their war (which was far less dangerous than this) with the Cimbri and the Teutones. Driven behind the walls of their towns and reduced like us by hunger, rather than surrender to the enemy they supported life on the flesh of those who were judged too old or too young for fighting.*

The structure of this speech will be found on analysis to be thoroughly rhetorical, but it is not complex or elaborate like the rhetoric of Cicero or Livy, and may be considered to be in the plain style. In general, Latin taste preferred a more florid eloquence. Yet the plain style had a very great influence on ancient prose, because it was something which was, or seemed to be, within the power of any writer who was prepared to take some pains with his writing. Cicero or Livy very few could hope to emulate. The average writer was content with a simpler manner, which busied itself more with what we should call grammar and syntax and the best order of the words than with flowers of speech and sonority of diction. This is better seen in Greek than in Latin prose, because Roman taste on the whole liked something louder and brighter than the Attic simplicity of a Lysias or a Xenophon. It helps us to understand the historical significance of Xenophon if we remember that he, perhaps more than any other Greek, produced a sort of standard prose, based on Lysias, which others could learn to write. It does not seem necessary to illustrate this by quotation, for the quotations would all, whatever subject Xenophon was writing upon, be in the same manner. We noted that Thucydides had two styles, one for the speeches in his History and another for the narrative. In Xenophon speeches and narrative are written in the same style—simple, natural, plain. To create an organ of expression like that—an all-purposes style—was a very great service to Greek literature.

*Bell. Gall. VII. 77.

CHAPTER TEN

THE ORNATE STYLE

Tᴴᴱ plain style had its day without becoming out of date. But after a time audiences began to hanker after something that would more completely fill the ear and satisfy the imagination. This was perceived by Isocrates. He was not much younger than Lysias but he long outlived him and came to see his own influence paramount; it remained paramount for a very long time after his death. He was scarcely a man of high genius or superior intellect. He believed that culture was another name for the kind of rhetoric he was prepared to teach. It was a new, if not quite an original, style. He invented or developed a more elaborate, at any rate a more smoothly elaborate, form of period than had hitherto been successfully constructed. It was indeed a wonderful structure, consisting of several parts or clauses all carefully balanced one against the other and yet all building up to a conclusion which gives them unity. Now a sentence of this kind, though difficult to make, is imitable because the rules for making it can be mastered. This largely accounts for its prodigious success. There were no rules for writing like Plato or Thucydides. Thus it may be said that Isocrates created an alternative style to that of Xenophon. Observe that neither was a practising orator. Their task—only half-conscious in the case of Xenophon—was to adapt the art of oratory to the art of literature, so as to produce a standard prose. Xenophon adapted the plain style; what Isocrates produced may be called the ornate style.

Instead of translating from Isocrates himself I will take a passage from Samuel Johnson which shows, as well as anything in English can, the form of the Isocratean sentence.

The reader will find here* no regions cursed with irremediable barrenness, or blessed with spontaneous fecundity, no perpetual gloom or unceasing sunshine; nor are the nations here described either devoid of all sense of humanity, or consummate in all private and social virtues. Here are no Hottentots without religion, policy or articulate language, no Chinese perfectly polite, and completely skilled in all sciences. He will discover, what will always be discovered by a diligent and impartial inquirer, that wherever human nature is to be found, there is a mixture of vice and virtue, a contest of passion and reason, and that the Creator doth not appear partial in his distributions, but has balanced in most countries their particular inconveniences by particular favours.

The antitheses and internal correspondences in sense and sound of this passage are Isocratean, though Johnson learned to produce them not by study of Isocrates but from those English and Latin authors who had absorbed the lessons of Isocrates. So potent and persistent can be a literary tradition.

In order to produce his balanced clauses Isocrates had often to multiply words, so weakening the force of the thought he wished to express. Again, the resemblance of sentence to sentence in general structure produces an effect of monotony. (We feel this monotony in Johnson and Gibbon when they are not holding us, as they generally are, by the interest of their matter.) The ancient Greeks were connoisseurs in the art of composition, and the incomparable skill of Isocrates in this could hold their attention much longer than it holds ours. But even their attention would flag at last. To move a popular audience some modification of his style became necessary. This was finally effected by Demosthenes, and his speeches enable us to see how it was done. He did not break up the symmetry of the Isocratean period but he destroyed its monotony. He has no superfluity of words because he does not pursue concinnity for its own sake by multiplying doublets and synonyms for that purpose, as

* That is in Lobo's *Voyage to Abyssinia*, to which Johnson is writing a Preface.

Isocrates and Cicero, the stylistic heir of Isocrates, too frequently do. Though his style is on the whole ornate and therefore Isocratean, he constantly varies his periods, quite in the manner of Burke, with short, stabbing sentences which often verge on the colloquial. He reasons too more closely than Isocrates and as it were more legalistically. Above all he pours into what he says an energy of passion and imagination quite beyond Isocrates. This is shown in his bolder use of figurative language and in the number and picturesqueness of his metaphors and similes. He is almost certainly the greatest of orators.

As it is wholly impossible to give an adequate notion of Demosthenes' style by brief citation, and as his positive influence on later prose was less than that of Isocrates and the more florid orators of the Hellenistic age, which immediately followed that of Demosthenes, I will say no more of him here but pass at once to Cicero, the principal master of Latin eloquence. It must be said of Cicero that he clearly perceived the supremacy of Demosthenes and owes a great deal to him. But Demosthenes was in a sense above imitation and he had lived three centuries earlier. It was not possible for Cicero to escape altogether the literary fashions of his own generation. Two were prevalent, and these were opposed to one another at every point. One was florid, diffuse, emotional—the 'Asianic' style; the other plain, concise, restrained—the 'thin' (*exilis*) or, if you wished to be polite, the 'Attic' style. The temperament of Cicero, mobile and immensely articulate, predisposed him in youth to favour the exuberant Asianic style. But he saw its faults and in time he acquired a style of his own, more diffuse and highly coloured than that of Demosthenes, a splendid medium for his emotional eloquence. In form it was Isocratean, like the Asianic style, which might be described as decorated or flamboyant Isocratean, but became increasingly restrained in the use of ornament, though still using it a good deal more lavishly than Demosthenes. Here is part of a famous passage—the peroration of the second speech against Antony.

Remember then that day, Marcus Antonius, on which you abolished the dictatorship. Set in your mind's eye the joy of the senate and the Roman people; contrast it with the monstrous traffic in which you and yours are now indulging; you will then perceive the gulf that lies between glory and gold. But as some people cannot enjoy their food because of some disease or insensitiveness of palate, so I suppose lustful, avaricious, unscrupulous men have no taste for the approval of decent people. Yet if such approval cannot tempt you to behave with honour, are you not deterred from your foul offences by your very fears? For the law you care nothing. If this is because you are innocent, I gladly accept your explanation. But if it is because you trust in force, do you not see what a man has to fear whose reason for not fearing the law is no better than that? If brave and high-minded patriots cause you no apprehension because your armed guard keeps them from your person, your own supporters, you may be sure, will not tolerate you any longer. But what sort of existence does a man lead who lives day and night in fear of his own friends? You can hardly pretend, can you, that you have attached them to yourself by greater obligations than those which the dead dictator bestowed on some of those who put him to death, or that you can be in any respect placed on an equality with him. Caesar was a man of genius, with great powers of memory and organisation, a scholar, a thinker, an administrator; his military achievements may have been disastrous to his country, but at least they were great; for many years he had prepared himself to exercise absolute power, and at the cost of great risks and great exertions he reached the goal of his ambition; by free shows, by new public buildings, by doles, by feasts he won over the mob. He put his friends under obligations to him by rewards, his enemies by a show of clemency; in short he succeeded in inducing a habit of submission to his personal rule in a free state half afraid of him and half acquiescent. I find it possible to compare you with him in your lust of domination, but not in any other respect. Yet the many searing evils inflicted by him on our country has had one good result: the Roman people has now learned how far this man or that deserves its trust and confidence, and of whom it must beware. Do you never reflect on that? Do you not understand that it is enough for men of character to have learned how noble the deed, how dear the benefit, how proud the fame of destroying a tyrant? If men could not tolerate him, will they tolerate you? I tell you that from now onwards there will be a rush of competitors for this work and that they will not wait too long for the opportunity to present itself.

Antonius, I implore you, have at long last some regard for your country. Think of the men from whose loins you are sprung, not of those with whom you are now living. With me deal as you please, but be friends, as once you were, with your native land. But it is your own affair; I shall say what *my* course of action will be. I defended the liberties of my country when I was young, I will not desert her in my old age. I scorned the swords of Catiline; I shall not be terrified by yours. Nay I am ready to offer my life, if by the sacrifice of that the freedom of my country can be re-established here and now, so that at last from the pangs of the Roman people may be born that with which it has been so long in labour. Twenty years ago I said in this very temple that for a man who had been consul death could not come untimely. How much more truly can I say it now that I am old! Two wishes and two only are left me now. The first is that with my dying eyes I may see the Roman people free; Heaven could not grant me a greater boon. The second is that the recompense of each of us may be measured by his service to our country.*

The influence of Cicero upon the history of prose far exceeds that of any other writer. What happened was this. The Greek orators had, during the fourth century before Christ, worked out a standard prose based on the principles of rhetoric. Each orator had a contribution to make; but, while they play their variations on the instrument, the instrument itself they received from one another. When Cicero began to write there was no such standard in Latin. He was the man who supplied it. Being by nature an orator, and having been

*Phil. II *ad finem.*

educated like other young Romans to admire and imitate the Greek masters of eloquence, he devoted himself to the reproduction in Latin of all the arts and graces of Greek rhetoric. He succeeded almost too well. In spite of the fact that there were always some critics and dissentients, in spite of the fact that the natural idiom of Latin is not that of Greek, he remained the model for most subsequent writers of studied Latin prose. In the seond half of the second century the chief educationist of his time, Quintilian, lent his authority to the view that all the merits of Latin eloquence could be found and should be studied in Cicero. Quintilian's great book, 'The Education of an Orator' (*Institutio Oratoria*), survived entire to furnish the principles which guided the reformers of education at the Renaissance. Consequently the new writers nearly all strive to be as Ciceronian in their prose as they can. They found this harder to do in English than in Latin—thus Milton's Latin flows more easily from his pen and is better constructed than his English prose—but in the end they succeeded. The difficulty arose from the fact that English is a very different language from Latin and loses its idiomatic quality when it is forced into conformity with the classical tongue. Why then should the attempt have been made to assimilate them? Because it was thought that the Latin classics, and above all Cicero, had set the model for *all* good prose. This doctrine was inculcated in the grammar schools and universities. It was therefore inevitable that lads proceeding from them should think, when they came to write themselves, that they must try to make their English prose look like Latin. Consider again the case of Milton. Here is one of the greatest of modern writers, with a genius for style which has rarely been equalled. Yet he can hardly write English prose for thinking about Latin.

True, Milton is not a representative figure. He is neither typical of the early Renaissance nor of the later (mostly Protestant) learning, but mingles elements of both in a proportion not elsewhere successfully achieved. And much in him is natively English. When we take a general survey of our literature before his time we shall find it learning indeed from Latin but learning to do without it. In the centuries between, and including, Bede and Matthew Paris it was the normal habit of authors to write prose in Latin. Thus vernacular prose had from the first a rival and a model, not only in classical authors but also and much more in this home-produced Latin, which indeed was generally thought to be the only prose which could be regarded as literature at all. Moreover, the first efforts of vernacular prose largely took the form of translation from Latin, as when Alfred translated Boethius and Orosius, and this could only increase the tendency of English-writing authors to assimilate their medium to the older language. And if before the Renaissance the pressure of ancient or modern style was strongly felt, with the coming of the Renaissance it was naturally intensified. But it was also resisted, and this is perhaps the most significant fact in the history of English literature. The Renaissance only brushed England with its wing on its way from other lands. Classical scholarship —almost the only kind of scholarship which was greatly esteemed, almost the only kind which even existed then—after beginning so well with Grocyn and More and Linacre fell below the level maintained in the rest of educated Europe. Elizabethan literature is essentially a product of the native spirit, only influenced by the classics.

Wholly untouched by the new enthusiasm for classical style it could not be. We see that style affecting the prose of Lyly's *Euphues* books and of Sidney's *Arcadia*, although the manner of neither could be called Ciceronian. The Ciceronian phase in England came later—it is, in spite of Hooker, rather Jacobean than Elizabethan—as classical learning revived, bringing with it a more perceptive admiration for that high-built polyphonic prose which derived from Cicero. It would be difficult to find more ornate writing than Donne's Sermons or Milton's *Areopagitica* or Browne's *Hydriotaphia*. All three have got more poetical minds than Cicero, but he has still much to teach them. Only Browne (and he not completely) has mastered the structure of the period; the other two constantly lapse into sequences of disjointed and sometimes doubtfully grammatical clauses. Or take the translators of King James's *Bible*. As long as they were translating they had the wisdom or inspiration to follow the tradition of simple idiomatic English which had been founded by Tyndale, and everyone knows the beautiful result. But when they combined to write a Dedication to the King they felt that they must use a more Latin style. So they produce a sentence like this, perhaps the best in the whole composition.

For whereas it was the expectation of many, who wished not well unto our *Sion*, that upon the setting of that bright *Occidental Star*, Queen *Elizabeth* of most happy memory, some thick and palpable clouds of darkness would so have overshadowed this Land, that men should have been in doubt which way they were to walk; and that it should hardly be known, who was to direct the unsettled State; the appearance of Your Majesty, as of the *Sun* in his strength, instantly dispelled those supposed and surmised mists, and gave unto all that were well affected exceeding cause of comfort; especially when we beheld the Government established in Your Highness, and Your hopeful Seed, by an undoubted Title, and this also accompanied with peace and tranquillity at home and abroad.

The structure of this sentence is very closely modelled on that of a Ciceronian period; in fact it is so closely modelled that it almost ceases to be an English sentence and looks like a rather dull translation.

Towards the end of the seventeenth century we find signs of a reaction against the ornate style beginning with Dryden, or even with Hobbes and Cowley, in the direction of a more idiomatic English. This movement continues into the eighteenth century carried on, for example, by Addison and Swift, both very 'classical' writers so far as the form and structure of their sentences go, yet both preferring the plain to the ornate style. But the ornate style never died out. We find it revived by Swift's friend Bolingbroke and, nearer the middle of the century, by Samuel Johnson, whose style is perhaps the most Ciceronian in the language. That style, as everybody knows, had enormous influence and—coinciding with the rise of journalism—it led to johnsonese, of which Johnson himself was rarely guilty. His true descendants are Robertson and Gibbon and Burke, although each of these imposed his own character upon it. The revived ornate style had, however, learned something from its rival. After Addison and Swift it was not possible to offer the public the ramshackle sentences of Donne and Milton; the syntax of Johnson and Robertson is impeccable. This was an immense, a transforming improvement; it produced standard ornate prose. The Romantic Movement felt itself out of sympathy with Johnson and his generation; yet the Romantics themselves favoured an ornate style. We have Landor and De Quincey; then later Ruskin, Pater, Stevenson. All these contrive the 'complex' sentence, the history of which goes back to Cicero.

CHAPTER ELEVEN

THE APOPHTHEGM

IN MATURE classical prose the typical sentence is the period, which we have now perhaps sufficiently described and discussed. One of its tendencies is that, throwing out in its tree-like growth symmetrical and corresponding branches, it may, as in Isocrates and in Cicero, proliferate too abundantly. But this tendency is not at all inevitable. The period can be controlled, its extension can be made intensive, it can pack more meaning within its limits than may be found in a string of simple sentences. Gibbon can put in a page what Macaulay puts in a chapter. In this respect (though not in others) Gibbon is the more classical author. Concentration is one of the great principles of classical art, hardly enough insisted upon in books of literary criticism, though abundantly recognized by the historians of ancient sculpture and painting. To simplify, to clarify, to concentrate meaning was a principal aim of the best Attic prose. Of the Attic writer that is true which Joubert says of himself. 'If there is a man upon earth tormented by the cursed desire to get a whole book into a page, a whole page into a phrase, and this phrase into one word—that man is myself.'* At any rate it is true in general and in spite of some notable exceptions, which perhaps are not true exceptions at all. Contrast Lysias or Demosthenes with Jeremy Taylor or Burke, Thucydides or Tacitus or Sallust with Macaulay or Carlyle or Grote or Froude.

It might be argued with a show of reason that the Greek love of a concentrated clarity was not, originally at least, artistic but had an economic cause. To write a book in the sixth or even the fifth century before Christ was for the ordinary man an

*Matthew Arnold's translation.

expensive business. He had to provide himself with a special kind of skin prepared in a particular way or with strips of papyrus imported from Egypt; and that cost money at a time when it was harder to earn a penny than it is now to earn a pound. He could not afford to waste an inch of his precious material. He had therefore an important incentive to brevity, and this would become even more important if he desired to make a more permanent record of his words on bronze or marble. But the true explanation is to be found not here but in the Greek artistic consciousness. To achieve his purpose by the fewest possible means is with the classical artist—architect, sculptor, potter as well as writer—a sort of instinct. It was there from the first. If it was once the habit to think of Homer and Herodotus as garrulous old men, a better-informed criticism does not think so now. Let anyone read Odysseus' tale of his adventures as he related them to king Alcinous or any of the stories in Herodotus, and he will marvel at their economy of words.

I use the word 'apophthegm' to denote a type of sentence to which Greek utterance naturally, though by no means inevitably, tends to adapt itself. It is a word one does not find much used now, but there seems to be no other that is not misleading. For the apophthegm is neither an adage nor an epigram, at least it need not be. It is just a saying of concentrated meaning. If it is humorous or witty, as it must often be, that is an accident, not a property, of the apophthegm. Phocylides of Miletus said, 'The people of Leros are bad—not one bad and another good, but all bad, except Procles. And Procles is a Lerian.' This drew from Demodocus the retort, 'The Milesians are no fools, yet they behave as if they were.' Here are two Greeks writing about six hundred years before Christ what may be the two best epigrams ever composed, the expression in the original Greek being supremely neat and elegant. The feeling for style they show takes one's breath away, just as the feeling for style in Homer takes one's breath away. Here is the classical style—the power of saying notable things in a crystalline way—in perfection from the very first.

The two apophthegms I have quoted happen to be amusing —they are epigrams. But to be amusing or even witty never seemed to the Greeks a very noble ambition, and this despite the fact that they were such witty and amusing talkers. Perhaps a better way of putting it would be to say that for them the important thing in an amusing writer was not so much what he said as how he said it. In this they were probably right; what delights us in Falstaff or Uncle Toby or Mrs. Gamp is the way in which they speak. It is certain that the Athenians admired Aristophanes less for his jokes—there were other comedians who made them laugh more or at least louder—than for his style with its Attic grace and quicksilver agility. Our business then in this chapter is with the apophthegm as an element of style, not with the wit or wisdom of its matter. And we must exclude the proverb because, although it may be regarded as a kind of apophthegm, it is found in all languages and is not particularly characteristic of the Greeks. Reluctantly I have also had to exclude the memorable sayings of unique persons as not sufficiently representative, for I can deal only with broad currents and general tendencies. I therefore omit the strangely impressive prose oracles of Heraclitus, which remind one only of themselves or, sometimes, of the aphorisms of William Blake. On the other hand Democritus, a philosopher less remote from the centre than Heraclitus, may be quoted. 'Happiness does not reside in flocks or in gold; the spirit that makes a man happy has its dwelling place in his soul.' A commonplace now perhaps, but not when Democritus said it. 'You must either be a good man or behave like one.' Is that true? If it is, it is an important contribution to ethics. An apophthegm, however, need not state a moral position, it need only be pregnant and memorable. Democritus said 'I came to Athens and no man knew me.' Could anything be simpler? Or harder to forget? When Aristippus, another philosopher, was asked why sages were seen at the doors of the rich, but the rich never at the door of a philosopher, he replied that this happened because 'the sages know what they lack and the rich do not'. This was not offered as a witticism but as the concise statement of a fact. The philosophers rather specialized in such pithy comments. I need not quote those attributed to Diogenes the Cynic, they are too well known. Perhaps the least well known to English readers is the most interesting. When asked what his 'mission' was Diogenes replied 'To deface the currency'—meaning no doubt by currency or coinage Greek conventional notions of right and wrong. 'If a mouse, finding nothing to eat, nibbled a hole in the bag, that is not news; if the bag ate the mouse, that is news.' It was 'Bion the Borysthenite' who said that, not some newspaper proprietor. Ariston of Chios said that those who neglected philosophy and went in for—shall we say popular journalism? —were 'like Penelope's suitors, who when they could not get the lady contented themselves with her maids'. When a proposal was made that gladiatorial games on the Roman model should be exhibited in Athens the philosopher Demonax rose in his place and said that, if the Athenians adopted the proposal, they should first 'pull down the altar of Pity'.

Some of these sayings have an epigrammatic look in modern eyes. Yet those who uttered them were not so much trying to be epigrammatic as to pack their meaning into the fewest and most expressive words. Greek art rather avoided than sought the modern type of epigram; it was the Romans who developed that. There is a famous anecdote about Alexander the Great which may illustrate the point. Alexander was offered extraordinarily favourable terms of peace in his war with Darius. His general Parmenio exclaimed, 'If I were Alexander, I would accept them.' 'So would I,' said Alexander, 'if I were Parmenio.' It sounds witty. But it is certain that Alexander had not the least intention of being smart or witty. Was he not Alexander? He was only stating, as plainly and briefly as he could, the difference between himself and Parmenio. His words are an apophthegm, not an epigram. Like the others I have quoted they reveal an instinctive dislike of diffuseness. This dislike we find everywhere among the best classical authors with, as I observed, some notable exceptions. But they are exceptions of the kind that proves the rules. The most eminent is Plato. There can be no denying that Plato is on the whole a diffuse, sometimes an exceedingly diffuse, writer. But then he is writing dialogues, in which he feels bound to aim at the effect of conversation, which is naturally diffuse. He had also to reckon with the unfamiliarity of general ideas to the public for whom he was writing. Socrates was almost the first man to discover that general ideas existed at all. A contemporary Athenian might speak of 'goodness', but what he meant by that was the goodness of such and such a man, a horse, a sword, a lyre; he had not asked himself whether there was such a thing as goodness in itself existing apart from the particular cases in which he recognized it. It was unspeakable the difficulty which Socrates had in driving into people's heads what he himself meant by 'goodness' or 'justice' or 'courage' as things in themselves. He had to use illustration after illustration, and to repeat himself over and over again, before he could get them to understand. Hence Plato's diffuseness. When he was telling a story he did not use more words than Herodotus. A similar explanation may be given of the diffuseness we often find in the orators. They were addressing popular audiences on matters in which they needed instruction or persuasion, and it is notorious that the only way in which even one new idea can be instilled into a popular audience is by iteration and reiteration. When the orators are dealing with known facts they are as concise as other people; the 'narrations' of Demosthenes are masterpieces of compression. The exceptions then are no exceptions.

It is necessary, however, to get two points clear, and I will take them in order. The first is this. The typical Greek apophthegm is not 'striking'; on the contrary it is unemphatic. It should no doubt be impressive, but it should be quietly impressive. This creates a difficulty, too often insuperable, for the translator; what is perfectly phrased in the Greek will in his version often seem commonplace. The apophthegm in fact depends on the truth or justice of what is said and not on any surprising or challenging way of saying it. Plato is one of the greatest of prose-writers and his works are voluminous, yet hardly any great writer is less quotable; he depends on the aptness, not the effectiveness of his words. And this is true in general of the best Greek prose. It has an aphoristic, an apophthegmatic, but not an epigrammatic character.

The other point which needs to be emphasized is that what I have been saying applies only to the best, the typically classical, prose. Such prose was always profoundly admired in antiquity and from time to time it was revived, Lucian being one of those who sought to revive it. But these movements were sporadic and could never be long maintained against the spirit of later ages. As early as the beginning of the fourth century before Christ if not earlier it was attacked by rhetoric; attacked and at last destroyed. It would be possible to describe the effect of this attack by saying that the apophthegm became the epigram. The transition was gradual and perhaps never quite complete. When Lamachus, who was a contemporary of Thucydides, said 'In war one is not permitted to make a mistake twice', when Aristotle about a century later said 'One swallow does not make a summer' and 'Education is learning to take pleasure in the right things', when Euclid a generation after Aristotle said 'There is no royal road to geometry', they were uttering apophthegms, not epigrams, because they were not trying to make a point. But when Tacitus makes the Caledonian leader Calgacus say of the Romans, *ubi solitudinem faciunt, pacem appellant*, 'where they make a solitude they call it peace', that is an epigram, because it has been carefully framed by a master of rhetoric to make you jump.

It was in fact Roman authors who were chiefly responsible for the change. It is too late to blame them now, if indeed they deserve to be blamed. For on occasion they made superb use of the epigram, and an author is always justified in practising what he does best. Certainly the epigram as Tacitus for instance uses it, for a satirical or tragic purpose, is a wonderful literary device, not exactly of his own invention, for we find it in a less subtle and perhaps even in a less poetical form in the poet Lucan. Literature is enriched by such expressions as *omnium iudicio capax imperii, nisi imperasset*, as *felix opportunitate mortis*, as *es immitior quod toleraverat* ('the more savage because he had suffered'), as the sentence about the ladies who called on Agrippina, the mother of Nero, after she had lost her influence at court, *nemo solari, nemo adire praeter paucas feminas, amore an odio incertas* ('none consoled her, none visited her except one or two women out of love—or hate'), as *praefulgebant Cassius atque Brutus es ipso quod effigies eorum non visebantur* ('The busts of Brutus and Cassius were conspicuous by their very absence').

The epigram, however, never became, even in Tacitus, the characteristic form of the dictum or apophthegm. That form is called *gnomé* in Greek, *sententia* in Latin. Very often it is a generalization crystallised in words the most few and apt. For the ancients loved to generalize just as the moderns love to particularize; they were interested in the type, we study the individual. We may say at least that this is broadly true, and it is with broad differences that this book must be concerned. It is therefore only to be expected, and it will be found, that ancient authors are full of *gnomai* and *sententiae* except in those genres, such as the mime, where a point is made of particularity. They do not appeal greatly to modern taste because, however neatly expressed in Greek or Latin, what they say has become obvious or even platitudinous. The ancient reader, however, was more interested in the form than in the substance of the *sententia*, which aimed at being 'what oft was thought, but ne'er so well express'd'. The critic who hopes to understand literature in its historical development and is not content merely to express his personal preferences must judge the *sententia* with this knowledge in his mind. He need not travel out of English literature to find it. It is at least as common in the Middle Ages and the eighteenth century as in Greek or Latin. If he cannot sympathise he can always try to understand. Why was the *De Consolatione Philosophiae* admired so much in the Middle Ages? Why was the *Rambler* admired so much in the eighteenth century? These are historical problems and the historian of literature must try to solve them. Readers were not more stupid then than now; probably as a whole they were less stupid, because only the comparatively intelligent could read. There has evidently been a change of taste, which may have been produced by a surfeit of 'sentences'. It is a change of taste for the form of expression rather than the thing expressed, though we see this better perhaps in poetry than in prose. The meaning of a piece of contemporary writing is generally not recondite when we have made it out. The eighteenth century sought for the clearest words; we search for the most suggestive.

It might give a false impression to quote a great many 'sentences', because the brilliant would outshine the more typical. It will be more instructive to give a continuous passage from an author in whose style the *sententia* has a special importance. Such an author is Seneca, for it was his 'sentences' which chiefly accounted for his very notable influence on mediaeval and Renaissance authors.

We ought not to raise our hands to heaven or wheedle a sacristan into letting us go close to the ears of the holy image as if that could give us a better chance of being heard. God is near you, is with you, is within you. That is what I say, Lucilius: a sacred spirit is lodged within us who keeps watch and ward over the evil and the good that befall us. He treats us exactly as He himself has been treated by us. Verily there can be no good man without a god. Can anyone

rise superior to fortune unless aided by Him? He supplies him with
high and noble thoughts. In every good man there 'dwells an unknown god, but a god'. If you come upon a thick forest of old trees
exceeding the average height and blocking out a view of the sky by
a roof of boughs which cast their shade over one another, the height
of the trees, the loneliness of the scene, awe of so deep and unbroken
a gloom in the open country will create in you belief in a divinity.
And if a mountain overhangs a cave where the rock has been deeply
eaten out—not an artificial grotto but a cavern hollowed out by
natural causes to that great depth—your soul will be pierced by a
religious feeling. We worship the head waters of great rivers. The
sudden uprush of a mighty stream from the depths has its altars; the
sources of hot springs have a ritual assigned to them; some lakes have
been sanctified by their gloom or their unplumbed profundity. If
then you see a mortal not terrified by danger nor seduced by
temptation, happy in adversity, calm in the thick of the storm, will
not a veneration for him steal over you? Will you not say *That is
too great and high a thing for us to believe that it is like the wretched body in
which we find it?* That divine power has entered the body from above.
The supereminent soul that controls its passions, that passes through
all experience as if it were of no great importance, and smiles at all
our hopes and fears, is animated by some celestial potency. So great a
thing cannot stand firm without the support of a god. For that
reason it has its being for the most part in that heaven from which it
has come down. As the rays of the sun do indeed touch the earth but
have their being in the luminary from which they are emitted, so the
great and holy soul, which has been let down into this body of ours
that it may have a closer view of things divine, associates indeed with
us, but clings to its source. By that it holds fast, towards that it looks
and strives; it moves in our world as a superior being. What then is
it? The soul, which looks for support to no good but its own.*

Seneca can go on like this for ever. Carlyle mischievously
called him the first Anglican bishop. There is some historical
justice in the observation, for it seems unquestionable that
Seneca had much influence on the development of the more

Epist. XLI.

literary type of Christian sermon. Let any reader who cares to take the trouble count the references—very often wrong—to Seneca in Chaucer's *Tale of Melibeus*, which is a translation of a French translation of an earlier composition more a sermon than anything else. The sermon was not a Christian invention but was used by the Church to inculcate the new religion.* No doubt a popular audience or congregation would find a Senecan discourse to be over their heads; but Seneca did provide a model of how to influence a cultivated audience. Any objection to quoting or imitating him was removed when the fiction was accepted that he had been converted by St. Paul. What made him so useful to the preacher was that for every moral, and most religious, sentiments he was sure to have some bright generalization. It is hardly credible how much the Middle Ages, or the monkish (which was also the literate) part of it, delighted in 'sentences', whether drawn from Tully or Seneca, from Cato or Publilius Syrus. For one thing they looked well in a sermon. Narrative prose was on the whole unaffected. But the didactic prose of which the Middle Ages seem to have been quite inordinately fond gets more and more sententious; it was the mediaeval way of being sophisticated. Cicero in his ethical treatises, Seneca in all his work, are more and more quoted and imitated. Style becomes more apophthegmatic. The tendency survived the Renaissance. We find Erasmus, the most influential of all the later scholars, making a great collection of what he called *Adagia*, drawn from Greek and Latin sources. These are proverbial or semi-proverbial sayings, which can hardly be described as apophthegms but are nearly all concise and pointed in the manner of the apophthegm. This collection was enormously popular and had a distinct influence on vernacular prose. But it in no way supplanted Seneca, whose fame on the contrary had been mightily increased by the discovery, or

*There were three words, *sermo*, *diatribe* and *homilia*—our 'homily'—all used to describe the kind of discourse to be heard from an ancient, especially a Cynic or Stoic, philosopher.

re-discovery, of his tragedies, which are at least as aphoristic as his prose. Of course, he had rivals in influence, even more powerful rivals, such as Cicero, who contributed far more even than Seneca to form the pattern of Renaissance prose. Yet the love of the pithy saying (which, of course, Seneca did not create but only reinforce and which is perhaps natively English) was by no means damped down by enthusiasm for the rounded Ciceronian period, and against Hooker and Sidney may be set Bacon and Jonson and Burton. In the upshot we get a style which aims at mingling the different virtues of the apophthegm and the period. It is the style of a good deal of Bacon (not the Bacon of the *Essays*), and later of Sir Thomas Browne and Burke.

And therefore, restless inquietude for the diuturnity of our memories unto present considerations seems a vanity almost out of date, and superannuated piece of folly. We cannot hope to live so long in our names, as some have done in their persons. One face of Janus holds no proportion unto the other. 'Tis too late to be ambitious. The great mutations of the world are acted, or time may be too short for our designs. To extend our memories by monuments, whose death we daily pray for, and whose duration we cannot hope, without injury to our expectations in the advent of the last day, were a contradiction to our beliefs. We whose generations are ordained in this setting part of time, are providentially taken off from such imaginations; and, being necessitated to eye the remaining particle of futurity, are naturally constituted unto thoughts of the next world, and cannot excusably decline the consideration of that duration, which maketh pyramids pillars of snow, and all that's past a moment.*

An examination of this passage will show that it is by no means purely Ciceronian in character, though it must be called Ciceronian in its structure and lineage. We do not expect, as we do not find, in Cicero so much that is sententious and

Hydriotaphia V.

aphoristic. When we read *Christian Morals* it is rather of Seneca we are reminded than of Cicero. We may say that Browne gets his effects by blending the two strains in such a way as to give scope to a more poetical imagination than belonged to either of the Romans.

Let me now quote a famous passage from Burke.

It is the love of the people, it is their attachment to their government from the sense of the deep stake they have in such a glorious institution, which gives you your army and your navy, and infuses into both that liberal obedience, without which your army would be a base rabble, and your navy nothing but rotten timber. Magnanimity in politics is not seldom the truest wisdom: and a great empire and little minds go ill together. If we are conscious of our situation and glow with zeal to fill our places as becomes our station and ourselves, we ought to auspicate all our public proceedings on America, with the old warning of the Church, *Sursum Corda*.*

It can be seen how between the first and last sentences, which are of some elaboration, there intervenes a *sententia*, expressed in two different ways, exactly in the manner of Seneca. It is not that Burke is imitating Seneca, or thinking of Seneca at all. But he is equally a master of the style we associate with the name of Cicero and of the style we associate with the name of Seneca, and he has learned to interweave them in a manner which mutually enhances them.

On Conciliation with America.

CHAPTER TWELVE

PHILOSOPHICAL PROSE

THE literature of a people reflects its mind, and this makes it necessary for the student of a literature to attend to the thought expressed in it; for unless we know what a man is saying we cannot judge how well he is saying it. There is a tradition of thought, permeating classical literature, which has come to permeate also mediaeval and modern literature, and that to an extent which is often inadequately recognized, at any rate by critics who dispense with the historical point of view. It is true that this country has made an original contribution to the general stock of European ideas. But a good deal even of that starts from positions already occupied by ancient speculation. We are, of course, not called upon to touch on the history of thought except so far as it has found expression in English prose. But to that extent we are bound to touch on it.

It seems right to begin with Plato, because he is the first European thinker about whom we have sufficient evidence, and because most subsequent philosophy is the result of agreement or disagreement with him.

It is probable that Plato's chief interest was in ethics. He desired in the Greek phrase 'to make men better in their cities'. The only question was how to produce this result. Plato thought it could be done by education—education of the soul. The ordinary Englishman feels like saying, 'Education of the mind, perhaps—but of the *soul*?' Plato did not feel this distinction. He had received from his old friend Socrates the doctrine that in some sense virtue is knowledge. You cannot be good unless you know how to be good. Out of this arises the question, 'What is knowledge?' If it is to be real knowledge, it must be knowledge of the truth, not of mere appearances. Of these we can *know* nothing. We may get impressions of them, we may form opinions about them, but know them we cannot. Now we live in a world of appearances; so the truth must be elsewhere. To the question, 'If we cannot know the truth about the world perceived by our senses unless we discard the evidence of the senses, what is it that we can know?' Plato replies, 'Objects *not* perceived by the senses'. To the ordinary unphilosophical man such a view seems merely paradoxical. But philosophers do not think it so, even when they do not accept it. And it has had a very great and remarkable history. We are therefore bound to consider it a little further.

Plato's own words will serve better than any explanation by another. Here is a passage from the *Phaedo*, a book which has had an incalculable influence both on philosophy and on religion, for it (and not the Bible) first gave reasons for believing in the immortality of the soul. The first speaker in my extract is Socrates—the *Platonic* Socrates.

'Do we say that there is such a thing as the just *in itself* or not?'
'Of course we say there is.'
'And such a thing as the beautiful and the good?'
'Certainly.'
'Now have you ever seen anything of the sort with your eyes?'
'No.'
'Well, did you perceive it by means of any other of the bodily senses? I mean perceive the *essence* in each case of all such things— size, health, strength and so on? Is the absolute truth of them perceived through the bodily senses? Or is it like this? Whoever among us has prepared himself in the most thorough and correct way to comprehend the essence of the thing he is studying will come nearest to knowing it?'
'I quite agree.'
'Then would not this be done in the most luminous way by the man who should grapple with each particular object as far as possible by the unaided intelligence without adding sight to the

credit side of his account in his thinking, or dragging after him any other of the senses along with reason, but by means of pure thought alone should seek to track down each object in its reality absolutely by itself, freed as far as may be from eyes and ears and in a word the whole body as a disturbing factor which does not permit the soul to acquire truth and wisdom when associated with it? Is such a man, Simmias, not more likely than another to touch reality?'

'What you say, Socrates, is exceedingly true.'*

Then after a little Socrates sums up in these words.

'Well then, must not the effect of all these arguments on men whose wisdom is genuine be that they come to form an opinion of the kind that leads them to say to one another something like this? *Surely there is some cross-country path which will bring us out? For, so long as we have this body of ours, and our soul is kneaded up with such evil in it, we shall never find ourselves sufficiently in possession of what we desire, and what we desire (say we) is the truth. Endless is the trouble which the body procures us, because it has to be fed; moreover, if we are attacked by ill health, our ailments hamper us in the pursuit of the truth. It infects us with fears and fancies of every kind and much silliness, so that really and truly it never gives us a chance, as people say, of thinking about the truth at all. For from the body and its passions we get nothing but wars and broils and battles. For all wars are the result of a desire to get money, which the body, in our slavery to its service, forces us to feel; the consequence of all this being that we never have time for study. The worst of all is that, if we get some respite from it and take to study, it always turns up again in our researches, troubling and disturbing and dismaying us, so that we cannot reach the truth because of it.'†*

How then are we to correct the distorting reflections cast by the senses? By the use, Plato says, of a faculty possessed by the human soul which operates independently of them—a faculty which resembles what we call reason. It is for instance by reasoning, not by looking or measuring, that a geometer proves that the square on the hypotenuse of *any* right-angled

Phaedo 65d.   †66b.

triangle is equal to the sum of the squares on the other two sides. For clearly he cannot measure every right-angled triangle. The philosopher is a man who has educated this reasoning faculty to such a degree that he has discovered more of these eternal truths than other people. These truths are not abstractions; they are truths *about* certain things, real things, in fact the only real things. These things Plato calls 'ideas'—which are therefore not what *we* mean by 'ideas'. And the best thing a man can do, thinks Plato, is to study these eternal, substantial forms—the 'Ideas of Plato'.

Now the natural sciences do not aim at this kind of truth; they are content to observe phenomena, which is simply Greek for 'things that seem', that is 'present themselves to our senses'. But these are the very things which, according to Plato, are not real and not true. Still some kind of existence they have, if only the existence of shadows; a shadow must be cast by something. It might have been expected that Plato, holding such views, would be disposed to think lightly of the physical sciences. In fact he gave much thought to them. Will not examining the reflection of a thing give one some notion of the thing reflected? He was of opinion, however, that scientists should not present their 'results' as if they were finally and absolutely true. When he himself wishes to indicate such results he prefers to do it through the medium of a 'myth', by which is to be understood a story that gives not the truth itself but an image of the truth. In telling it he employs a special style, touched with archaism and poetry, suggestive of the old religious myths and strangely beautiful and majestic.

Instead of attempting to translate such language I quote a passage from the *Somnium Scipionis* of Cicero, which is a myth in the Platonic manner composed by a great, if inferior, master. The speaker is Scipio Africanus the Younger, who relates what he heard in a dream from the spirit of the Elder Africanus now dead, which he met (in his dream) in a heavenly region among the stars.

I gazed on these things with amazement and, when I had recovered my senses, 'What', said I, 'is this overpoweringly strong and enchanting music that fulfils my ears?' 'It is', said he, 'that which, divided by unequal and yet proportionately separated intervals, is produced by the onward rush and movement of the orbs themselves and, combining high notes with low, makes a harmony of varied sounds; for not in silence may such mighty motions go on, and it is in the order of things that the extremes should give forth a high note on one side and a low note on the other. Wherefore that highest star-bearing movement of the heavens, the revolution whereof is more rapid, moves with a high and lively sound, but this lunar and lower sphere with a sound that is very deep. For the earth, which is the ninth sphere, abiding unmoved remains ever steadfast in one station, occupying the central place of the universe. But those eight revolving spheres, of which two have the same speed, produce seven distinct notes, which number may be called the mystic knot of almost all things; and musicians imitating this movement on harp and in song have opened for themselves a way back to heaven, as have others, men of genius who in their human lives have pursued divine studies. With this sound filled full the ears of men have grown deaf to it; nor is there in us any duller sense, as we find exemplified in that race, dwelling near where the Nile casts himself down from towering mountains at the place called the Cataracts, which by reason of the loudness of the sound has lost the sense of hearing. Similarly on earth so loud is the sound of the whole universe in swift revolution that men's ears cannot take it in, in like manner as ye may not gaze directly upon the sun, but the sharpness of your vision is overpowered.*

I had another reason for quoting this passage. It was here that later ages found that doctrine of the music of the spheres which interested them so deeply. But the whole *Somnium Scipionis*—it is very short—has had an extraordinary influence. It appears to have started the literary Dream or Vision which, developed by Boethius and advancing through the Middle Ages, culminates in the *Divina Commedia* and the *Roman de la Rose*, though it by no means ends with them. As for the matter

*Somn. Scip. 5.

of the *Somnium*, it is only partly Platonic. (The music of the spheres is a Pythagorean notion and older than Plato, who uses it for his own purposes.) It reflects Stoic thought, but Stoic thought influenced by Platonism. We have also to take into account the fact that the *Somnium* came to the Middle Ages embedded in an extensive commentary by Macrobius, a scholar working about A.D. 370. Macrobius had a leaning towards Neoplatonism and has interpreted the *Somnium* along the lines of that. Since his commentary was received in the Middle Ages with the same unquestioning credence as the text, a kind of Platonism mixed with a good deal of unplatonic speculation was propagated through what used to be called the Dark Ages. For it was Plato rather than Aristotle who influenced the mind of Europe in these earlier centuries. It was only with Albertus Magnus and his pupil Thomas Aquinas that the influence of Aristotle began to prevail, and it did not wholly prevail till the fourteenth century.

There was a revival of Platonism at the Renaissance, beginning (so far as the West was concerned) in Italy, at Florence, where a Platonic 'Academy' was founded. Here was developed an aspect of Platonism which had not been considered to any serious extent in the Middle Ages: indeed the evidence (which is found for the most part in the *Symposium*) was not then accessible. In his *Symposium* Plato introduces a long discussion of love, and this was taken up by the new Academy. Now therefore and for long after European literature is full of discussions of and references to Platonic Love. What was understood by this it would be hard to say; what Plato meant is explained in the *Symposium* where the belief is expressed that the soul of the lover could beget beautiful conceptions in the soul of the beloved. This belief should be viewed in the light of Plato's conviction that truth was more like to be won from the earnest converse of mind with mind than by the solitary enquirer. That was one main reason why his writings took the form of dialogues.

F

The dialogue as a literary form was apparently not invented by Plato, but it was he who showed what could be done with it. In his hands it becomes the vehicle of almost every movement of the human spirit—wit, irony, humour, indignation, intellectual rapture, intellectual subtlety. None of his successors could boast that range of expression. Lucian, who writes largely in dialogue, is content to be amusing and satirical, and it is the Lucianic type of dialogue which on the whole has been most successfully practised among the moderns. But the more serious (and difficult) type of dialogue has also been cultivated. In particular the more literary-minded philosophers, seeing how Plato used the medium, were tempted to try their own hands at it. Berkeley in his later writings, after he had been making a special study of Plato, used the dialogue form with the happiest results. Hume used it too, not unskilfully. And not only philosophers; authors with a turn for reflection, Dryden in his essay *Of Dramatick Poesie*, Landor in his *Imaginary Conversations*, Fitzgerald in his *Alciphron*—these with others have transplanted the dialogue into English literature, though not always directly from Plato. But directly or indirectly it comes from him. Just as without Herodotus history might never have become a branch of literature, so but for Plato it might not have occurred to later philosophers that they need trouble themselves about the form in which they expressed their views. It has not occurred to some of them even yet.

Plato's influence can never be measured with accuracy because so much of it has been indirect. Thus the Fourth Gospel, with all that has flowed from that source, is strongly tinctured here and there with Platonism. So is the *De Consolatione Philosophiae*, which the Middle Ages reverenced next to the Bible. Who can estimate the effect of all this? It may be seen in English literature as least as early as Chaucer. In Chaucer's time, however, Plato was hardly known in his own writings except through an inadequate Latin version of the *Timaeus*, which gives in mythical form what he thought a probable account of the creation of the world and of man. This the Middle Ages accepted without much or any criticism. Then came the Renaissance and, with it, a far more exact and extensive knowledge of what Plato actually said. Three dialogues in particular were found impressive: the *Phaedo*, which spoke of the immortality of the soul—it was studied, it will be remembered, by Lady Jane Grey under Ascham's tuition; the *Republic*, first and greatest of Utopias; the *Symposium*, which treated of love. Ficino's Latin commentary on the *Symposium* was studied in England, and to England came the Platonist Giordano Bruno, the friend of Sir Philip Sidney. Galileo and Michael Angelo were both platonically disposed. In this country Spenser wrote his platonic *Hymnes*. In the seventeenth century we find a school of 'Cambridge Platonists'. The universities began (and continue) to produce a succession of learned students and expositors of Plato. All this could not but affect our writers. Wordsworth is affected, Coleridge is affected, Shelley is strongly affected. In prose Ruskin, Matthew Arnold, and Pater without being Platonists reflect the influence of Plato. He has given a new direction to the thoughts of men.

For many centuries his influence was conveyed through Latin channels, mainly of course translations of his work. We have seen how strong and continuous it has been. But Plato is the philosophers' philosopher; for the plain man he is too lofty and difficult. The plain man's philosopher was Cicero. Although in ancient times he owed his reputation to his oratory, it was his philosophical writings that attracted the Middle Ages. For in them Cicero was discussing topics of absorbing interest to mediaeval men in language they could understand. Here is the opening of the third book of the *De Officiis*, a treatise on moral obligations in the form of an open letter from the writer to his son Marcus, then a student at Athens.

My dear Marcus, there is a passage in Cato which says that Publius Scipio—the Scipio who was first called Africanus and was a somewhat older contemporary of the author—was in the habit of saying that he was never busier than when he had nothing to do, and never less alone than when alone. It was a grand saying, worthy of a great and wise man, signifying that it was his custom in moments of leisure to plan what he was to do and when he was alone to hold debate with himself, the consequence being that he was never idle and did not need sometimes to talk over things with another person. In this way two things which bore the rest of us—leisure and solitude—were to him a stimulus.

You see with what art the reader is lured to read on. And he did read on, for this book, known to our forbears as *Tully's Offices*, had a vast popularity from the Dark Ages to the nineteenth century. Its opinions entered into the general consciousness of Europe and have helped to form modern standards of conduct. Cicero was the first great man of letters to write on philosophical subjects without claiming to be himself a philosopher. How many have followed his example, especially in this country, where so many of our best thinkers have wished to be thought no more than amateurs of philosophy! This has resulted in their being taken too readily at their own estimate in countries where philosophy is more formidably technical. But literature has gained, because the amateur of philosophy generally tries to write in a style free from the jargon of the profession. So we have not many better prose-writers in the language than Bacon and Hobbes and Berkeley and Hume.

Next perhaps to the *De Officiis* in its influence upon the mediaeval mind was the treatise *De Divinatione*, which discusses the question whether it is possible to foresee the future. Quintus Cicero, the brother of the orator, argues that it is and quotes some anecdotes in support of his belief. The Middle Ages loved these anecdotes. The one I shall now extract is perhaps the best known, because it was versified—though apparently not from Cicero—in Chaucer's *Nonne Preestes Tale*.

There is another dream which admits of a perfectly clear interpretation. Here is the story. Two close friends, Arcadians, who were travelling together, came to Megara. There one of them took up his quarters with an innkeeper, while the other went to stay with a host. After dinner they went to bed. There in his first sleep the friend who was a guest dreamed that the other appeared and begged him to come to his aid because the innkeeper was plotting his death. The first action of the terrified sleeper was to get up, but then after collecting his wits he decided that the dream must be disregarded, and went back to bed. He had fallen asleep when his friend again appeared and begged him, since he had not come to his help when he was alive, not to let his death go unavenged, explaining that after he was murdered he had been flung by the innkeeper into a cart and had dung thrown over him, and he asked his friend to go in the morning to the city gate before the cart could get out of the town. This dream did strongly impress the sleeper, and in the morning he met the carter at the gate and asked him what was in the cart. The other fled in terror, the dead man was extricated and, the truth being revealed, the innkeeper was executed.*

The *De Officiis* and the *De Divinatione* were within the capacity of anyone who could read Latin at all. But other parts of Cicero's philosophical works are harder. In these he undertook the very difficult task of making more refined and abstruse speculations intelligible to persons who found it beyond them to understand these in the original Greek. By his time two systems of thought had succeeded, without superseding, Platonism, which in fact outlived them both. These were Stoicism and Epicureanism. There is remarkably little difference that we can see in the practice of the good Stoic and the good Epicurean, for each aimed at serenity of mind and sought happiness in helping his fellowmen. But they differed widely in theory. To the Epicurean it appeared that the world was composed of atoms, which could only obey their own laws and the mechanical forces acting in conformity with these. Gods there

*I. xxvii. 57.

might be, but he could find no evidence of divine intervention or even interest in human affairs. The Stoic (with whom on this point Cicero wholly sympathises) could not bear that thought. He held that the world *was* ruled by God—an intelligent, beneficent God. This sounds quite Christian; but when a Stoic was questioned further he gave some curious answers. God, he said, governed the world by penetrating it like a kind of subtle fire, so that he necessarily conformed in shape to the world, which was globular. Listen to an Epicurean in Cicero who fastens on this point.

You Stoics are also in the habit of asking us what sort of life the gods live and how they pass the time. Truly their life is such that nothing happier or richer in every blessing can be imagined. For God, as we believe, does nothing, is involved in no activities, labours at no tasks, rejoices in his own wisdom and goodness, has full assurance that he will be in enjoyment of the greatest pleasures for ever. Such a god we aver to be truly happy, while yours we maintain has a most laborious existence. For if your god *is* the world, what can be less restful than to turn without a moment's intermission about the axis of the sky with astounding rapidity—now nothing restless can be happy—or if he is *in* the world, a god who rules and governs it, keeps the stars in their courses, preserves the changes of the seasons and the ordered alternations of events, and contemplating all lands and seas keeps watch over the welfare and lives of men, surely he is involved in troublesome and toilsome affairs. We Epicureans on the other hand lay it down that the happy life is found in peace of mind and freedom from all active duties.*

And here is part of a Stoic answer.

Also you found fault with those who, when they had looked upon the universe itself and its members, the sky, the lands and the seas, with their ornaments the sun, the moon and the stars, and had come to know the maturities and changes and alternations of the seasons, had from these majestic and glorious works drawn the conclusion

*De Nat. Deorum I. xix.

that there existed some surpassing nature which had created these things and moved, regulated and guided them. Even if they are wrong, I can see the line of reasoning which they follow. But what mighty and excellent work can *you* point to, which you regard as the creation of a divine mind, leading you to infer that gods exist at all?*

It will be observed that these are rather rhetorical questions than arguments, and I am afraid that is the tendency of a good deal of Cicero's philosophical writing. Yet it was a great work he did—historically considered, a work of inestimable value. By the mere force of events, by the turn taken by human history, he became the chief interpreter of ancient thought not only to his Roman contemporaries but to the whole Latin-speaking world, to the Dark and the Middle Ages, to modern times up to and into the eighteenth century. From him the mediaeval philosophers drew much of that terminology which they have transmitted to the modern—words like 'quantity' and 'quality'—and even Voltaire, even Hume speaks of him with respect. The historian must take note of these facts; he is not concerned with the value of Cicero's contribution to European thought but with the extent of it. And that can hardly be overestimated.

It is now somewhat the fashion (at least among historians) to depreciate the achievement and even the character of Cicero, who can easily be made to appear a vain and garrulous person and an ineffective politician. But there is such a thing as a history of historians, and when we study that we find that the opinion commonly, though far from universally, entertained now about Cicero differs widely from that held of him by our ancestors. And it is their opinion, right or wrong, which a book of this kind must take into account. We note then that up to the nineteenth century he was generally reverenced as a wise and good old man. This was in the main due to his philosophical works, above all, it may be conjectured, to his

*Nat. Deor. I. XXXVI.

little treatises or essays on Friendship (*De Amicitia*) and Old Age (*De Senectute*). It is true that the sentiments which found favour in the *De Senectute* were taken to be the sentiments of the author himself. The little book was so widely read that an extract from it will help to complete the picture of the man in literary history.

I do not see why I should not make bold to tell you what I myself think about death, for I believe that the nearer I am to it the better view I have of it. Your father, Publius Scipio, and yours, Gaius Laelius, men of the highest distinction and firm friends, are in my judgment still living, and living that life which alone deserves the name. For as long as we are shut up in the prison of this body of ours we are performing a task and heavy service imposed on us by natural law. For the soul is a heavenly being which has been thrust from its high home and as it were plunged to earth, the region that is opposed to the divine nature and to eternity. It is my faith that the immortal gods gave each human body a soul in order that men might view the earth and, as they gazed on the orderly motion of the heavenly bodies, might imitate that in the consistent and orderly conduct of their own lives. And I have not been driven to this conclusion by reason and reflection alone but also by the authority of great and eminent philosophers. When I was a student I used to be told that Pythagoras and the Pythagoreans, who were at one time called the 'Italian' philosophers and might be regarded as compatriots of ours, never doubted that our souls were drops from the fountain of the divine intelligence that pervades the universe. I also had explained to me the arguments which Socrates, whom the oracle of Apollo declared to be the wisest of all men, used on the last day of his life concerning the immortality of the soul. In short I convinced myself and still feel that, since the soul possesses such mobility, such a memory of things past and foreknowledge of things to come, so many arts and sciences and new ideas, it is impossible that such a substance, naturally possessing such qualities, should be mortal; that, since the soul is always in movement without anything to set it moving, because it moves itself, it will not have an end to its movement, because it will never be parted from itself; that, since it is in its very nature one, without intermixture of anything unequal or unlike to itself, it cannot be broken up, and if it cannot be broken up, cannot be destroyed; and that a strong proof that men are in possession of much knowledge in a pre-natal state may be found in the fact that when a child is old enough to learn a difficult subject he picks up countless facts so quickly that it is obvious he is not hearing them for the first time but is recollecting or remembering.—These are, roughly, the arguments we find in Plato.*

As Cato says, this is Platonic teaching. The truth is that Cicero had no settled or systematic philosophy of his own. That probably did him no harm with English readers, who have never been enamoured of philosophical systems. He is chiefly engaged, either by way of criticism or commendation, in expounding the tenets of Stoicism, which in his day was the most influential system or creed among the more intellectual circles of Roman society. One says system or creed because it is possible to regard Stoicism as either or both. After Cicero its chief Latin expositor was Seneca. He was hardly less of an amateur, but he had a good deal of Cicero's literary skill and dexterity. In style, however, he is very dissimilar. He does not compose in rounded periods but in short, antithetic, rather epigrammatic clauses somewhat loosely strung together—'his mortar is all sand' was the criticism of the mad, witty emperor Caligula. It is a somewhat teasing style, at any rate to English readers, who prefer a more restful manner—perhaps a national prejudice, for Seneca has always pleased the Spanish and the French, and has had a great influence on their writers. Even on English literature his influence at certain periods has not been small, and that not simply in the development of Tud- or and Elizabethan tragedy. It was the Seneca of the moral treatises for whom the Middle Ages had most regard, and such influence as he had on English prose was a consequence of this admiration. It was as a moralist too that his reputation

*De Sen, XXI,

maintained itself as late as the eighteenth century. Consequently we must say something about him in that capacity.

Here is a fairly typical example of his manner. His subject is 'tranquillity of mind', which we should now rather call 'serenity of spirit'. It was what the Stoic most desired to have.

Yet nothing can give us such heartfelt pleasure as a loyal and dear friendship. What a blessing it is when we have someone to receive us with open arms, one to whom we may safely confide every secret, whose intimacy you fear less than your own self-knowledge, whose words soothe your anxiety, whose opinion helps you to make a decision, whose cheerfulness scatters your gloom, the very sight of whom makes you glad! It should be premised however that we shall as far as possible choose for our friends men who are free from the lusts and desires. For the vices stalk us and then spring upon the nearest victim. Their touch is dangerous. Accordingly, as during a plague we must be careful not to sit beside persons who have already contracted the disease, and in whom it is taking its course, because we shall be exposed to the danger and suffer from infection, so in our choice of friends we shall pay attention to their characters, so that those we adopt as such may be as stainless as possible. To mingle the healthy with the sickly is the beginning of illness. This does not mean that I am advising you never to seek or attract the friendship of anybody who is not a wise man. For where will you find that ideal being whom we have been looking for through all the ages? Instead of the best man we must be content with the least bad. It would hardly be possible for you to choose anyone better than that, if you were to seek for good men among the Platos and Xenophons and that famous brood that came from the Socratic nursery, or if it were given you to make your choice from the generation of Cato, which produced very many who were worthy of being born in the age of Cato just as you would find many worse men born then than at any other time; for Cato needed a large number of both kinds to bring out his qualities. He needed to have both good men whose approval he could win and bad men to test the force of his character. Today, when good men are so rare, we must not be too fastidious in our choice. But above all we should avoid gloomy and pessimistic people who never miss an opportunity of ventilating a grievance. A companion of that nature may be steadily loyal and kind, but he is an enemy to our peace of mind with his unrelieved distress and depression.*

These observations are more sensible than profound. But an author is entitled to be judged by his intention; he must not be condemned for not doing something which his critic would have preferred him to do. The *De Tranquillitate* might be described as a lay-sermon, and so judged it is admirable. A lay-sermon must not be over the heads of those who hear it, and yet must be striking enough to hold their attention. A writer who can thus combine brilliance and intelligibility will always have readers, and therefore Seneca always had them. It would have been easy for him to be more 'profound', for he was a very clever man and could make a great show of his very considerable reading. There is a good deal of the essayist in him, and he, next to Plutarch, contributed most among ancient writers to form that climate of the mind, favourable to free speculation on moral and personal problems, which made possible the *Essais* of Montaigne and the *Essays* of Bacon.

The lay-sermon had long been cultivated under the name of *diatribe*, first perhaps by Cynic philosophers but later also by Stoics. Seneca brought it up to date and made it fashionable, often disguising it in the shape of letters to friends. What follows is part of a celebrated letter.

Nature rules this visible kingdom of hers by means of change and succession. Cloudy is followed by fine weather; storm succeeds a calm at sea; one wind blows and then another; day comes after night; one part of the starry heavens rises, another sets; the eternity of the world is established by its internal oppositions. To this natural law we must adjust our minds; this they must follow, this obey; and let us believe that whatever happens was bound to happen, and not hurl abuse at Nature. It is best to endure what cannot be

De Tranq. Animi VII.

cured, and without murmuring to follow God, from whom all things flow. He is a bad soldier who follows his commander with a grumble. So let us vigorously and cheerfully take our orders and not leave the ranks in the marshalled movement of this glorious creation of which all that we suffer forms an essential part, and let us address Jupiter, by whose pilotage that mighty ship is steered, in the eloquent verses addressed to him by our Cleanthes. I may be allowed to translate them by the example set by the eloquent Cicero. If you like them, I can only say thank you; if you don't, you will know that I have here followed Cicero's example.

> Lead me, O father and lord of the lofty heavens,
> Wherever it has seemed good to thee. There is no delay in
>   my obedience;
> Here am I, eager to do. Suppose me reluctant, yet shall I
>   follow groaning.
> Fate leads the willing, drags the unwilling wight,
> And if bad I shall suffer what if good I might have suffered.*

One cannot but admire the skill with which Seneca presents these far from original moralizations. He had in a very high degree what the Elizabethans meant by 'wit'. Perhaps more than any other ancient author he (though now so little read) taught later ages how to treat a moral topic. On that account they felt profoundly indebted to him. Whenever a mediaeval author preaches or moralizes you are pretty certain to find many references to Seneca and borrowings from him. But we can discover or reasonably surmise much later traces of his influence. Portia's speech on Mercy is astonishingly like a Senecan *diatribe*. Even Hamlet's most famous utterance is not unlike a Stoic discussion of suicide. It is in the highest degree improbable that Shakespeare read the prose of Seneca; he was only dealing, on these two occasions, with an ethical topic in a more formal manner than was usual with him—a manner which had become naturalized in English literature but had been learned in the main from Seneca. In the same way the

Epist. CVII.

passion for moralizing, so characteristic of the Middle Ages, was not inspired by the classical moralists but was guided by them into certain channels of expression, by Seneca more than most. What it comes to is just this, that a writer who had been admired for centuries, numbering good intellects among his admirers, was bound to have an indirect as well as a direct influence.

We have already had to speak of Plutarch's *Lives*. But Plutarch was a philosopher as well as a biographer, and a considerable body of philosophical studies or essays has come down to us under the title of *Moralia*. Most of them, as the title suggests, treat of human behaviour. They are, at least to us, of very unequal interest, but the best of them are admirable—less perhaps for what they say than because of the man who says it, Plutarch having the essayist's gift of communicating his personality. But even if the intrinsic value of the *Moralia* were less than it is, we are bound to take notice of their influence. This was chiefly exerted after the coming of the Renaissance, when Plutarch was translated. A translation of the *Moralia* was made in 1603 by Philemon Holland, from which I quote this passage in the essay *On Superstition*.

As for the superstitious person, evill he is, but not able, to joy and take pleasure: for his heart is much like unto that city which Sophocles describeth in these verses:

> Which at one time is full of incense sweet,
> Resounding mirth with loud triumphant song,
> And yet the same doth shew in every street
> All signs of grief, with plaints and groans among,

he looketh with a pale face, under his chaplet of flowers upon his head; he sacrificeth, and yet quaketh for fear; he maketh his prayers with a trembling voice; he putteth incense into the fire, and his head shaketh withal; to be short, he maketh the speech or sentence of Pythagoras to be vain and foolish, who was wont to say: That we are then in best case when we approach unto the gods and worship them. For verily even then it is when superstitious people are most wretched and miserable, to wit, when they enter into the temples and sanctuaries of the gods, as if they went into the dens of bears, holes of serpents and dragons, or caves of whales and such monsters of the sea. I marvel much, therefore, at them who call the miscreance and sin of atheists impiety, and give not that name rather to superstition. And yet Anaxagoras was accused of impiety; for that he held and said that the sun was a stone: whereas never man yet called the Cimmerians impious or godless because they suppose and believe that there is no sun at all.

What say you then? Shall he who thinketh that there be no gods at all be taken for a profane person and excommunicate? and shall not he who believeth them to be such as superstitious folk imagine them, be thought infected with more wicked and impious opinions? For mine own part, I would be better pleased and content if men should say of me thus: There neither is nor ever was in the world a man named Plutarch, than to give out of me and say: Plutarch is an unconstant man, variable, choleric, full of revenge for the least occasion that is, or displeased and given to grieve for a small matter; who, if when you invite others to supper, he be left out and not bidden, or if upon some business you be let and hindered, so that you come not to his door for to visit him, or otherwise do not salute and speak unto him friendly, will be ready to eat your heart with salt, to set upon you with his fangs and bite you.*

One expects a lighter touch from our essayists now, but Plutarch must be seen in his own time and place. It will then appear how admirably he employed this kind of writing. Compare it with the moralizing prose of Chaucer, who is not only one of our best but one of our wittiest writers. Compare it in respect of readability even with Boethius, who is so good in other ways. By the side of these later men Plutarch is modern and 'civilized'. If his essays now bore us a little, the sixteenth and seventeenth centuries found him far from boring, and that is the kind of fact of which we are bound to take cognizance.

Contemporary with him or a little younger was Epictetus,

*From the essay *On Superstition* in Plutarch's *Moralia*.

who has always been a favourite with 'thoughtful' readers and has often been translated, a certain proof of popularity. There are few more sympathetic figures in ancient history. By birth perhaps a Greek-speaking Phrygian, he was brought to Rome, apparently as a slave, where he served in the household of a freedman of Nero. Somehow he got enough education—the freedman would be a rich and clever Greek—to make him acquainted with the subtle disquisitions of the Stoics; and he obtained his freedom. His intelligence and the beauty of his character attracted notice and he acquired a circle of pupils and admirers, who listened to what he said. When the emperor Domitian banished the philosophers from Rome, Epictetus settled at Nicopolis in Epirus. Here too he found a group of friends and disciples to console him for his exile and lameness and poverty. There is a reference to him by Matthew Arnold in a sonnet which acknowledges his deep indebtedness to Epictetus—

> *that halting slave who in Nicopolis*
> *Taught Arrian, when Vespasian's brutal son*
> *Cleared Rome of what most shamed him.*

Epictetus was a Stoic with a dash of Cynicism, which, of course, is very different from cynicism. But he does not greatly insist on the importance of dogma; for him the important thing is conduct. The reader is often surprised to note how close he comes to the sentiments and even the language of the New Testament, which was taking form in his lifetime. That no doubt has helped to commend his words to many.—What follows is taken from a passage on 'Providence', a typically Stoic conception.

You should not be surprised if the lower animals have all their bodily wants supplied—not only meat and drink but a place to sleep in, and no need of shoes or bedding or clothes, all of which superfluities are necessary to us. They were not created for their own sake but for our service, and nothing was to be gained by creating them with extra needs. Consider what it would mean for us to take thought not only for ourselves but for sheep and donkeys, how they are to be clothed, how they are to be shod, what sort of food they are to have, what sort of drink. A commanding officer finds his men already supplied with boots, uniforms and arms—it would be a sorry business if the colonel had to go about fitting his regiment with boots and regimentals. In the same way nature has created the animals born for our service so as to be already provided with all they need without requiring any more attention. This is why a single urchin drives a flock of sheep with nothing more than a stick. But as it is we dismiss the idea of being thankful that we have not to pay the same attention to them as to ourselves and blame God for not taking care of us. And yet surely to goodness any one natural fact is all a reverent and grateful man needs to give him a sense of Providence. I am not now asking for important illustrations of this; only look at the way milk is made out of grass, and cheese out of milk, and wool got from skin—who has done and thought of all that? 'Nobody', you are told. What a want of modesty and intelligence! . . .

If we were reasonable beings wouldn't it be our duty both public and private to sing hymns to the Deity, to laud Him and recount the sum of his benefits? Wouldn't it be our duty when we were digging or ploughing or eating to sing the hymn to God? 'Great is God for that He hath furnished us with these tools wherewith we shall till the ground; great is God for that He hath given us hands, a gullet, a belly, the power of growing imperceptibly, of breathing in our sleep.' We ought to sing a hymn of that sort on every occasion and follow it up with the greatest and holiest hymn thanking Him because He has bestowed on us the capacity to comprehend these blessings and to use our way of logical reasoning. What! Seeing that most of you are blind, was it not necessary that some one should perform the duties of this post and sing the hymn to God on behalf of all men? What else can I do, old and lame as I am, but sing the praise of God? To be sure if I were a nightingale, I would be doing what a nightingale does; if I were a swan, what a swan does. As it is I am a rational being—praise God I must. This is my function, I do just this, and I will not leave my post so long as it has been assigned to me; and you also I invite to join me in this song.*

*Discourses 16, de Providentia.

One catches from these words some of the thrill which this great moral genius must have communicated to his followers. Now perhaps he is little more than a name except to scholars. But it is a great name in moral philosophy, and something ought to be known about a man who seemed important to a long line of English authors from the learned divines of the seventeenth century to Matthew Arnold. He is part of our classical inheritance.

The next representative of ancient philosophy whose influence on literature has been too considerable to be passed over in silence is Plotinus, the founder of what is called Neoplatonism.* This influence was not exerted directly on Western thought but through the medium of such Latin authors as Augustine, Macrobius and Boethius. It is therefore our business to consult them and not the original (and very difficult) Greek of Plotinus himself. A very little may be said by way of introduction. Plato had argued in favour of the belief that the human soul is (so far) divine and akin to God. But the human soul is also implicated in human personality, and the question then arises how, without losing its individual character, it is to find its true self and completion in God. Plato had left the question open. Plotinus expressed the belief that the human soul could achieve union with God through a process which he calls 'ecstasy' and we now prefer to call the mystical experience. This belief is not unlike that which Paul entertained when he spoke of the *psyche* or 'soul' becoming *pneuma* or 'spirit'. At any rate the teaching of Plotinus was not out of harmony with Christian theology and had in fact a good deal of influence upon Augustine, who in turn exerted a deep and lasting influence on the religious thought of the Church.

A passage may be quoted from Macrobius which describes the transition from Platonic to Neoplatonic doctrine on the subject of death, natural and self-inflicted. It is given not on its merits as literature but for this reason, that it was read with

*His dates are given as A.D. 205–270.

passionate attention and interest throughout the Middle Ages as an authoritative pronouncement on matters which they considered of inexpressible importance to them.

But in this same dialogue Plato says both that death is to be desired by philosophers and also that philosophy itself is the practice of how to die. Now these two statements are on the face of them contradictory. But it is not really so. For Plato knows two deaths of a man. I am not for the present repeating what has been said above, that there is a death of the soul and a death of the animal; what he is asserting is that there are two deaths of the *animal*—the human animal—one of which is caused by nature, the other by virtue. For a man dies when the soul leaves his body after it has suffered dissolution by the law of nature; but he is also said to die when, his soul being still in his body, it is taught by philosophy to despise the allurements of the body and to divest itself of the pleasant snares of lust and all the other passions, and this is what we indicated above to be a consequence of the second order of virtues, which are meet only for those who are students of philosophy. This then is the death which Plato says should be desired by the wise; but the former—that which nature determines for all—he says should not be enforced or inflicted or invited, teaching us that we ought to wait for nature to act and explaining the grounds for this ordinance in language which he borrows from the business of life, which forms the staple of our daily conversation. He maintains that a man who has been thrust into prison by an exercise of official power ought not to seek to escape from it until the power itself which imprisoned him has permitted him to leave; for a secret flight does not mean the avoidance but the increase of his punishment. He adds that we are in the service of our masters the gods, by whose protection and providence we are guided, and nothing must be taken away against the master's wish from his possessions in the place where he has stored his own; and just as he who takes the life of another man's slave will not be void of guilt, so he who has sought his own end before his master bade him does not meet with acquittal but with prosecution. These suggestions of the Platonic school are developed by Plotinus. The soul of a man, says he, should be found after his death free from the bodily passions, but the man who violently thrusts it out of the body does not suffer it to be thus free. For he who inflicts death upon himself comes to this either because he is utterly weary of fate or from fear or hate of something—emotions which are all counted among the passions. Consequently, even if the soul was formerly pure from these defilements, it becomes defiled when it is thus expelled from the very body from which it issues. Secondly, death ought to be a liberation of the soul from the body, not an attachment to it; but a soul which has made a forced issue is more and more attached to the body. And surely for that reason souls thus forced out haunt the body or the burial ground or the place in which the violent deed was done; while on the other hand those souls which in this life free themselves by death from the bonds of the body are placed, even in their bodily life, in heaven and among the stars. And so he gives it as his opinion that of voluntary deaths only that is laudable which is contrived, as we said, by philosophic reasoning, not a weapon; by wisdom, not poison. He adds that the only natural death is when the body leaves the soul, not the soul the body.*

It is not easy for a modern man to keep present to his mind the absorption of the mediaeval intellect in questions about the life to come and about the nature and destiny of the soul. It haunts nearly all its serious literature and art. Of course, certain books of the Bible, notably the *Apocalypse*, answered these questions up to a point. But it was not thought heretical (though it might be dangerous) to seek further enlightenment from Plato and Aristotle, from Cicero and Seneca and the Neoplatonists. Yet the mysticism of Plotinus was easily perverted into a kind of spiritualism or even necromancy; and this met with the severest criticism from Augustine. Here is what he says about this development as he found it in the teaching of Porphyry, the pupil and biographer of Plotinus.

For Porphyry goes on to promise a sort of purification of the soul by means of magic (though hesitatingly and with a shamefaced kind of argument) while at the same time he declares that this art does not procure for anyone the return of the soul to God, so that you can

*Comm. Somn. Sc. I. xiii.

see him wavering in alternate opinions between the vice of unholy curiosity and his profession of philosophy. For at one time he warns us against this art as fallacious and as dangerous in actual practice and by law prohibited, while at another time, giving way to those who commend it, he says it is useful for cleansing a part of the soul—not the intellectual part, which grasps the truth of intelligible things, which have no resemblance to the body, but the 'psychic' part, which conceives images of corporeal things. The latter, he says, can by means of certain magical rites, which he calls 'initiations', be made fit and apt for the raising of spirits and angels, and for seeing gods. Nevertheless he admits that from magical initiations there comes no purification to the intellectual part of the soul to make it fit to look upon its God and perceive the truth of the things that really are. Finally he says that the rational, which he prefers to call the intellectual, soul can make its way to the upper regions, even if the psychic part of it has not been previously purified by any magic; the psychic soul, he goes on to say, is purified in some measure by the magician but not so far as to enable it to reach immortality and eternity. But although he distinguishes in this way angels and demons, arguing that the regions of air belong to the demons and the regions of aether or the empyrean belong to the angels, yet while recommending us to take advantage of some demon's friendliness, by whose upward pull anyone after death may be raised even a little from the earth, and while maintaining that the way of the angels to the upper regions is different, he does testify by a kind of forced confession that we ought to beware of associating with demons when he says that the soul after death in paying the penalty of its sins shudders at the worship of the demons by whom it used to be surrounded. Nor could he deny that the very magic which he commends as a means of winning the favour of angels and gods has dealings with such agencies as either themselves hate the purification of a soul or serve the arts of men who hate it.*

This, though a polemical, may be taken as a not unfair statement of certain notions entertained by Porphyry, a good and learned but somewhat muddle-headed man. He was not a Christian; indeed he wrote against the Christians; but he

*De Civit. Dei X. 9.

shared their interest in angels and demons. A belief in such beings was disseminated, from Persia and other Zoroastrian centres, centuries before the time of Porphyry and had come to be widely accepted, at least through all the eastern parts of the Roman Empire. Porphyry tried to harmonize it with Neo-platonism. A somewhat similar attempt was made in a book attributed to Dionysius the Areopagite, who according to the author of the *Acts of the Apostles*—that is Luke—met Paul in Athens. The book is very much later than Dionysius but, as its attribution was accepted by Christians, it was treated with the respect denied to Porphyry. Though it contains much dele-terious nonsense, it had for a surprisingly long time a power-ful influence on many minds in the Middle Ages and even later. For this reason it cannot be overlooked by the historian. It was one of the main sources of that angelology and demonology which we are continually encountering through all that tract of time. Even the Elizabethan, Jacobean and Caroline ages were exercised over the problems of angels and devils, and the possibility of witchcraft and magic. This comes out, some-times quite strongly, in their literature, and there are traces of it in Shakespeare himself.

The last name for which room can be found in this chapter is far from the least important; it is the name of Boethius. No book (except, of course, the Bible) influenced mediaeval thought so long as the *De Consolatione Philosophiae*. There must have been reasons for this, apart from the intrinsic merit of the book, and some may be suggested. One is the date of Boethius, which brings him to the verge of the Dark Ages. He was therefore nearer them, and the subsequent Middle Ages, than was Macrobius or Augustine, and in consequence closer to them in spirit. At the same time it was full of information about what the ancients said and thought, and this was precious to them, for they felt their ignorance. Also it made for edifica-tion, and this commended it to the monasteries, where most readers were to be found. These were almost accidental advantages. But, even if they had not existed, Boethius deserved to be read for his own sake. He was prevented by his subject from being very original—for what could be said about it that should be both new and true?—but he presents his matter with force and eloquence in excellent, if not quite 'classical', Latin. He is, besides, a charming lyric poet, imitative no doubt and 'literary', but genuinely, if not strongly, inspired. For one of the curious things about his book—I mean the *De Consolatione*, for, although many other works are attributed to Boethius, I can only speak of the most famous—is that it is divided into sections of prose separated by interludes in verse composed in a great variety of metres. It was the prose, however, that appealed to mediaeval readers, who were not at home with the classical metres. Thus we find Chaucer translating the verses of Boethius into prose; indeed they have been written as prose in the manuscript from which he was translating.

The *Consolatio* has the character of an allegorical Dream or Vision, a form more delightful to the mediaeval than the modern mind. Philosophy appears to Boethius as he languishes in prison bemoaning his fate.

Having silently revolved these things in my mind and used my pen to record my tearful plaint, it seemed to me that there stood before me towering over my head a woman of a very majestic countenance with eyes glowing and piercing beyond the common power of men, of a brilliant complexion and unexhausted vigour, though she was so full of years that in no wise could it be believed that she was of our generation. Her statue was of variable proportions; for at one time she contained it within the common measure, at another she appeared to strike the sky with the towering summit of her head; and when she raised her head thus higher she pierced the very sky itself, mocking the sight of mortals who gazed upon her. Her vesture was of the finest threads subtly wrought and made of an indestructible substance; and this vesture, as I afterwards learned from her own lips, she had woven with her own hands. A certain dimness due to long neglect, such as we see on smoke-grimed statues, had covered its surface. On the lower hem of it could be read the Greek letter *pi* embroidered; on the upper, *theta*. There were also to be seen clearly pricked out steps as of a ladder ascending and descending to either letter, whereby it was possible to mount from the lower to the higher. Yet that same vesture had been rent by the hands of certain violent men, who had carried off such little fragments as each could. Moreover in her right hand she carried certain rolls, but in her left hand she bore a sceptre.*

Philosophy is here an allegorical figure, but as Boethius presents her throughout his Dream she is a supernatural *person*, whose words and actions seem as operative as those of the Emperor. At any rate that was the impression she made on mediaeval readers, so that she is not truly comparable with the personifications which are so common in Silver Latin or eighteenth-century verse. The Middle Ages had no place in their art for mere abstractions. The virtues and vices become for them Virtues and Vices, superhuman persons. In this respect Boethius must have done much to create the taste by which he was enjoyed. For, although he could believe that he was only following the example of Cicero in the *Somnium Scipionis*, he was in fact introducing into literature the mediaeval type of allegory. He had to some extent been anticipated in this by Prudentius and others, and his contemporary Martianus Capella was allegorical enough in his 'Marriage of Philology and Mercury' (*Nuptiae Philologiae et Mercurii*). But Prudentius influenced only the poets, while the *Nuptiae* does not succeed as a work of art, and the *Consolatio* does. In considering the history of a literary form we must not count the failures.

The *Consolatio* is a dialogue between the prisoner and his visitant, which tends to become a monologue spoken by Philosophy. They discuss the nature of Fortune, Boethius complaining of her, the other justifying her ways to men on the ground that Fortune herself is God's minister. Fortune was at least as real a person to the Middle Ages as Philosophy. Indeed

*I, *Prosa* i. *pi* is the first letter of *practical*, *theta* of *theoretical* (wisdom).

centuries before Boethius a sort of Fortune-worship had become almost all the religion that the average citizen of the
Empire possessed. Juvenal had protested:

> nos te,
> nos, Fortuna, deam facimus caeloque locamus.*

Naturally the Christians also protested; but however much they
denied her divinity, they were slow to deny her existence. There
grew up an elaborate mythology about her.† Boethius and
Philosophy have both a perfect faith in the existence of Fortune
as a superhuman person; the only question between them is
whether she is benevolent or not. Philosophy argues that she is
and finally convinces Boethius, thus consoling him in his
troubles, which were not imaginary or sentimental but in fact
ended in his execution. Here is part of what she says:

It is certain that the entire globe, as you have learned from
astronomical proofs, must be reckoned as a point in comparison with
the extent of the sky; that is to say, if it is compared with the
immensity of the celestial globe, yours must be judged to occupy no
space at all. Now of this region, so exiguous a component of the
universe, only about a quarter, as Ptolemy has proved to you, is
inhabited by creatures known to us. If from this quarter you
remove in thought all that is covered by seas and lakes, and the whole
extent of the waterless desert, there will be left the tiniest area for
men to inhabit. Well then, confined and shut within this point, so to
speak, of a point, do you men dream of the spreading of your fame,
the publicizing of your name? What grandeur or magnificence can
belong to a glory bounded within such narrow and tiny limits?
Add that even this pinpoint of a narrow dwelling is inhabited by a
goodly number of nations, differing from one another in language,
customs and their whole way of life, to whom both by reason of the
difficulty of the journeys thither, of the diversity of their speech and
the rareness of our commerce with them not only the fame of

---

*'It is we, it is we who make a goddess of thee, Fortune, and put you in heaven.'
†It is summarised, a little grotesquely but not unfairly, by Fluellen in *Henry V* (III,
6): 'Fortune is painted blind', etc.

individuals but even of cities cannot come. Even in the age of Cicero, as he himself in a certain passage declares, the fame of the Roman republic had not crossed the Caucasus; and yet that fame was then full grown and to the Parthians and the other races of that part of the world even formidable. Seest thou not then how narrow, how limited is that glory which you men labour to extend and advance? Thinkest thou that the celebrity of one Roman man will advance where the glory of the Roman name can proceed no farther? Consider too that the different nations have diverse customs and institutions, so that what in one is judged to be worthy of praise is judged to be worthy of punishment in another. And so it comes to pass that, if any man is delighted by the proclamation of his fame, it in no wise serves him to seek the publication of his name among a multitude of peoples. Thus everyone will be content with the extension of his renown among his own people, and that glorious immortality of fame will be confined within the bounds of a single nation.*

It is not certain whether or not Boethius was a Christian. There is nothing either in the *De Consolatione* or in his other books inconsistent with Christian teaching, and by the Middle Ages (which may have preserved some tradition about him) his Christianity, if not his othodoxy, seems to have been taken for granted. It is true that he does not quote the Christian scriptures or look for comfort to them, but this has been explained by the consideration that he was discussing a philosophic, not a religious, problem and therefore restricted himself to philosophical arguments, which cannot be proved by an appeal to authority. We must say, however, that if Boethius was a Christian he was of a different temper from the Latin Fathers of the Church whom he might have been expected to resemble. He had read the ancient philosophers sympathetically, whereas the Fathers for the most part quote them only to denounce them. In this way Boethius performed for the Middle Ages the inestimable service of keeping them in touch with the genuine philosophical tradition, which otherwise

*II *Prosa* vii.

they might have lost. Anyone who read the *De Consolatione*—as Dante for instance did and Chaucer—would get a fair, though of course a far from complete knowledge of the true history of speculation, especially ethical speculation, in antiquity.

In Boethius the element of allegory has had so much historical importance that we are bound to pick up the threads of that subject again. Philosophers who considered a good deal in Homer to be morally indefensible had begun even before the end of the sixth century before Christ to explain away the objectionable passages by calling them allegorical. Although this method was repudiated by the best Homeric scholars, it found favour with many Stoic philosophers and, later, with many Neoplatonists, some of whom, notably Porphyry, carried it to extravagant lengths. Nor was it applied only to Homer. Philo of Alexandria, a Greek-writing Jew, who lived about the time of Jesus, applied it to the Old Testament, and was followed in this by some of the Christian Fathers. Before the dissolution of the Western Roman Empire allegory had become a literary fashion, whether in verse, as in the *Psychomachia* of Prudentius, or in prose. The fashion persisted up to the time of Martianus Capella with his *Nuptiae Philologiae et Mercurii* and of Boethius. Thereafter it took possession of the Middle Ages.

A history of literature must to some extent be a history of taste, and should therefore contain some discussion of the taste for allegory. It may be true that nobody cares for allegory now unless the story which embodies it is interesting in itself, so that the reader—for this is what it comes to—can forget about the allegory. But it was not always so. In the *Canterbury Tales* when Chaucer is called upon for his contribution he begins what is clearly a parody of the metrical romances in which the earlier Middle Ages had taken boundless delight. *Sir Thopas* is abundantly silly but it is also, in places, rather charming to a modern taste. But the Pilgrims will have none of it. Thereupon Chaucer says (in effect) 'Very well, then I will give you something you are sure to like' and proceeds to deliver a prose

allegory, *The Tale of Melibeus*, which is received by the cavalcade with pleasure or at least without protest, though to us a
thing of infinite tedium. It was just that they liked an allegory.
The *Consolatio* is only one, though no doubt the chief, source of
the interest shown by the later Middle Ages in the prose allegory.
That it was earnestly studied then is shown among many other
proofs by Chaucer's translation. No doubt the *Consolatio* is
not merely or even mainly an allegory. It is partly a piece of
the writer's autobiography, partly a contribution to what the
ancients called 'protreptic' philosophy (that is philosophy
designed to encourage the practice of virtue) and partly a
'myth' in the form of a dream like the *Somnium Scipionis*. But
inasmuch as the principal speaker is the personified or deified
Philosophy, the *Consolatio* has an allegorical character.

Since the allegory is nearly always a myth—though a myth
need not be an allegory—we must pay some attention to what
may be described as the allegorizing myth. It has had a great
influence on our own literature, which it is impossible here to
do more than indicate. To trace its development it is necessary
to begin with Plato. His works, as everyone knows, contain a
considerable number of myths, and these are often of an
allegorical nature. They present us with the same kind of
problem as the Homeric Poems do in the history of epic poetry;
the best comes first, the progeny is scarcely worthy of the progenitor, although prose allegory has its Bunyan just as epic
has its Milton. Of the allegorical myths in Plato most are too
long for quotation, but one (perhaps the shortest) may be
given. Plato has sketched in outline the structure of his ideal
state. But how is its permanence to be secured? It is half-
humorously suggested by Socrates that it would greatly help
towards this if all classes in the state could be led to believe
the fable which he now proceeds to relate.

'I shall try to persuade first of all the rulers themselves and the
warrior class, and then the rest of the citizens, that they were not in

actual fact brought up and educated by us in the way they supposed
—that was a kind of dream they had. In reality they were all the
while in the bowels of the earth being fashioned and reared, while
at the same time their arms and the rest of their accoutrements were
being wrought. Finally, when they were quite ready, Earth like a
childing mother brought them into the upper air. So now they have
a duty to consult and defend the interests of the land in which they
dwell as their mother and their nurse, and in all their plans to think
of their fellow-citizens as brothers born of the same Earth-mother.'

'No wonder you have been so long in finding the resolution to
come out with so bold a fiction!'

'Quite so; but you must listen to the rest of my tale. Developing
our romance we shall say to them, "All you, citizens of this state,
are brothers; certainly. But there is more than that. The god who
made you put an ingredient of gold into the composition of all
those among you who have the qualifications for being rulers, so
that they are your most valuable citizens; into those who are to fight
for you he put silver, and into the husbandmen and artisans iron and
copper. Now your children will for the most part be like their
parents; but, since you are all of one stock, now and again a silver
child will have a gold father or *vice versa*, and so on throughout the
possible variations. This therefore is the first and greatest commandment of the god to the rulers, that they shall be good and vigilant
guardians of nothing so much as the admixture of gold or silver
or copper in the souls of the children, and if one of their own
class is born with copper or iron in him, they are to harden their
hearts and thrust him among the artisans or husbandmen, thus
assigning to him the rank appropriate to his natural endowment.
But if it is the other way round and a child is born of the working
classes with gold or silver in his soul, they are to promote him to be
a ruler or a soldier, whichever he may be judged worthy to be,
alleging the existence of an oracle which prophesies the ruin of the
state if an iron or copper ruler shall rule over it.'*

Socrates calls this a myth or even a 'fiction'; but it may also
be called a parable or allegory. The description matters little so
long as we perceive that the telling of the story moves on two

*Republic III. 414d–415c.

planes, one on the surface and the other beneath the surface. It has implications beyond its immediate implication, and this gives it a parabolic character. Now many, and perhaps the grandest, of the Platonic myths are like that. An excellent instance is the myth in the *Phaedrus*. It would in fact be unintelligible if we did not know that it was an allegory. The soul, according to the Platonic Socrates, is immortal and therefore divine. But it is not uniform throughout and may be taken as divided—though not separated—into three parts: that which feels the bodily desires, that which experiences the nobler emotions, such as courage and 'righteous indignation', and that which is capable of reasoning. In the *Phaedrus* myth the soul appears as a composite creature with the form of a charioteer driving two winged horses, one good and the other vicious. The details of the myth may be left to the reader, but we can say at once that they form an elaborate parallel to, or metaphor of, what happens to a human soul in this life. We may say much the same of the famous simile of the cave in the *Republic*. It is an imaginative picture of human life and of what happens to the philosopher in it.

The myths of Plato have qualities which put them above imitation. But as they have always been admired, so they have often been imitated. Of ancient imitations the most successful no doubt is Cicero's *Dream of Scipio*. Whether it is strictly speaking an allegory is much to be doubted; it is rather an apocalypse, the revelation by a spirit of the true nature of the universe. But it was treated as an allegory by the commentator Macrobius, who preserved the *Dream*, and the Middle Ages read it with the eyes of Macrobius. The *Dream* has one feature, not derived from Plato, which is of extreme historical interest and importance; the myth (as the title implies) takes the form of a dream. In this Cicero was followed by Boethius, while Boethius, we may almost say, was followed by everyone who composed an allegorical tale in the Middle Ages. The device has certain obvious advantages, especially impressive in times

when it was believed that divine secrets were sometimes revealed to the dreamer. It might happen that a secret of the
next world was revealed (whether in a dream or not) by a
ghost or angel revisiting the land of the living or by someone
who had been apparently dead, like Er in the myth of Plato's
Republic. In any case it is necessary to take the Platonic myths
into account if we are to obtain a just view of the origin
and development of the story which implies more than it
avows.

But not only do we find the professed allegory; many
fictions, not originally meant as allegory, were given an
allegorical interpretation. We have seen that even in antiquity
this form of criticism was applied to Homer. But it came to be
applied to other authors and other stories than the Homeric.
The method may be illustrated by a quotation from Bacon,
who is here treading in the footsteps of some ancient critics.

They say that Narcissus was exceeding fair and beautiful, but
wonderful proud and disdainful; wherefore despising all others in
respect of himself, he leads a solitary life in the woods and chases,
with a few followers, to whom he alone was all in all; among the
rest there follows him the nymph Echo. During this course of life, it
fatally so chanced that he came to a clear fountain, upon the breast
whereof he lay down to repose himself in the heat of the day; and
having espied the shadow of his own face in the water, was so
besotted and ravished with the contemplation and admiration thereof, that he by no means possibly could be drawn from beholding his
image in the glass; insomuch, that by continual gazing thereupon, he
pined away to nothing, and was at last turned into a flower of his
own name, which appears in the beginning of the spring, and is
sacred to the infernal powers, Pluto, Proserpine, and the Furies. This
fable seems to show the dispositions and fortunes of those, who in
respect either of their beauty or other gifts wherewith they are
adorned and graced by nature, without the help of industry, are so
far besotted in themselves as that they prove the cause of their own
destruction.

Bacon, it will be observed, does not accept the story on its own terms as a popular explanation of why the wild jonquil grows beside pools in which it seems to be admiring the reflection of its own beauty; he turns it into an allegory. In this he was in no way singular among writers either before or since, but especially before, since the passion for allegory had run through the Middle Ages like a forest fire. It may be seen in the *Gesta Romanorum*, which resembles the Bacon passage in this respect, that stories gathered from all quarters are treated there as allegories of Christian life or doctrine. I do not quote the *Gesta*, because it has had no influence on the form of literature, having no form itself. But we cannot pass over in silence the fact of its prodigious popularity, for what sinks into men's minds must colour what they say. Of course, it does not stand alone. The allegorizing or Christianizing of classical (and not only classical) stories is a regular feature of mediaeval sermons and homilies. There was even an *Ovide Moralisé*, and it takes some ingenuity to moralize Ovid. We may say that the monasteries considered that the Devil ought not to have all the best stories and sought to baptize them. But this cannot be the whole explanation. The love of allegory was a *vera causa* outside the monasteries. We need that to explain the *Roman de la Rose*, the *Faerie Queene* and much else.

What of Bunyan? It is clear that his reading was almost confined to the Bible. Yet the *Pilgrim's Progress* is just as clearly in the tradition of the *Reuelacion to a Monke of Eushamme* (1196) and *Piers Plowman*. It is an allegory in the form of a dream. The modern distaste for allegory is not operative for the *Pilgrim's Progress*, because the story is so good a story in itself and the telling of it so vivid. Something of the same interestingness is felt when one reads Morris's *News From Nowhere* or *The Dream of John Ball*. To *The Pilgrim's Progress* we must add *The Holy War* and—still better—*The Life and Death of Mr. Badman*, which is an allegory drawn from life itself. Bunyan would not be conscious of any debt to former writers. But he was infinitely familiar with sermons which made use of moral anecdotes and apologues with a good deal of Heaven and Hell in them, and the idea of telling one of these stories in greater detail was bound to suggest itself to a man with such a genius for just that sort of thing.

Bunyan is not imitable and in any case was not imitated, for his works were thought to fall beneath the dignity of literature. The most significant allegories which follow him tend to be in verse, like *The Hind and the Panther* and—though this comes somewhat later—Mandeville's *Fable of the Bees*. As we are treating of prose we must pass these by, though it is worth noting that allegory in a more or less explicit form is rife in nearly all forms of literature in the age of Dryden and Pope. This helps to explain the success of *A Tale of a Tub* and Arbuthnot's *History of John Bull*, though we find the allegory rather teasing now and concentrate on the satire and the style. In Addison the tone is less contemporary, at least in allegory, where he is as classical as Lucian and almost as Plato. No essay of his was more admired than the *Vision of Mirza*, though one rarely sees even a reference to it now. It is a simple allegory of human life, seen as a ruinous bridge over which we all must pass, but it is written with that exquisite delicacy of style in which Addison embalms the obvious. It had a great influence and was much imitated through most of the eighteenth century, though later masters of the classical allegory tried to be a little less obvious. In this they succeeded, or partly succeeded, by giving a flavour of irony or satire to their fables. It may be enough to mention *Rasselas*, which, of course, is fundamentally an allegory or parable like *Candide*, and perhaps Goldsmith's *Asem*. (The inspiration of Beckford's *Vathek*, so far as it is not original, is rather French than English, and at all events not classical.) After this the interest in allegory begins to fade.

Or perhaps it has only taken a subtler form. We may call this symbolism or use some other name than allegory, but the thing meant is not very different. The consideration of this would, of course, lead us much too far. But since we are restricting our enquiry here to prose, and since the novel has become so important in modern prose, I may permit myself a word or two about that. And first I think that many who would not admit that poetry is 'a criticism of life' might think that the novel was or should be. But a criticism of life involves the capacity to rise from the particular to the general; we cannot look for it in a writer wholly immersed in the matter of his writing. We need not then be surprised to find in many of our best novelists a tendency in the direction of the allegorical, the symbolical, the 'general picture'. Thackeray must have felt this when he called his most brilliant novel *Vanity Fair*; and his moralizing, like that of Fielding, is haunted by the ghosts or moral personifications. But we lose the sense of this in the truth and vivacity of their detailed observation. Are not the stories in the Christmas books of Dickens allegories, though such as only Dickens would have composed? *The Picture of Dorian Gray* is an allegory, and so is *Dr. Jekyll and Mr. Hyde*. There is at least something symbolic in *Wuthering Heights*. One might go on adducing instances. Is not the reason why novelists like Galsworthy and Bennett and George Moore appear to have receded, while Henry James and Conrad have not, largely this, that intelligent readers become discontented with stories which carry all their significance on the surface and prefer those which suggest the ambiguity of life itself? Even the best detective stories do not derive all their interest from the process of detection or the strangeness of the incidents. The tale related for its interest as a tale will never be superseded, but it is accompanied by the narrative of undertones and remoter references. A lesson, a point of view is insinuated. There is even concealed, or half concealed, propaganda. Some of the ablest of contemporary novelists have as much of a design upon our consciences as any mediaeval fabulist. The desire to edify is still a source of stories.

G

CHAPTER THIRTEEN

PROSE SATIRE

PROSE satire was hardly a distinct genre—though verse satire was—either in Greek or Latin, mainly for the reason (surprising to a modern) that it was felt to be on the whole a branch or application of philosophy. That is why a chapter upon it may logically enough succeed a chapter on philosophical prose. In this as in that we must begin with Plato. No doubt there was a kind of prose satire before him; but, as it no longer exists, we can do no more than speculate about it. We know, however, that Plato took it up, refined it, transformed it; and prose satire for us begins with him. It begins with him and in him it achieved at once a finer quality than was ever quite attained by later satirists. The full compass of it obviously could not be exhibited except at great length, and the two excerpts I shall now give must simply be taken as indications.

My first quotation is from the dialogue called *Protagoras*. The hero—at any rate the subject—of the dialogue, Protagoras himself, was the most eminent of the Sophists. These were 'experts' in various branches of knowledge, on which they discoursed or lectured for a fee. Socrates would never have taken a fee for imparting any knowledge he possessed, but then he never professed to have any. On the other hand he was unable to satisfy himself that the Sophists had any either; what they had was the appearance without the reality of knowledge. Plato accepted this estimate of the Sophists. He also believed that as a class they were given to arguing for the sake of argument. Protagoras was no ordinary Sophist and Plato recognized that in his way he was a great man. When the news ran about Athens that the celebrity was actually in the city, staying with the wealthy Callias, the Athenian intelligentsia were quite excited. A friend brought Socrates along, and this is what happened:

When we reached the porch we stopped and continued our discussion of a point which had arisen on our way to the house. As we did not want to leave it unsettled before going in, we halted and argued the matter between us until we had reached agreement. Now the porter had evidently overheard us, and he must have been put in a bad temper by the stream of visitors—all of them Sophists. At any rate when we knocked at the door, he opened it and after one look at us said 'Ugh! Sophists!—Not at home.' And with that he furiously banged the door shut with both hands as hard as he could. We knocked again, and without opening the door he said, 'You there! Didn't you hear me say that Callias was not at home to you?' 'But, my dear man,' said I, 'we are not calling on *him* and we are not Sophists. Don't be alarmed. It's Protagoras we have come to see. So do take in our names.' Then at last the man opened the door.

When we entered we found Protagoras walking up and down the portico accompanied on one side by Callias with his half-brother Paralus and Charmides, and on the other by Xanthippus and Philippides and Antimoerus, who is Protagoras' most distinguished pupil and is studying his art with the view of becoming a professional Sophist. These were followed by a crowd of people who were trying to catch what was being said. Most of them had the look of visitors to Athens —Protagoras leads a band from every city he passes through, charming them with his voice like Orpheus, while they follow at his call—but some of the train were native Athenians. A sight that gave me particular pleasure was the careful manner in which they avoided getting in the way of Protagoras. I could not help admiring the graceful regularity with which these listeners divided their ranks to right and left whenever he made a turn with his companions. The way they wheeled round every time and then fell in behind was the prettiest sight in the world.*

The satire is unmistakable, though it does not go much beyond amusement spiced with what the French understand

*Protagoras 314c–315b.

by *malice*. But in the passage I am about to quote there is something far more dangerous. It is directed by the speaker (who is represented as an influential politician) against Socrates, who was in fact later put to death at the instigation of such men. The words of Callicles are therefore not to be taken as banter. He is fencing with the blade which was afterwards used to kill. Where then lies the satire? It lies in the revelation which Plato makes of a mind which he wishes us to hate. In other words it is not Socrates who is satirized by Callicles, but Callicles who is made to satirize himself. This is how he does it:

Some philosophy is all right for purposes of education; it is no disgrace for a lad to study it. But when a man now getting on in life goes in for philosophy, the thing becomes a farce, Socrates, and I have much the same reaction towards philosophers as I have towards people who lisp or engage in the amusements of children. When I see a small boy, at an age when it is still suitable for him to speak in that way, lisping or at play, I am pleased and think it nice and like a young gentleman and appropriate to his time of life. (When it comes to an urchin chopping logic I hate to hear *that*; it grates upon my ears to listen and I think it shows a lack of the right spirit.) But when I hear a grown man lisping or see him at some children's game, I consider it contemptible and unmanly, and I feel like kicking him. Anyway that is how I feel about the philosophers. When I notice a lad making progress in philosophical studies I am filled with admiration, it appears to me a suitable thing for him and I believe that such a youth is on the way to be a scholar and a gentleman, whereas the youth who has no command of philosophy seems to me to be on a different level and unlikely ever to rise to any fine or gallant achievement. But when it is an elderly man I see who has not shaken himself clear of philosophy but goes on practising it—that, Socrates, is a man who in my opinion ought to get a sound thrashing. As I said just now, he can't, even if his talents are of the highest order, help turning out an unmanly character when he keeps away from the centre of affairs in the life of the city and from those meeting places in which, as Homer has it, men win distinction; his fate is to spend what is left of his life in seclusion whispering with three or four beardless boys in a corner, and never uplift his voice in a single frank or lofty or spirited utterance. . . .

Do you not agree that matters are as I think they are in the case of yourself and the others who carry on with philosophy too long? Suppose yourself or any one else of your sort were to be arrested at this moment and marched off to prison charged with some offence of which you are not guilty, you would certainly not know how to conduct yourself, but would stagger about open-mouthed without knowing what to say. And when you appeared in court, if your prosecutor happened to be an unscrupulous rascal, you would be executed if he should choose to demand the death penalty.*

Callicles is thought to be a type, not an individual, as we hear of no politician of that name in the time of Gorgias or Socrates. If Plato invented him, his satirical intention is still more obvious. It is important, however, not to confuse the satire of Plato with his irony, although of course irony may invade his satire. The great prose satirists in English have generally been masters of irony as well—the capital instance is Swift. But the combination is not essential. It can, however, be of great value. A sense of the ironical will save a piece of satire from becoming mere invective; it is probably a deficiency in this sense which prevents Burke and Ruskin from being masters of satire, as they undoubtedly were masters of invective.

Plato is beyond successful imitation, and satiric writers in Greek prose who followed him could do so only at a distance and in one or in another of the directions in which he led the way. An original satirist did appear towards the end of the third century before Christ. This was Menippus of Gadara. His own writings are lost, but they influenced authors whose work has survived, or survived in part, such as Varro, Seneca, Petronius and Lucian. In form it was a medley of prose and verse. To Greeks who inherited the old classical tastes that must have seemed a startling, perhaps a shocking, innovation,

Gorgias 485a–486b.

for it was mixing two different mediums. But it caught on in a world now full of Greek-speaking Syrians and Mesopotamians and Egyptians. It would seem that Menippus (a Syrian) was a Cynic philosopher, and his satires may have been intended for so many popular sermons, for an ancient Cynic was a good deal more like John Knox than Lord Byron. But the truth is, we do not know.

The Romans liked to think that they had a natural turn for satire. Certainly the modern world has learned a great deal from their satirists both in verse and in prose. We must therefore deal with their prose satire at suitable length. There is not much evidence until we come to Cicero. His powers of ridicule and invective have always been recognized; but satire is to be distinguished from these. Not but what there is plenty of satire in Cicero. Here is an attack on the more paradoxical tenets of Stoicism softened by the critic's personal regard for the youthful Cato—so virtuous and so devoid of humour—who maintained them.

There was a man of immense intellectual power called Zeno, whose original ideas have been eagerly adopted by the philosophers who are called Stoics. He delivered himself of certain apophthegms and precepts such as these. 'The truly wise man is never moved by gratitude, and never forgives an offence committed by anyone.' 'A man should refuse to listen to arguments or appeals.' 'Nobody except an unwise and frivolous person is compassionate.' 'The wise alone are beautiful, wealthy, kings, even if they are most ill-favoured, most beggarly, slaves.' (On the other hand we who are not wise are runaway slaves, exiles, public enemies and, to crown all, mad.) 'All sins are equal; every offence is a wicked crime, and the man who twists the neck of a farmyard cock without necessity is just as guilty as the man who has strangled his father.' 'The wise man never merely "supposes", never feels remorse, is never deceived, never changes his opinion.' Our brilliant young friend Cato was induced by learned authorities to embrace this teaching not, as most do, as something to argue about but as something on which to model his

own life. The farmers-general make a request. 'Take care that
favouritism carries no weight with you.' Some poor unfortunates
come in the guise of suppliants. 'You will be a criminal scoundrel
if you take any action from a motive of compassion.' A man will
confess that he has done wrong and ask pardon for his offence. 'It is
a crime to pardon.' But, it may be said, the offence was trifling. 'All
sins are equal.' You have said something. 'It is fixed and decided.'
You were led to say it not by the truth but by an opinion. 'The wise
man has no "opinions".' You have made a mistake of fact. He
considers that you have slandered him. That is the teaching which
gives us sayings like these. 'I said in the senate that I would indict a
man who was a candidate for the consulship.' But you were angry
when you said it. 'The wise man,' says he, 'is never angry.' But you
simply took the chance to speak. 'It is characteristic of a bad man,'
he says, 'to deceive by a falsehood; to change one's settled view is
dishonourable, to let oneself be won over is a crime, to pity is a
scandalous thing.' Now the teachers who have influenced me—for I
will confess to you, Cato, that I too in my young days sought the
aid of instructors because I distrusted my own powers—my teachers,
I say, the famous successors of Plato and Aristotle, men who observe
the mean and moderation, affirm that the wise man is on occasion
capable of feeling gratitude; that it is characteristic of the good man
to feel pity; that there are distinct kinds of offences and different
penalties; that there is a place for pardon in the heart of a consistent
man; that the wise man actually does sometimes form an opinion
on a matter of which he is ignorant, that he is sometimes angry, that
he is not inexorable but placable, that he sometimes goes back on
something he has said, if that seems the fairer course, that he occasionally changes his views, that all the virtues find their direction in the
observance of a certain mean. If Fortune had wafted you, Cato, with
your natural endowments to these masters, you would be not indeed
a better or braver or more continent or juster man—that is impossible—but a little more inclined to gentleness. You would not be
bringing an accusation against a man uninfluenced by any personal
enmity to him, in no way wronged by him—an honourable gentleman of the highest position and respectability; you would consider
that, since fortune had placed Murena and yourself in charge of the
same year, you had been in a manner linked to him by this bond

attaching you to the state; the very strong language you held in the senate you would either not have uttered at all or you would, if you could, have put a milder interpretation on his actions. I will add that you yourself, now so passionate and impulsive, carried so high by the force of your temperament and genius, and full of enthusiasm freshly kindled by our instructors, will, so far as I can judge of the future, soon be rendered moderate by experience, mollified by time, softened by the passage of the years. To be sure these your instructors and teachers of virtue seem to me themselves to have pushed the limits of our duties beyond what nature intended in order that after we had struggled and strained to the utmost we might get a firm footing where we ought to have it. 'You must forgive nothing.' Yes, something, though not everything. 'You must do nothing out of favouritism.' Rather, resist favouritism when duty and honour call. 'Do not be moved by pity.' Yes, when you are relaxing strictness; besides, some commendation is due to sympathy. 'Hold by your opinion.' Certainly, unless it is surpassed by another and better opinion.*

This perhaps is little more than badinage—the tone of it almost reminds one of Matthew Arnold—but when Cicero is really embittered his satire can be almost Swiftian. I give one of his attacks on Antony.

But what a thing was that return of his from Narbo! He positively asked *me* why I returned so suddenly when I was actually on the road. The reason for my return I explained to the senate the other day. I was anxious if possible to render some service to my country even before the first of January. As for your question, Antonius, about the *manner* of my return, this is my answer. In the first place I came back in daylight, not in the dark; secondly, wearing boots and a toga, not brogues and a cloak.—Why, you are now actually looking at me with what I am afraid is an angry expression! As a matter of fact you would make up to me again if you knew how ashamed I am of that rascality of yours for which you feel no shame yourself. Of all the scandals I have seen or heard of not one has been so

*Pro Murena XXIX, XXX, XXXI.

disgraceful. You who imagined yourself to be Master of the Horse, who were a candidate, or rather a petitioner, for the consulship of the year to come, scuttled in brogues and cloak through the municipalities and colonies of Gaul for whose support in our candidature we used to ask in the days when there were candidates for the consulship and not petitioners. Look, gentlemen, at the frivolity of the man! After arriving at Saxa Rubra about the tenth hour of the day he hid in a public house and there, keeping out of sight, drank steadily till evening. He then drove furiously to the city in a cab and went to his house with a hood pulled over his head. 'Who are you?' said the man who used to answer the door. 'Post from Marcus.' He was instantly conducted into the presence of her for whose sake he had come, and handed her a letter. When she began to cry as she read it—it was expressed in very loving terms, the gist of it being that he would have nothing more to do with that actress from now on; that he had withdrawn all his love from that quarter and now transferred it in overflowing abundance to herself—as madam wept copiously our soft-hearted gentleman could stand it no longer; he flung the hood from his head and made a jump for her neck. The blackguard! What other description can I give of him? Certainly none so appropriate. So, just that you might spring a pleasant surprise on a female by giving her an unexpected sight of a degenerate like yourself, you created a panic in the city that night and an alarm throughout Italy which lasted for days? To be sure you did have at home a motive in your amorousness. But out of doors you had an even more disgraceful motive in your fear that Lucius Plancus would auction the properties for which your securities had paid. When a tribune gave you leave to make a public speech, in which you said in answer to a question that you had come to Rome 'on private business', you caused the very populace to utter witticisms at your expense.*

It is interesting, and in a way important, to observe a change in manners. A modern reader will be apt to have at least a sneaking sympathy with Antony, especially as the lady in the case was his wife. But there was a strong feeling in antiquity

*Philip. II. 30, 31.

that it was disgraceful for a man no longer young to be in love, and particularly disgraceful if he was a magistrate. The objects of satire change with every change of moral sentiment. If a satirist were now to sneer at minor poets for their poverty it would be exceedingly ill received; but Pope does it. We must allow for the contemporary point of view. It does not matter whether we agree with Cicero or not, since all we are considering is the literary quality of what he writes. And clearly he had the power of expressing contempt, sometimes kindly and sometimes not. Macrobius has left us a few anecdotes which exhibit this form of satire.

When he was dining at the house of Damasippus and his host, setting a wine of very mediocre quality before the guests, said 'Drink this Falernian, it is forty years old', Cicero observed 'It carries its age well'. Again, noticing his son in law Lentulus, who was quite a little fellow, girt with a long sword, 'Who', said Cicero, 'has tied my son in law to a sword?' Even his brother Quintus was not spared the sallies of his biting wit. Observing in the province which Quintus had administered a representation of his brother on the heroic scale in the usual form of a bust framed in a circular background— Quintus, be it remembered, was low in stature—Cicero remarked 'The half of my brother is greater than the whole'. In the consulship of Vatinius, which lasted only a day or two, a notable witticism of Cicero's went the rounds: 'A miracle has happened in Vatinius's year, for in his consulship there has been neither winter nor spring nor summer nor autumn'. Pompey could not abide the *mots* of Cicero. Here are some which were repeated at the time. 'I know whom to avoid but not whom to follow.' When he joined Pompey at the latter's camp and found people saying that he had been long in coming, 'On the contrary', he retorted, 'I have come too soon, for here, I see, nothing is ready'. Afterwards when Pompey said to him 'Where is your son-in-law?' 'With your father-in-law'* was the retort. And when Pompey had bestowed the Roman citizenship on a Celt who had deserted from Caesar, 'Here's a fine fellow', said

*Caesar.

Cicero, 'promising Gauls the citizenship, which does not belong to them, and he not able to give it back to us, to whom it does belong.' No wonder Pompey said 'I wish Cicero would go over to the enemy, so that we might give him a scare'.*

So far as we can judge from what is left of Latin prose literature, Cicero did not bequeath his wit to his immediate successors; we must wait until we come to Seneca, a century later, who composed a 'Menippean' satire which is a parody of the process called 'apotheosis', whereby a Roman emperor was made a god after his death. This accounts for the title of the little piece—*Apocolocyntosis*.† It need not be inferred that Seneca condemned apotheosis in every case; he only condemned it in cases like that of Claudius, the emperor who is the object of his satire. Claudius is represented as being refused admission to heaven after his demise upon earth and being assigned an ignominious function among the common dead instead of his hoped-for deification. It is a good comic idea, and it is not hard to imagine what play Aristophanes could have made with it. But Seneca was no Aristophanes. He dwells upon the physical disabilities of Claudius.

The news came to Jupiter that there was a new arrival, 'rather tall, rather grizzled; there was the suggestion of a threat, for he was perpetually nodding his head; he dragged his right foot'. The messenger had asked what nation he belonged to; the newcomer made an unintelligible answer in an inarticulate growl; the messenger did not understand his language, which was neither Greek nor Latin nor the speech of any known people. Then Jupiter told Hercules, who had roamed all over the world and was supposed to know every race in it, to go and find out which the person belonged to. Hercules went, saw and got a shock, for there are *some* monsters he has not yet braved. When he looked at that queer new face and odd gait, when he heard that voice unlike any earthly animal's, hoarse

Saturnalia II. iii. 2.
†The colocynth was a sort of gourd or pumpkin with real or fancied medicinal properties.

and thick like a seal barking, he imagined that his thirteenth labour had arrived. However, on looking more closely, he perceived that it was a sort of man.*

This again illustrates a change of manners. It is not thought witty now to jeer at a man's physical defects. But we are not to suppose that Seneca's *jeu d'esprit*—it is no more—seemed to his contemporaries, or indeed to any but exceptional persons till towards the end of that eighteenth century in which Pope was ridiculed for his deformity, to be in such bad taste as we now feel it to be. And it may be admitted that, though in bad taste, the squib is clever. It is written in colloquial (but not slangy) Latin, which is more fresh and interesting than formal Latin prose had become and is not at all like Seneca's usual style. Nor is it a mere curiosity. It has influenced later writers. Erasmus took from it the idea of his *Julius Exclusus*, which tells how Pope Julius II was excluded from heaven for his bellicosity. Byron's *Vision of Judgment*, though directly suggested by Southey's effusion of the same name, develops the theme of the *Apocolocyntosis*, whether Byron had read the original or not.

But now we come to an undeniably great satirist, whom we have met before, Petronius 'Arbiter'. His unique book is in nothing more unique than this, that it cannot be classified. However regarded, it is pervaded by a spirit of satire. We see this in the first of the surviving fragments. It is a very just and sensible attack upon the sort of rhetoric which had come to infest Latin literature.

But are our students of oratory pursued by the same sort of Furies? You hear them intoning 'These wounds I got defending the liberties of my country'. 'This eye I have freely given on your behalf.' 'Give me a guide to lead me to my children, for the sinews of my knees are cut and can support my limbs no more.' Such things would be tolerable in themselves if they did pave the way to

*Apoc. 5.

eloquence; as it is, by this bombastic matter and empty rattle of periods they only succeed in making their practitioners, when they speak in public, imagine that they have been wafted into another world. That leads me to think that boys are made very silly in our schools of rhetoric, for they never see or hear anything that we have in real life—only pirates in chains standing on the beach, and tyrants writing ukases in which they order children to cut off their fathers' heads; only oracles given to deal with a pestilence enjoining the sacrifice of three or more virgins; only pills compounded of honeyed words and everything that is said or done peppered as it were with seeds of poppy and sesame. Young persons educated in such an atmosphere can no more have common sense than people who live in a kitchen can have an agreeable smell. Give me leave to say, you professors of eloquence have been the first to ruin your subject. With your frivolous and meaningless utterances you have made a mockery of it, with the result that oratory has been losing its sinews and its strength. Young men were not confined within the limits of such declamation at the time when Sophocles or Euripides invented a diction which they were bound to use. The private tutor had not yet killed native genius when Pindar and the Nine Lyric Poets took good care not to chant in Homeric metre. And without even calling the poets in evidence I see no proof that Plato or Demosthenes went in for this sort of training. A great and (if I may use the word) modest oration is not puffed up with swellings and tumours, but rises in natural beauty. This windy and measureless verbosity* emigrated from Asia to Athens, where like some ill planet it blasted the aspiring impulses of youth, while at the same time the true model of eloquence was destroyed, halted and silenced.†

But the triumph of Petronius' satiric art is the figure of Trimalchio, the self-made man, the ex-slave become plutocrat. No doubt it is a caricature, but a caricature of genius, as legitimate a creation as Uncle Toby or Mrs. Gamp. That is to say, he is larger than life, but he is alive, more alive than many

*_ventosa et enormis loquacitas_—a good phrase.
†_Satirae_ 1.

of us now drawing breath. He is ineffably vulgar and stupid and conceited, but there is something almost touching about him too—he is so vulnerable. He stands out of the canvas grotesque, monstrous, but not inhuman; nor is his creator entirely merciless. One has a feeling that he almost likes Trimalchio.

Here is the poor man giving himself away on the subject of Greek mythology. But I can give no more than the general sense of what he says, for he speaks in an illiterate gabble, the meaning of which is sometimes only to be guessed.

Ascyltos started to answer this abuse, but Trimalchio, delighted with the eloquence of his fellow-freedman, said 'Come now, no backchat! Better let's have no ill feelings and you, Hermeros, don't be hard on the kid. His blood is boiling, it's up to you to keep calmer. This is a game in which the loser is always the winner. You too when you were a cockerel were all cock-a-doodle-doo and had no sense. So let's start some new fun—that's a better idea—and watch a charade by the Homerists'. Immediately in came a troupe banging on shields with spears. Trimalchio himself sat up on his couch and, while the 'Homerists' bandied Greek verses in their pretentious way, he began to read in a high-pitched voice from the Latin crib. He stopped for a moment to say 'Do you know the plot? Diomede and Ganymede were two brothers. Helen was their sister. Agamemnon carried her off and sacrificed a deer to Diana to take her place. So Homeros now tells us as how the men of Troy and the men of Paris start a fight. Agamemnon won, you know, and married his daughter to Achilles. That put Ajax off his rocker—you'll see in a minute how it all worked out'. Trimalchio had no sooner spoken than the Homerists raised a yell, and through the middle of the scurrying servants was carried on an enormous platter a boiled calf which actually had a helmet on its head. The calf was followed by 'Ajax', who drew a sword and hewed it in pieces like mad. Then, brandishing his blade now up and now down, he picked up the pieces on the point and served up the veal to the admiring company.*

*Cena Tr. 59.

When Petronius made the novel—so far as the *Satyricon* is a novel—the vehicle of satire as well as of character-drawing he started a tradition which is carried on in Fielding, in Smollett, in Jane Austen, in Thackeray and others whose names will occur to the reader. Petronius had, of course, no thought of starting any such thing. He wrote as he wished and as he could. But in literature it is often the unintended effects that prove most powerful.

We may now turn to Lucian. A Syrian of the second century, he taught himself to write Attic Greek, mainly from books which had been written four or five centuries before he was born. It was therefore inevitable that there should be some artificiality about his style. But the ease and brilliance of it are extraordinary. Lucian is one of the most entertaining of ancient writers, so that the critic has to harden his heart a little if he questions, as I think he must, his title to be enrolled among the really great satirists. He has been likened to Voltaire, but he could not fairly be said to have the intellectual force, the incomparable style or even the wit of the Frenchman. Nor has he succeeded in giving, as Swift and Juvenal give, the impression of a burning conviction, such as is probably necessary if a satirist is to carry his point with readers. All this we may allow and yet make good the claim of Lucian to be regarded as one of the great originating forces in the history of literature.

The most frequently imitated section of his work has been no doubt his *Dialogues of the Dead*, perhaps because the subject —conversations with the famous dead—offers the satirist so fine an opportunity. Some of the humour is rather trivial, but on occasion it has a touch of macabre poetry. Here is a snatch of conversation between the god Hermes, whose office it was to conduct the dead to the lower world, and Menippus, the inventor of this way of writing.

M. Where are the beauties, male and female, Hermes? Be my cicerone, I am a newcomer.

H. I haven't the time, Menippus.—But you may take a glance to your right, where Hyacinthus is, and Narcissus, and Nireus, and Achilles, and Tyro, and Helen, and Leda, and all the beauties of the olden time.

M. I see nothing but bones and fleshless skulls, one much the same as another.

H. Well, these bones you evidently despise *are* what the poets rave about.

M. All the same, show me Helen, for I could not tell her from the rest.

H. This skull is Helen.

M. What, was it for this that the thousand ships from the whole of Greece were manned, and so many Greeks and Barbarians fell, and so many cities have been laid waste?

H. Ah, Menippus, you did not see the lady while she lived. Even you would have said that it was pardonable

'For such a woman long to suffer pain',

for if a man should only look at the flowers when they are withered and have lost their colour, they would certainly appear ugly to him, yet when in bloom and retaining their hue very lovely.

M. What surprises me, Hermes, is that the Greeks did not see that their labour was all about a thing so short-lived and ready to fade.

H. I am too busy to philosophize with you, Menippus.*

This is hardly a typical passage from the *Dialogues of the Dead*, which as a whole are written in a lighter tone. English writers who have felt their attraction include such great figures as Swift (in *A Voyage to Laputa*) and Fielding (in *A Journey from this World to the Next*). Yet in the quoted passage we hear a note struck which sounded through the Middle Ages and the Renaissance—the note of the Triumph of Death, of the *danse macabre*. There is indeed a difference in tone; it is the rarest thing to find a mediaeval or even a Renaissance author making a jest of death and the decay of youth and beauty. Yet Lucian is not misanthropic, as Swift was or became; he does not feel strongly enough about the matter for that. And it must not be inferred that he influenced the Middle Ages, whose thoughts on this theme were dictated by the *meditatio mortis*, which entered so largely into their religion. Indeed they hardly knew of Lucian except as the author of an allegorical piece about Calumny, the subject of Botticelli's picture, and of a supposed attack on Christianity, which led to his being regarded as an 'infidel' and therefore not to be read. This prejudice was not immediately dispelled when the Renaissance caused his work to be better and more fully known. But a more liberal, or better informed, spirit was now abroad, and we find men like Erasmus and Thomas More delighting in him. Yet no doubt they were moved by a feeling deeper than amusement when they read a passage like this, where Lucian rises for a moment above his usual mocking self. (Hermes has carried Charon from the Underworld to a high mountain, from which he can look down upon the earth.)

H. You see the human multitude, Charon—at sea, at war, in the law-courts, tilling the soil, borrowing, begging.

Ch. What I see is a motley scene of activity, an existence full of confusion, cities like bee-hives, in which everyone has his own sting and stings his neighbour, while some like wasps harry and plunder the weaker. But what is that cloud of creatures flying about them unseen?

H. Hopes, Charon, and fears and ignorances and pleasures and greeds and angers and hates and things like these. Ignorance mingles with them there below and enters into their public life, yes and hatred and rage and jealousy and stupidity and dubiety and avarice, while fear and hopes fly over them, the former sometimes swooping down on them and terrifying them, sometimes making them actually cower beneath it, the latter floating over their heads; then just when one expects them to settle upon them they fly up and away, leaving them agape with disappointment, just as you see

Tantalus in the Underworld disappointed by the retreating water. And if you look very hard you will also see the Fates on high there weaving the destiny of each man on their spindles, from which all are suspended by slender threads. You see the threads descending like spiders' filaments?*

Erasmus owes much to Lucian; the debt is clear in his 'Praise of Folly' (*Encomium Moriae*) and in many of the *Colloquies*, in one of which Charon himself appears. Erasmus in his younger days had in collaboration with More translated a good deal of Lucian into Latin, and that could not but have had its effect on both the collaborators. The *Utopia* is in spirit and substance more Platonic than Lucianic, but it bears strong traces of the Lucianic manner too. In his 'True History' (*Vera Historia*) the Greek satirist gives the account of an imaginary voyage to the west, in the course of which the travellers arrive at the Islands of the Blest and similar places, all described with an air of candour and veracity such as we associate with *Robinson Crusoe* and *Gulliver's Travels*. I translate here what is said about the Isle of Dreams.

After a short time we came to the Island of Dreams, quite close but indistinct and hard to make out. It was subject also to a phenomenon such as we experience in dreams, for it drew farther off as we approached, retiring deeper and deeper into the background. But we did make it at last and sailed into Slumberhaven (as it is called), passing near the Ivory Gate, where is the temple of St. Gull, and landed at dusk. Passing into the city, we observed many varied dreams. But first I want to say something about the city, because no one else has written about it, unless you count a brief mention by Homer, whose account is not quite accurate. All round it stands a wood, the trees of which are tall poppies and mandragoras, on which there roosts a multitude of bats—the one bird that the island produces. Close by runs a river called by the natives Nightford, and beside the city gates are two springs, called respectively Fastasleep

*Charon 15, 16.

and Nightlong. The wall which girdles the town is many-coloured
like the rainbow and high. The gates are not two, as Homer has said,
but four: two looking towards the Plain of Idlesse, one of them
made of iron, the other of earthenware—said to be the quarter of the
dreadful, the murderous and the cruel—and two facing the harbour
and the sea, one of horn—this was the gate by which we entered
—and one of ivory . . .*

Now here is More's account of his meeting with Hythlodaeus (hythlos is Greek for 'nonsense') who tells him about
Utopia. It will be seen that More employs the Lucianic method
of plausible realism.

In the meantime I betook myself, as my business required, to
Antwerp. While staying there I was often visited by, among others
but as welcome as any, Peter Giles, a native of that town, who holds
a place of great trust and honour among his own people and is
worthy of the most honourable, as a young man not more learned
than virtuous. I happened to see him one day in St. Mary's—a
beautiful church much resorted to by the people—talking with an
elderly stranger, who had a sunburnt complexion, a long beard and
a cloak hanging loose from the shoulder; from his looks and dress I
took him to be a sea-captain. Peter noticed me and came up and
greeted me. As I returned the greeting he drew me aside a little and
said, 'Do you see that man?'—at the same time pointing to the person
with whom I had observed him in conversation—'I was just going
to bring him from here straight to you'. 'He would have been very
welcome,' said I, 'for your sake.' 'Nay rather for his own,' said he,
'if you knew the man. For there is no living mortal who can tell you
so much as he about unknown men and lands, and I know that you
have a passion for hearing about such matters.' 'Well,' said I,
'my conjecture was not so far out, for at the first glance I saw that he
was a sea-captain.' 'For all that,' he replied, 'you were very wide of
the mark; he has to be sure sailed the sea, but in the rôle of Ulysses,
not Palinurus; indeed I might say he has voyaged like Plato.
For Raphael there—he is called Raphael, though his surname is

*V. Hist. II. 32, 33.

Hythlodaeus—in his eagerness to see the world attached himself to Amerigo Vespucci, and in the last of his three famous voyages he was his constant companion.'*

This is admirably conceived and cannot but make some of us regret that the author has not left us more in that style. As it is, the great intermediary between Lucian and the moderns is Erasmus. He like More is entitled to be quoted here because they wrote in classical Latin, carrying as it were the classical tradition in writing directly from Cicero to their own day, almost as if the Middles Ages had never existed. In fact there was a good deal of the Middle Ages in both of them, but especially in More; which rather adds to than detracts from their interest and importance. And if they wrote in classical Latin—more classical in the works of Erasmus than in those of his friend—they applied their style to modern subjects and in this way taught their successors how to handle these subjects in English prose. The rather long extract which I now propose to give is from the *Naufragium* or 'Shipwreck' which is one of the *Colloquies* of Erasmus. Readers of Rabelais, of the *Tempest*, of *The Cloister and the Hearth* will get some idea of the influence exerted by this brilliant and vivid piece of writing on vernacular prose. The conversation in the *Naufragium* is between Antonius and Adolphus, Antonius questioning and Adolphus replying.

Ad. The darkness was beginning to lift, and at the top of the mast, in what I believe is called the crow's nest, stood a seaman keeping a look-out for land, when a ball of fire proceeded to attach itself to him. This in the view of sailors is a very bad sign if single, though lucky if the flame is twofold. The twin flames were believed by the ancients to be Castor and Pollux. *An.* What have *they* to do with sailors, seeing that one of them was a horseman, the other a boxer? *Ad.* I am only telling you what the poets fancied. The master (who was at the tiller) said 'Mate'—it is the name sailors use

Utopia I. 26.

when they address each other—'do you see what sort of a friend you have sticking by you?' 'I do,' he answered, 'and I hope to God he's a lucky one.' Presently the fiery ball slid down the rigging and rolled along to the skipper's feet. *An.* Wasn't he scared to death? *Ad.* Sailors are accustomed to queer things. The ball stayed there for a little and then rolled round the bulwarks of the whole ship; after which it slipped through the scuppers and disappeared. Towards noon the storm got worse. Have you ever seen the Alps? *An.* Yes. *Ad.* Those mountains are warts compared to the waves of the sea. As often as the ship lifted you could have touched the moon with your finger; as often as we dipped we seemed to go through a gap in the earth straight into Hell. *An.* What fools are those who trust themselves to the sea! *Ad.* As the sailors vainly struggled against the tempest, the captain at last came on deck as white as a sheet. *An.* I augur some great disaster from that paleness of his. *Ad.* 'My friends,' said he, 'I have lost all control of my ship; the winds have beaten me; it only remains to put our trust in God and for everyone to prepare for the worst.' *An.* A grim speech indeed! *Ad.* 'First, how-ever,' he said, 'the ship must be lightened—so hard necessity commands. It is better to consult our safety by jettison of our goods than to perish with them.' There was no resisting the logic of facts, and a great many containers full of valuable merchandise were flung into the sea. *An.* This was making a sacrifice indeed. *Ad.* There was an Italian on board who had been on a diplomatic mission to the Scottish court; he had a portmanteau packed with vessels of silver, rings, cloth and silk garments. *An.* He refused to accept a settlement with the ocean? *Ad.* Yes; he wished to sink or swim with his dear wealth. So he voted against the proposal. *An.* What said the master to that? *Ad.* He said, 'So far as we are concerned you might perish along with your property if you were by yourself; but it is not fair that we should all run the risk of our lives for the sake of your portmanteau; so unless you agree with the rest we will throw you head first into the sea, portmanteau and all. *An.* A truly seamanlike speech! *Ad.* So the Italian too made the sacrifice, with many curses upon heaven and hell because he had trusted his life to so unfeeling an element. *An.* I recognise something Italian in the expression. *Ad.* Soon afterwards the gale, not in the least appeased by our gifts, broke the cordage and split the canvas. *An.* Dreadful! *Ad.* Back came the shipman. *An*. To deliver a speech? *Ad*. He hails us: 'Friends,' says he, 'the circumstances urge every one of us to commend his soul to God and prepare for death.' Questioned by some experienced travellers how long he thought he could keep the ship from perishing, he replied that he could make no promises, but that he could not keep her more than three hours. *An*. This was an even grimmer speech than the former. *Ad*. After uttering it he ordered all the ropes to be cut away and the mainmast to be sawn through where it was stepped in its box and tumbled into the sea along with the yards. *An*. Why? *Ad*. Because after the sail was split or carried away the mast was a hindrance, not a help, to the vessel; the rudder was all we had to trust to. *An*. And meanwhile what about the passengers? *Ad*. You would have witnessed a sad state of affairs; the crew, chanting *Salve Regina*, were praying to the Virgin Mother calling her Star of the Sea, Queen of Heaven, Lady of the World, Haven of Safety, and flattering her by many other titles which the Scriptures nowhere ascribe to her. *An*. And what has She, who never, I believe, sailed in a ship, to do with the sea? *Ad*. In olden days Venus watched over seafarers, because it was believed that she was born of the sea: since Venus has ceased to do that, the Virgin Mother has taken the place of the No-Virgin Mother. *An*. That is your little joke. *Ad*. Some fell upon the boards to do reverence to the sea, pouring all their oil upon the waves, soothing it exactly as we do an angry potentate. *An*. What did they say? *Ad*. 'O gentle sea, O gracious sea, O rich sea, O beautiful sea, be peaceful, save us!' Such was the tenor of their litany to the deaf sea. *An*. Absurd superstition! And others? *Ad*. Some could do nothing but vomit, most made vows. There was an Englishman among us who promised untold gold to Our Lady of Walsingham if he got ashore alive. Some made a world of promises to a wooden cross in such and such a place, others to a wooden cross in such and such another place. The vow to the Virgin Mary was the same, but they think it ineffectual unless one expressly names the place. *An*. Absurd! As if divine beings do not live in heaven. *Ad*. There were some who promised that they would be Carthusian monks. One man swore that he would visit St. James, who lives at Compostella, barefoot and bareheaded, his body clad in nothing but an iron shirt, and begging his food as well. *An*. Did nobody think of Christopher?

Ad. I was amused to hear one fellow who in a voice loud enough to be heard vowed to the Christopher in the high church at Paris, who is more like a mountain than a statue, a wax candle as tall as himself. As he kept repeating this as loud as he could bawl, a crony who happened to be standing beside him nudged him and hinted 'Mind what you promise; you couldn't pay for that if you were to auction all you are worth'. Then the other in a lower voice, presumably that Christopher might not catch what he said, muttered 'Shut up, you ass; do you think I mean it? Let me once set foot on dry land, and I won't give him a farthing dip.'*

Nobody who has read Lucian can doubt from whom Erasmus learned to write like that. And how 'modern', how competent it is compared with anything written at that time in English prose! The explanation is certain. Erasmus was using a medium of which all the resources had been exploited, while the English writers had no such advantage. They had to teach themselves, and they taught themselves largely out of Erasmus, on whose *Colloquies* they were educated at their grammar schools. It was impossible that clever boys should not pick up from a book so familiar to them the Erasmian method of satiric observation. It needs very little critical sagacity to detect the seeds of drama and the novel already germinating in the passage I have quoted.

As Erasmus is so important in this connexion, it is perhaps right to exhibit him in a more serious mood, though still a satirist. We have seen what Charon says in Lucian; here is what he says in Erasmus, speaking to Alastor, a devil.

Ch. Why in such a hurry, Alastor? *Al.* Well met, Charon; I was hurrying to you. *Ch.* What's the news? *Al.* I have news that will give Proserpine and you the utmost pleasure. *Ch.* Out with it, then; discharge your cargo. *Al.* The Furies have managed their business with a success proportioned to its grimness; there's no part of the

*Colloq. Naufragium.

world which they have not infected with the evils of hell—controversies, wars, rapine, plagues—to such an extent that they have made themselves bald by hurling at their victims the snakes which they had for hair and are going about without a drop of poison left them, looking everywhere for any viper or asp that may remain, for they are as smooth as an egg and have not got a hair on their heads nor any efficacious poison in their breasts. So get your skiff and oars ready. Presently there will be such a multitude of ghosts arriving that I am afraid you won't be able to take them across. *Ch.* What you say had not escaped my notice. *Al.* How did you know? *Ch.* Rumour brought me the news a couple of days ago. *Al.* How that goddess outstrips everything else! But in that case why have you left your boat and why are you hanging about here? *Ch.* The fact of the matter is that I have come here to get me a strong trireme, for my craft is now rotten with age and leaky and will prove inadequate to this job, if what Rumour told me is true. Though what need was there for Rumour to tell me? I am forced to believe the facts, for I have been shipwrecked. *Al.* To be sure you are dripping wet; my conjecture was, you were coming from a bath. *Ch.* No, I have saved myself from the Stygian lake by swimming. *Al.* Where have you left the shades? *Ch.* They are swimming with the frogs.

Since what we are considering is the influence of Erasmus on the history of our literature, something is gained by seeing how he appears in the language of the seventeenth century. I will therefore discontinue my own translation of what follows and append that of Sir Roger L'Estrange—very free but getting the general sense and spirit well enough.

Alastor. But what says *Fame**★ upon the whole matter?

Charon. She speaks of Three Great Potentates, that are mortally bent upon the ruin of one another, insomuch that they have possessed every part of Christendom with fury of *Rage* and *Ambition*. These Three† are sufficient to engage all the lesser Princes and States in their quarrel; and so *wilful*, that they'll rather perish than yield.

★Or Rumour.
†Charles V, Francis I, Henry VIII.

The *Dane*, the *Pole*, the *Scot*, nay, and the *Turk Himself*, are dipt in the broil and the design. The contagion is got into *Spain*, *Britany*,* *Italy* and *France*; nay, besides these feuds of hostility and arms, there's a worse matter yet behind: that is to say, there is a malignity that takes its rise from a diversity of *opinions*, which has debauched men's minds and manners to so unnatural and insociable a degree, that it has left neither *faith* nor friendship in the world. It has broken all confidence betwixt brother and brother, husband and wife; and it is to be hoped that this distraction will one day produce a glorious Confusion, to the very desolation of mankind. For these controversies of the *tongue* and of the *pen* will come at last to be tried by the *sword's point*.

Alastor. And *Fame* has said no more in all this than what these very ears and eyes have heard and seen. For I have been a constant companion and assistant to these *Furies*, and can speak upon knowledge, that they have approved themselves worthy of the name and office.

Charon. Right, but men's minds are variable; and what if some Devil should start up now to negotiate a peace? There goes a rumour, I can assure ye, of a certain scribling fellow (one *Erasmus* they say) that has entered upon that province.

Alastor. Ay, ay: but he talks to the deaf. There's nobody heeds him nowadays. He writ a kind of *Hue and Cry* after Peace, that he fancied to be either *fled* or *banished*; and after that an *Epitaph* upon *Peace Defunct*, and all to no purpose. But then we have those on the other hand that advance our *cause* as heartily as the very *Furies themselves*.

Charon. And what are they, I prithee?

Alastor. You may observe up and down in the courts of Princes certain Animals; some of them tricked up with feathers, others in *white*, *russet*, *ash-coloured frocks*, *gowns*, *habits*; or call 'em what you will. These are the instruments, you must know, that are still irritating *Kings* to the thirst of *War* and *Blood* under the splendid notion of *Empire* and *Glory*: and with the same art and industry they inflame the spirits of the *Nobility* likewise and of the *Common People*. Their *sermons* are only *harangues* in honour of the outrages of *Fire* and *Sword* under the character of a *just*, a *religious*, or a *holy war*.

*Britain.

And which is yet more wonderful, they make it to be *God's Cause* on *both sides. God fights for us,* is the cry of the *French* pulpits; *and what have they to fear that have the Lord of Hosts for their Protector?—Acquit yourselves like men,* say the *English,* and the *Spaniard, and the victory is certain*; for *this is God's cause, not Caesar's.** As for those that fall in the battle, their souls mount as directly to Heaven, as if they had wings to carry 'em thither, arms and all.

Charon. But do their disciples believe all this?

Alastor. You cannot imagine the power of a well dissembled Religion, where there's *youth, ignorance,* and a *natural animosity* to work upon. 'Tis an easy matter to impose, where there is a previous propension to be *deceived*!†

Change the historical allusions, change a little the phraseology, and that might be the cry—might it not?—of a contemporary writer.

Our prose satirists, at least from Swift to Peacock, were nearly all versed in both Lucian and Erasmus. Swift prided himself on not borrowing from other authors; but a man cannot jump out of history any more than off his own shadow. In his *True History* Lucian parodies the nautical details—notes of latitude and changes in the weather—which figured so prominently in tales of sea-travel; and Swift does the same. When Lucian's hero reached the Islands of the Blest, where the famous dead live again in an earthly paradise, he questioned some of them and got answers very different from those current upon earth. Here, for instance, is his interview with Homer.

After a day or two I went up to Homer when we had nothing else to do and began to question him. In particular I wanted to know where he came from, that being the point that is discussed more than any other nowadays. 'I myself am well aware', said he, 'that some think that I was born in Chios, others that I am a native of Smyrna,

---

*The Kaiser, Charles V.
†*Coll. Charon.*

and a good many that I come from Colophon. The truth is I am a Babylonian and my name in Babylon was not Homer but Tigranes —it was later, when I became a hostage in Greece, that I changed it.' My next question was about the lines in his poems that are condemned as spurious by the critics—did he write them? 'Yes,' he said, 'every one of them.' This then gave me a very poor opinion of the taste exhibited by scholars like Zenodotus and Aristarchus. After he had satisfied me on these points I asked what made him start the *Iliad* at the Wrath of Achilles. He said that he had not given two thoughts to the matter—the idea just occurred to him. I next wanted to know whether he wrote the *Odyssey* before the *Iliad*, as most people say. He answered no. I did not have to ask whether he was blind—another thing they say about him—for I could see with my own eyes that he was not.*

In the island of Glubbdubdrid, which is 'extremely fruitful', Gulliver is introduced to the Governor, who is a necromancer. To please his guest the Governor calls up some of the famous dead, with whom Gulliver converses, eliciting from them confessions which did not in the least accord with the accounts of them found in the historians. He meets Homer.

Having a desire to see those ancients who were most renowned for wit and learning, I set apart one day on purpose. I proposed that Homer and Aristotle might appear at the head of all their commentators, but these were so numerous that some hundreds were forced to attend in the Court and outward rooms of the palace. I knew and could distinguish those two heroes at first sight, not only from the crowd, but from each other. Homer was the taller and comelier person of the two, walked very erect for one of his age, and his eyes were the most quick and piercing I ever beheld . . . I soon discovered that both of them were perfect strangers to the rest of the company, and had never seen or heard of them before. And I had a whisper from a ghost, who shall be nameless, that these commentators always kept in the most distant quarters from their principals in the lower world, through a consciousness of shame and

*V. Hist. II. 20.

guilt, because they had so horribly misrepresented the meaning of those authors to posterity. I introduced Didymus and Eustathius to Homer, and prevailed on him to treat them better than perhaps they deserved, for he soon found they wanted a genius to enter into the spirit of a poet.*

Here, it is obvious, Swift did borrow an idea from somebody else. Indeed it seems very probable that the general conception of *Gulliver* came, perhaps half-consciously, from Lucian's *True History*; at any rate it is the same conception. However, in everything that matters Swift is entirely original, and if we are to discover evidence of real imitation we must go elsewhere—to Fielding, to Fontenelle, to Peacock, to H. D. Traill, whose *The New Lucian* should not be allowed to disappear from the record of English literature.

This chapter would hardly be complete without some discussion of the place of satire in history. The dictum of Aristotle that poetry is more philosophical than history is no doubt very true, but it does not mean that history is not philosophical at all. On the contrary, it differs from the chronicle in looking for some nexus between events, in looking (according to the simple phraseology of the old writers themselves) for 'the causes of things'. The ancients are always doing that, some no doubt better than others; and, since it is human beings whose actions they are recording, they must have some view of human life and human nature by which to judge them. They all have such a view, even if very often they have not clearly stated it even to themselves. This gives a moralizing turn to their writing, which in consequence often becomes pessimistic or censorious or satirical. For that is a frame of mind only too frequently produced by the study of history.

I have said that it is not always easy to distinguish satire from invective. But it helps to do this if we take it as broadly true that satire is directed against types and invective against

Laputa VIII *ad init.*

individuals. The satirist attacks, or professes to attack, some vice or failing embodied in an individual; it is supposed that there is nothing 'personal' in his attacks. Now the historian is under an almost irresistible temptation to see the characters in his story as so many embodiments of certain tendencies or policies, some of which he may consider weak or wicked. So there is apt to be a satirical undercurrent in what he writes about these men. It is possible to exaggerate the significance, it is not possible to deny the presence, of a satirical vein in Tacitus or Gibbon or Carlyle. Whether it has any right to be there or not, there it is; and it tends to appear in just those historians who are of most importance for literature.

It appears as early as Herodotus, who finds it difficult to write without satire about the Ionians. He tells how the Ionian fleet, having to fight a vastly superior enemy, put itself in the hands of a noted admiral, Dionysius of Phocaea. Thereupon, Herodotus says,

Dionysius, their Phocaean commander, made a speech among them to this effect. 'Men of Ionia, our fortunes are now balanced on a razor's edge, while it is undecided whether we are to be free or slaves, and slaves, so to speak, who have run away. Now therefore if ye be willing to encounter hardships, for the moment indeed it will be painful for you, but ye will be able to overcome the enemy and have your freedom. But if ye show a womanish and disorderly spirit in all ye do, I have no hope that we shall escape the penalty that we must pay the King for our revolt from him. Nevertheless follow my counsel and entrust yourselves to me, and I warrant you, if the gods deal fairly between us and them, either the enemy will not meet us in battle or meeting us will be heavily defeated.' When the Ionians heard this, they put themselves in the hands of Dionysius. But he made them put to sea every day with their ships in column, exercising the men at the oar in breaking through each other's lines, and the fighting men on deck at their arms; and for the rest of the day he would keep the ships at anchor, and the Ionians had no respite from toil all the day long. Now for seven days they obeyed their orders and did that which was commanded, but on the eighth day, being unaccustomed to such labour and worn out by their sufferings and the heat of the sun, they said one to another, 'What god have we offended that we endure these things? We had left our senses and gone out of our wits when we committed ourselves to the charge of a Phocaean braggart, who provides but three ships. And he took us and torments us with extreme torments, yea many of us have fallen sick and many others think to do the like. Better were it for us to suffer anything whatsoever than these evils and to endure whatever slavery shall be our lot than continue in our present bondage. Come, let us obey him no more.'*

Good-humoured satire, if you like; but satire all the same. In general, however, Herodotus is not a satirical person. Nor is Thucydides. There is a very brief passage in the second book of his history† in which he describes Spartan incompetence in naval matters. Some readers have felt or suspected a touch of satire there; but if it is there at all it is only a touch. He has some chapters which describe with overpowering truth and insight the deterioration of public morality in Greece under the stress of war. But in these he is not so much accusing as describing, whereas satire must attack somebody or something. On the other hand it does look as if satire were an element in the *Philippica* of Theopompus. This historian wrote about the middle of the fourth century before Christ. According to a very probable conjecture of Gilbert Murray's he was a Cynic or sympathetic with Cynicism. The Cynics were constantly preaching against the absurdity as well as the corrupting power of wealth. Here is a version of one of the fragments which are all that is now left of the voluminous work of Theopompus.

What city or what tribe of Anatolia did not send ambassadors to the king of Persia? What among the fruits of earth, or what beautiful or expensive production of art was not conveyed to him for his

*VI. 12.
†Ch. 84.

acceptance? Masses of valuable tapestries and mantles, some crimson, some parti-coloured, some white; a multitude also of tents, woven of gold thread and furnished with all things needful; a multitude of vestments and couches, together with much money. Add to this silver plate and gold plate finely wrought, and goblets and mazers, some of which you might have seen studded with gems, others exquisitely finished and of rich workmanship. Then there were more arms than one could count, both Greek and foreign, and any number of baggage animals, and victims fattened for the knife; there were sauces by the gallon, piles of bags and sacks, reams of paper and everything heart could desire, and such a quantity of junk that people travelling from a distance thought they were coming up against hills and mountains.

This is in the very accent of the Cynic preacher, the barefoot friar, and it must be satirical—must have been so at least in the ears of Greeks, who disliked nothing so much as vulgar ostentation.

Any influence that Theopompus could have had on English historians could only be at second hand through the influence he had on certain Roman historians. It is the Roman historians who are our direct concern. Now the moralizing tendency is strong in them, and it is not qualified by that power of critical detachment which strikes, which almost startles, us in Greeks like Thucydides and Polybius. We are therefore prepared to find a satirical element in their writing. It is true that the Romans had a great notion of 'the dignity of history', and this disposed them to adopt the attitude of the censor rather than the satirist, a less impersonal character. Yet impersonality is a common enough assumption of the satirist too. So when Tacitus avers that he is not moved either by likes or dislikes we cannot doubt that he believes this himself, but we remember that Juvenal and Dryden, that Swift and Pope say much the same.

Among Roman historians Sallust is so ambiguous a character that it is hard to be certain how far, if at all, he means to be satirical. One feels that sometimes he is, but one desires clearer evidence. On the other hand Livy is so ingenuous that satire appears foreign to his nature. The master of history as satire is Tacitus. Him no sensitive reader would accuse of insincerity or conscious partiality. But he suffers from a spiritual wound which makes him describe things and people as if they hurt him. What caused the wound is now past finding out; he half confesses that he is hurt in conscience because he had not protested more boldly against the tyranny of Domitian. Whatever the cause, he is almost without hope, angry with the world yet with no plan for reforming it. Give a man like this an exceptional feeling for words, and he is almost bound to be a satirist. And the very fact that we cannot doubt the sincerity or question the character of Tacitus gives a terrible weight to his insinuations. Take this passage about the accession of the unhappy Tiberius.

But at Rome consuls, senators, knights—they all took the plunge into slavery. The more eminent the person, the greater his haste and hypocrisy. Their features carefully arranged that they might not betray too much joy at the death of one emperor or too much gloom at the accession of another, they mingled tears with smiles and laments with flattery. Sextus Pompeius and Sextus Appuleius the consuls were the first to take the oath of allegiance to Tiberius Caesar, and with them Seius Strabo and Gaius Turranius, of whom the former was commander of the imperial guard, the latter responsible for the food-supply, and immediately after these the Senate, the army, the people. For at first Tiberius did everything through the consuls, as in the days of the Republic, in the pretence that there was still some question as to whether he was to be emperor; the very edict by which he summoned a meeting of the senate he published simply under the title of the tribunician power which had been conferred upon him in the reign of Augustus. The edict was short and phrased in terms of great moderation. In it he promised to consider what honours should be done to his father, but explained that in the meantime he could not leave the body, that being the one public duty which he insisted on performing in person. For all that, after the death of Augustus he had given the imperial guard their countersign as commander-in-chief of the Roman armies; he had his bodyguard, his armed attendants, all the paraphernalia of a court; a detachment of soldiers attended him to the forum and the doors of the senate house. He sent dispatches to the armies which implied that he was now their prince; nowhere did he show any hesitation except when he was addressing the senate. His principal motive was fear lest Germanicus, who commanded so many armies, a vast body of allies serving with them and unbounded popularity among the civilian population, should prefer to have the empire now rather than wait for it. Tiberius also thought that he must try to conciliate public opinion by making it appear that he had been invited and chosen emperor by a free state rather than that he had crept into power through the intrigues of Livia, who had induced her elderly and uxorious husband to adopt him. Another reason for his assumed hesitation was his desire to penetrate the real intentions of the governing class, whose every word and look he misconstrued and remembered against them. But the truth about this did not come out till afterwards. . . . Their supplications were now all directed to Tiberius. His reply touched on various points—the immensity of the empire, his own limited abilities. 'Only the genius of Augustus could cope with such a burden: when he had been invited by the emperor to undertake a share of his duties he had discovered by experience how difficult, how much exposed to the assaults of fortune was the burden of governing the world. So many distinguished men helped to support the state that they ought not to put all the responsibility on the shoulders of one person. By co-ordinating their efforts more would administer the functions of government with less difficulty than one.' It was an impressive speech but hardly a sincere one. Whether as the result of some congenital incapacity or from habit the words of Tiberius, even in matters where he was not seeking concealment, were always hesitating and obscure, but on that particular occasion, when he was struggling to repress his deepest feelings, they tended to be more than ever ambiguous and involved. But the senators, whose one fear was that they might give the impression of understanding him, burst into lamentations, tears and prayers. As they stretched out their arms in appeal to the statues of the gods, the image of Augustus, the knees of Tiberius himself, he caused a document to be produced

H

and read. It contained a record of the total resources of the state—a complete list of Roman citizens and allies under arms, of the fleets, associated kingdoms, provinces, direct and indirect taxes, charges on the treasury and bounties paid by it—all of which Augustus had written out in his own hand, adding a recommendation to keep the empire within its existing limits, whether he really feared its extension or grudged it to a successor.

While the senate was sounding the depths of self-abasement in its protestations Tiberius happened to say that, while he was not equal to the whole burden of public business, he would undertake the care of whatever part of it should be entrusted to him. Thereupon Asinius Gallus said, 'May I ask you, Caesar, what part you should wish entrusted to you?' Startled by this unexpected question, he did not answer at once. Then, recovering his self-possession, he replied that he must be excused the invidious task of choosing or declining a part of that which he would prefer to have nothing to do with as a whole. Judging by his expression that he was deeply offended, Gallus went on to say that the question was not put with the object of breaking up what could not be divided but of proving by Tiberius' own admission that the body politic was one and must be ruled by the mind of one. He proceeded to deliver a eulogy of Augustus and reminded Tiberius himself of his victories in the field and his successes in civil administration over so long a period. But he did not thereby appease the anger of the new emperor, to whom in fact he had long been an object of dislike for having married Vipsania, the daughter of Agrippa, who had formerly been the wife of Tiberius, for aspiring to the position of emperor and for reproducing the outspoken spirit of his father, Asinius Pollio.*

Is not this satire rather than history? At least it is not pure history, for even if the facts were as Tacitus says they were, he presents them in such a way as to make the persons concerned —both senators and emperor—odious and contemptible. And that is satire. Whether it is justified or not is an irrelevant question, though historians are now inclined to believe that

*Annales I. 7, 11, 12.

the feelings of Tiberius were pretty much what he professed them to be. Yet Tacitus is not always satirical; the remark of Merivale that the *Annals* are 'all satire' is absurd. No historian is more deeply or quickly touched by a heroic deed or a trait of moral dignity. Only they came so rarely! And he has some prejudices.

Accordingly Polyclitus, one of the palace freedmen, was sent to see with his own eyes the posture of affairs in Britain, Nero having great hopes that his commissioner would be able not only to use his influence in restoring friendly relations between the general and the procurator but in pacifying the spirit of revolt among the natives. Polyclitus did not fail so far as burdening Italy and Gaul with a long retinue went and, after he had crossed the Channel, causing alarm and despondency among our troops as he proceeded on his way. But to the enemy he was a ridiculous object, for the flame of liberty even then burned brightly among them and they had not yet discovered the power that may be wielded by the sons of slaves; they could but marvel that a general and an army that had brought a great war to an end should obey a serf. However his report to the emperor put matters in a less serious light than that in which they had been represented, and Suetonius was kept in control, though after losing a few ships with their crews on a beach he was ordered to hand over his army to Petronius Turpilianus, whose term of office as consul had now expired, on the ground that the war was not yet over. The new governor, neither attacking nor attacked by the enemy, gave this cowardly inaction the honourable name of peace.*

It will be observed that Polyclitus carried out his special mission with success, relieving a dangerous situation which had developed under the rule of Suetonius. But then Polyclitus was only a 'freedman', a whole or half foreigner, at any rate not a Roman gentleman; and for these reasons he was to be looked down upon. That is not history. Or let us say, more justly, that

*Annal. XIV. 39.

it is history, but history as presented by a satirist. The same perhaps may be said of this account of the brief emperor Vitellius, though the feeling here is less unworthy of the historian.

After the capture of the city Vitellius was carried in a sedan through the back regions of the palace to his wife's house on the Aventine, hoping that, if he could avoid detection during the day by hiding there, he would make good his escape to Tarracina, where his brother was in command of some companies of the imperial guard. But being of an irresolute character and thinking (as frightened people do) that the situation he was in was worse than any other— though he feared all others too—he went back to the palace, which he found desolate and deserted, even the meanest of his slaves having slipped away or avoiding every occasion of meeting him. The solitude and silence of the place terrify him. He explores closets, he shudders in empty rooms. Worn out as he wandered unhappily up and down, he hid in a boothole. It was from here that he was dragged out by Julius Placidus, who commanded a cohort. They tied his hands behind his back; they led him along, a disgusting figure in rags, abused by many, wept over by none; the ugliness of his end made pity impossible. A soldier from one of the German armies got in front of him and aimed a blow, whether in anger or to free him the sooner from insult was never known; it may have been an attack on the tribune, whose ear he cut off. This soldier was killed on the spot. Vitellius they pricked with their swords to make him hold up his head and expose it to their insults, once to watch his statues being hurled from their pedestals, more than once to look on the rostra and the spot where Galba was killed. Finally they pushed him up to the Gemonian Steps, where the body of Flavius Sabinus had lain exposed. One thing he was overheard to say which proved him not utterly ignoble. In reply to some insult of the tribune he said 'Yet you have been my subject'. At last he fell under a shower of blows. The mob cursed the dead man with a malignity equal to the servility they had shown to him while he lived.*

*Hist. III. 84, 85.

The sense of tragedy which mingles with the contempt expressed in this passage saves it from being all satire, but it is satirical enough. It is extraordinary how the example of Tacitus has taken hold of later historians; it would seem as if all the good writers among them wanted to write like that. His persuasiveness, his power over the emotions, the vividness of his style have together proved almost irresistible. It is the way Carlyle writes history; and although this may be mainly due to a similarity of temperament, nevertheless Carlyle had the example of Tacitus before him. The case of Gibbon is less disputable. Gibbon no doubt learned much from Voltaire and Hume in the art of giving expression to irony in narrative. But his real master is Tacitus.

The character of the prince who removed the seat of empire, and introduced such important changes into the civil and religious constitution of his country, has fixed the attention, and divided the opinions, of mankind. By the grateful zeal of the Christians the deliverer of the Church has been decorated with every attribute of a hero, and even of a saint; while the discontent of the vanquished party has compared Constantine to the most abhorred of those tyrants who, by their vice and weakness, dishonoured the Imperial purple. The same passions have, in some degree, been perpetuated in succeeding generations, and the character of Constantine is considered, even in the present age, as an object either of satire or of panegyric. By the impartial union of those defects which are confessed by his warmest admirers, and of those virtues which are acknowledged by his most implacable enemies, we might hope to delineate a just portrait of that extraordinary man, which the truth and candour of history should acknowledge without a blush. But it would soon appear that the vain attempt to blend such discordant colours, and to reconcile such inconsistent qualities, must produce a figure monstrous rather than human, unless it is viewed in its proper and distinct lights by a careful separation of the different periods of the reign of Constantine.*

*Decline, ch. XVIII ad init.

Compare that with the character of Augustus at the beginning of the *Annals*.* It will be obvious where Gibbon found the
inspiration and method of that character of Constantine. Moreover Gibbon is almost as great a master of innuendo as Tacitus,
who uses it, as Gibbon uses it, with an effect which we generally
feel to be satirical.

No later Roman historian approached the eminence of
Tacitus as an artist. But Ammianus Marcellinus, who wrote in
the fourth century, ought not to be passed over unremarked,
for he is perhaps the last ancient historian who has some claim
to be called great, even if his influence has been rather small.
What he did was to carry into the Dark Ages something of the
method and spirit of Tacitus, who had ceased to be read. This
is his account of the scenes in Rome at the election of Pope
Damasus.

His successor was an ex-quaesitor of the palace, Viventius, an
honest and sensible Pannonian, whose administration was peaceful
and undisturbed, overflowing with supplies of every kind. Yet he
too was terrorised by the murderous riots of the contentious
populace, culminating in the affair which I shall now describe.
Damasus and Ursinus, whose eagerness to seize the papal throne
went to inhuman lengths, met in the fiercest conflicts of party hate,
while their supporters carried the quarrel to the extent of inflicting
wounds and death. Viventius, not being in a position to punish or
moderate this frenzy, yielded to force and retired to his suburban
residence. It was Damasus who came out victorious from the
struggle at the head of the party which favoured him. It is known
that in a single day there were found in the basilica of Sicininus,
where the Christians meet to perform their rites, one hundred and
thirty-seven bodies of men who had been killed, and that it was only
with difficulty and after a long time that the passions of the infuriated
mob were calmed.

When I consider the splendour of the Roman scene I am not
disposed to deny that men who are ambitious of obtaining such a

prize ought to strain every nerve in the effort to win it, seeing that, when they have got it, they will be sure to be enriched by the offerings of matrons, and to ride in state in carriages dressed carefully in their vestments, and to provide banquets expensive beyond the means of royal tables. And yet they could be sincerely happy if, disregarding the immensity of Rome, which they offer as an excuse for their vices, they should frame their lives on the model of certain provincial bishops, whose spareness in eating and extreme moderation in drinking, together with the inexpensiveness of their clothes and the way they fasten their eyes on the ground, recommend them to eternal God and His worshippers as pure and modest persons.*

The native language of Ammianus was Greek and he never learned to write Latin with any feeling for its idiom; his style is turbid and rather excessive. As a result he had no effect on the form of literature, but he kept history in the mould into which it had been cast by Tacitus. In fact he designed his own work to be a continuation of the *Annals*. He confirmed the view that the historian is concerned not merely with facts but with their moral significance. This is the classical view, and it prevailed among English historians until quite recently.

Let me add one brief quotation from Ammianus, writing about the emperor Constantius:

Christianam religionem absolutam et simplicem anili superstitione confundens; in qua scrutanda perplexius quam componenda gravius excitarat discidia plurima; qua progressa fusius aluit concertatione verborum, ut catervis antistium iumentis publicis ultro citroque discurrentibus per synodos (quas appellant), dum ritum omnem ad suum trahere conantur, rei vehiculariae concideret nervos.†

Now here is Gibbon's translation:

The Christian religion which, in itself, is plain and simple he confounded by the dotage of superstition. Instead of reconciling the

Hist. XXVII. 3, 12.
†XXI. 16.

parties by the weight of his authority, he cherished and propagated by verbal disputes the differences which his vain curiosity had excited. The highways were covered with troops of bishops, galloping from every side to the assemblies, which they call synods; and while they laboured to reduce the whole sect to their own particular opinions, the public establishments of the posts was almost ruined by their hasty and repeated journeys.*

This is clearly satirical. That is why it delighted Gibbon.

*Decline, ch. XXI.

CHAPTER FOURTEEN

CHARACTERS

THE genre to be discussed in this chapter gets its name from a particular book, the *Characters* of Theophrastus. But the psychology of human types had interested the Greeks long before Theophrastus.

It has already been remarked that one of the distinctions between English and the classical literatures is that, while English is interested and excels in the characterization of individuals, Latin and Greek are interested and excel in the delineation of types. For long the distinction scarcely appears; our mediaeval writers are as fond of types as any Greek. But a change may be observed at least as early as Chaucer. The Knight and the Squire in the *Canterbury Tales* are types, but the Reeve and the Miller, Harry Bailly and the Wife of Bath are individuals. It was perhaps Shakespeare who first decisively tilted the balance in its present direction, and it took even him some time to do it. The characters in the *Comedy of Errors* and in *Titus Andronicus* are rather types than individuals; when we come to *Romeo and Juliet* we get characters as individual as the Nurse and Mercutio. This did not prevent Ben Jonson and Restoration Drama from reverting to types. There is in fact a large body of English literature which has carried on the classical tradition in this way.

Since we are treating of prose, we need not go farther back than Plato.—It is essential in philosophy to define the general terms and concepts which it uses; Socrates had made a special point of this and Plato follows him here. There is nothing to be gained by arguing about justice unless your opponent is prepared to accept your definition of it. But justice is embodied in the just man. We must therefore have a clear notion of what we mean by 'the just man'. In other words we must describe that *type*. And, of course, many other types as well. Thus in his *Republic* Plato is led to describe various forms of political constitution—the oligarchic, the democratic and so on. But, since it is human beings who operate these constitutions, he feels it incumbent on him to describe the typical oligarch, the typical democrat and so on. Here is his description of how the democratic type is evolved from the oligarchic. (It is Socrates who speaks.)

The process, I think, generally takes some such form as this. A young man is brought up in the way we have described, that is in an illiberal and stingy manner; he tastes the honey of the drones,* and associates with fierce and dangerous animals of the human species who can provide him with pleasures of many sorts and kinds and varieties. In such conditions you will find, believe me, the beginning of a change from the oligarchic constitution within him to the democratic. In the state the change began when one of the parties was helped by an accession of supporters from beyond its borders who identified themselves with it. That is just the way in which the young man changes when he in turn receives within his soul the help of a class of passions similar and akin to the passions already there. And if the oligarchic element within him is reinforced against these intruders by admonitions and denunciations from his father, perhaps, or others dear to him, then you have civil war, in which the lad is divided against himself. There will be occasions when his democratic instincts yield to the oligarchic; then some of his desires are killed and others expelled, because a sense of shame is still alive in the young man's soul; and so order is restored. But at another time no doubt, thanks to the ignorant way in which his father brought him up, another set of desires akin to the banished are secretly nourished till they multiply and grow strong. These wrench the lad back into his old associations and, secretly copulating with his old desires, beget a multitude of new ones. At last observing that the citadel of the young man's soul is empty of that finer knowledge and those loftier pursuits and true principles which best

---

*Anti-social persons who prey on the rest of the community.

keep watch and ward in the souls of men dear to the gods, those false and presumptuous principles and opinions rush up to the citadel and seize it in their place. And now he is back among the Lotos Eaters and lives openly with and among them. If his family send succours to the thrifty part of his soul, those usurpers bar the gates of Government House and will neither admit this active alliance nor listen to the friendly representations of older men speaking for themselves. They are the winners in the fight for control, and they thrust into banishment and disgrace modesty, which they call silliness, and self-control, which they call unmanliness, expelling it with insults, while moderation and reasonable expenditure, which according to them are rusticity and meanness, they chase beyond the frontier with the aid of many unprofitable desires. Yes, they sweep the soul clear of those instincts by which it was possessed and purify it by great ceremonies of initiation, and then and not till then they bring back with dancing and singing Insolence and Anarchy and Profligacy and Shamelessness in the glare of torches and crowned with garlands, while their conductors shower on them praises and pretty names, calling Insolence 'a distinguished manner', Anarchy 'liberty', Profligacy 'magnificence', Shamelessness 'a manly spirit'. It is in some such way as that, don't you think, that a young man brought up strictly changes to a loose-living character who gives rein to unprofitable and unnecessary desires. Thereafter he spends quite as much money and time and energy on unnecessary as on necessary pleasures. No doubt if fortune is kind and he manages to keep within some bounds in his excesses, he may find as he gets older that the wild uproar has passed by, and may take back certain elements of the exiled qualities, refusing to give himself up entirely to the invaders. He then arranges his life on the principle of treating all pleasures as equal, handing over the control of himself to the first comer as if he were the prize in a lottery and, when that is glutted, to another, rejecting none but assigning the same rations to each. Yet if somebody says (quite truly) that there are two kinds of pleasure, one consisting in the gratification of good and noble desires, the other derived from the satisfactions of evil desires, and that he should cultivate and honour these, but chastise and chain up those, he will not listen to so reasonable a suggestion or admit it into his citadel. No, he shakes his head at all this, declaring all pleasures to be equal and worthy of the same esteem. And so he spends his days gratifying each desire as it presents itself, now drunk with wine and exciting music, now slimming and drinking water; today in training, to-morrow idling and utterly slack, or again going in (apparently) for science. Every now and again he takes an interest in politics, jumping up and saying or doing whatever comes into his head. Suppose he conceives an admiration for the professional soldier—off he goes head-long into that profession; if it be business men he admires, he rushes into business. Neither order nor necessity governs such a life, yet he persists in leading it, calling it delightful and free and heavenly.*

That is the picture of a type, and there are many such types depicted in Plato. It is clear that he believed in the value of such studies and probable that he encouraged members of the Academy to pursue them. Among these were Aristotle and Theophrastus. But while Plato could communicate his interest he could not communicate his literary genius. The character sketches of the pupils are, compared with those of the master, uninspiring. But, though they cannot like him speak with the tongues of angels, their work in this field is sufficiently remarkable. I begin with Aristotle, to whom, after the death of Plato, Theophrastus looked as to a second master.

By a great-souled or superior man we mean one who claims, and is entitled to claim, high consideration from his fellows. Of course a man who makes such a claim on insufficient grounds is a silly fellow. . . . The superior man must have a particular object in view. What is it? When we say somebody or something has 'worth' or 'value' we are thinking in terms of external goods. The greatest of these we take to be that which we assign as their due to the gods and which is desired by eminent persons and awarded as the meed of victory in the most glorious contests, namely honour. For honour is the greatest of external goods. The superior man then has the right attitude to honours. . . . By them he will be gratified if they are distinguished and are bestowed by estimable persons—but gratified only up to a point, because he will feel that he is getting no more

*Resp. VIII. 559d–561e.

than his due, or rather less, for no honour can be enough for perfected virtue. Nevertheless he will accept such honours on the ground that they are the highest these persons have it in their power to bestow. But honour from men with nothing special to recommend them, and proffered for unimportant reasons, he will not consider for a moment; that sort of thing is altogether beneath him. And dishonour he will treat in the same way; for dishonour and he can never be justly connected. But while it is true that honour is the grand sphere of the great-souled man's activity, still he will also deal in the right spirit with riches, power, every form of good and bad fortune, as it may befall him. And when he meets with good fortune he will not be overjoyed, nor will he be unduly depressed when he meets with bad. For even honour does not arouse in him these strong emotions, even if it is the chief of external goods. For while power and riches are desirable, it is for the sake of the honour which surrounds them. At all events the holders of these advantages hope that they may be honoured because of them. Accordingly the man who sets little store even by honour will set little by these things. It is for this reason that the superior man gives the impression of superciliousness.

Doubtless it is a common belief that advantages of fortune do something to confirm the great man's sense of his merits. People do look on high birth and political power and wealth as proper objects of respect, because those who possess them have something more than others, and that which has the superiority in some good is always more honoured. Therefore such advantages increase the great man's sense of superiority. For he is receiving honour on their account—honour from a certain class of persons. But in truth only the good man is to be honoured. No doubt if a man is prosperous as well as virtuous he wins an accession of honour. But those who possess the advantages we have mentioned without being themselves virtuous cannot fairly make any large claims to respect and are improperly described as superior men; for true superiority complete virtue is a *sine qua non*. . . . They are like the superior man in looking down upon other people, but do not, like him, act in the character of the perfectly good man. And, if the superior man does contemn the rest of the world, it is with justice and because he has a correct view of his relation to it. But of these merely lucky people most have no special reason for assuming such airs at all.

The superior man will not run petty risks, nor indeed risks of any kind if he can help it, because there are so few things which he considers worth while. But he rises to meet a crisis and, while that lasts, he will put his life in peril for the cause, since he is not the man to purchase life at any price. It is also part of his character to confer benefits. But he hates receiving them. This is because the former action implies superiority, the latter inferiority. When he does repay a service it is with interest, for in this way the original benefactor will become the beneficiary and debtor in his turn. Again, the superior man is suspected of having a better memory for benefits conferred than benefits received—the recipient in such a relation is in the inferior position and the great man covets the superior rôle—and likes to be reminded of what he gave and not of what he got. . . . Another mark of the superior man is his refusal or reluctance to ask anyone to help him, though always anxious to bring help himself. And he stands on his dignity with those who are high in public esteem or favourites of fortune, but does not assume airs in his dealings with persons of no great distinction, because to maintain one's superiority in the company of notabilities is not easy and impresses others, so that here a haughty manner is not unbecoming of a gentleman, though in the worst of taste when one is dealing with humble people—as bad as hustling the weak. He will not enter the lists against ordinary competitors for distinction, or where he has no chance of the first prize; and it is in his way to make no effort, or to hang back, except when some really great honour or achievement is open to him. He will rarely undertake anything, and if he does it will be something great and glorious. Since it is a sign of fear to conceal one's feelings, the superior man is bound to be open in his likes and dislikes, and to care more for the truth than for what people may think, and to be straightforward in word and deed. He must live his own life uninfluenced by anyone, unless perhaps a friend, since to permit such influence would involve some degree of complaisance. He is not a gushing person, because nothing strikes him as really important. He does not nurse resentment, for it is not like a superior man to remember things against people, especially the mischief they have tried to do him—he tends to overlook all that. He does not care for personal talk, being indisposed to speak either about himself or anyone else. He is not interested in compliments to himself or in uncomplimentary remarks about his neighbours, although this does not mean that he is himself given to paying compliments. For the same reason he is not given to recrimination, even against his ill-wishers, unless he *means* to be insulting. In troubles which are unavoidable or of no great consequence he is not pathetic or appealing, for that would be to give them too much importance. He prefers his possessions to be beautiful and of no profit to him rather than profitable and useful, for this indicates that he is sufficient to himself. Add that he never hurries—or so people believe—and has a deep voice and a deliberate way of speaking. For the man who is convinced that there is little or nothing worth getting excited about will not be given to hurrying or be high-strung and, as a result, shrill in his tones and bustling in his movements.*

Most English readers have a feeling that, if they met a gentleman of this sort, they would dislike him extremely. But they will not meet him. In real life, as Aristotle knows perfectly well, characters are mixed. He is describing the great man as he would be if he had no endearing weaknesses; in real life he would have at least one. In other words he is a type and not an individual. Aristotle in his ineloquent way—it should be remembered that he was not writing, as Plato was, for readers but giving a course of lectures to students—is doing the same kind of thing in his portrait of the superior man that Plato had done in his portrait of the budding democrat. It is therefore absurd to speak, as too many do, as if the 'character' had been invented by Theophrastus.

What Theophrastus gave was the name. The title of his book—*Characters*—means in Greek things 'engraved' or 'stamped', especially the impressions on coins. In English we say 'traits' of character. As the book stands it can hardly have been meant for publication; it is a notebook containing a selection of thumb-nail sketches of various types of men observable in Athens during the residence of Theophrastus there. There are some thirty of them, each exhibiting some

*Nicom. Ethics IV. 1123b–1125a.

weakness or fault of character. Theophrastus does not concern himself with virtuous types, and there must have been a reason for that, though it is now past finding out. Yet the *Characters* does not strike us as cynical, and it is certainly amusing. This comes out even in a translation in spite of the fact that translation is almost impossible. Practically never is there an exact English equivalent for a Greek word denoting a moral excellence or defect. But though we cannot find names for the types of Theophrastus, we recognize them without difficulty. Every reader must instantly feel the truth of the following 'character'—its truth to human nature—though there does not seem to be a good name for him in English.

The inopportune or tactless man is the sort of person who goes up to a busy man to make some communication to him, or gate-crashes his sweetheart's flat when she has a temperature, or approaches a man who has already forfeited his deposit in a court of law and presses him to make a statement that he (the speaker) will stand surety for him, or when he has to give evidence turns up after judgement has been delivered in the case, or when he has been invited to a wedding party delivers a tirade against the female sex, or when people have just arrived after a long journey invites them to come for a walk. Then he has a genius for introducing to somebody who has completed a sale a man who is prepared to offer a better price, or for getting up in a committee and explaining all over again a point they have already heard and understood. He eagerly takes in hand the business of a man who (though he does not like to say so) does not wish it to be done. Again, when people are having a feast on the meat of a sacrifice which has cost them a good deal of money he is apt to ask for a slice. Or if a slave is being flogged in his presence he will be sure to tell a story of how a slave of his own had hanged himself after being flogged like that. Or if he is present at an arbitration, and both parties are anxious to get the dispute settled, he will bring them into collision. Or when he has a mind to dance he will seize the hand of another man, who is still sober.*

*Charact. XII.

It will be seen that Theophrastus has dispensed with the philosophical or psychological framework in which Plato and Aristotle had set the passages I have quoted from them. But that is all. His originality, so far as it goes, consists in letting the details speak for themselves. But how fresh and well chosen they are! No doubt he learned a good deal from the New Comedy, which flourished at Athens in his time. Not much of that has survived, yet enough to show that it had a particular aptitude for, and delight in, just such traits of character as we find in Theophrastus. There is no evidence that he relied on anything except his own observation, but it may fairly be said that almost any of his 'Characters' could have formed the psychological basis of a comedy such as Menander used to write. It is therefore an error to suppose that there was much that is unique and original in the talent and method of Theophrastus.

But we must, in view of his later influence, give another excerpt from his little, almost tiny, book.

The stupid man may be recognised by traits like the following. He works out an addition sum with the help of pebbles and when he has made out the total he asks the man beside him 'How much is it?' When he is defendant in a law-suit and due to appear before the magistrate, he forgets all about it and goes off into the country. When he is one of the audience at the theatre, he is left behind asleep when everybody else has gone away. When after a heavy meal he gets up in the night to visit the outside lavatory, he gets bitten by his neighbour's dog. He obtains something, puts it away himself—and then can't find it. When somebody brings him the news that one of his friends is dead, he looks sad, sheds tears and then says 'Well, here's luck!' When he is being *paid* back money owing him, he is a wonder for bringing witnesses to the transaction. In the middle of the winter he will start a row with his servant for not buying figs. He compels his young children to run and wrestle until he makes them ill from sheer exhaustion. When he is in the country, he will make his own porridge and put salt in twice, so that the mess is

uneatable. If somebody says to him, 'How many funerals do you
think passed the Sacred Gate?' he will answer, 'As many as you and
I would like.'*

Although the *Characters* must always have found admirers—
Cicero was one—it did not come fully into its own till the
Renaissance. Of the modern followers of Theophrastus the
most eminent was no doubt La Bruyère. But he had his English
followers too. The first in time was Joseph Hall, who published
his *Characters of Virtues and Vices*—you see he knows the
meaning of 'characters'—in 1608. He was able to make use of
the great edition of Theophrastus published in 1592 by Isaac
Casaubon. About the time of Shakespeare's death appeared the
Characters of Thomas Overbury. In 1628 there was published
at Oxford *Microcosmographie*, the author or principal author of
which turned out to be John Earle, afterwards Bishop of
Salisbury. It is the best of its kind in English and it had considerable influence. But it was the essayists who most effectively
carried on the work of Theophrastus, who was almost an
essayist himself. Sir Roger de Coverley, Will Wimble, Dick
Minim, Beau Tibbs are 'characters', and from such there is no
doubt that the early novel learned a great deal. Goldsmith
indeed was both essayist and novelist.

There is however a book which for a very long time had a
far wider influence than Theophrastus. It is a treatise on rhetoric
addressed to an unknown Hereunius. The writer was long
believed to be Cicero, and this led to the inclusion of the
treatise among the authentic works of Cicero on rhetoric, which
it apparently antedates. From this book, as from 'the horse's
mouth', it was thought one could acquire the secret of good
writing, and for this reason it was most assiduously studied in
mediaeval universities and indeed much later. One of the
things inculcated by the treatise is 'characterization'. Already,
in the passage I shall now quote, we can see an advance from

*XIV.

the thumb-nail sketch of Theophrastus to something like the full-length portrait of a type. We may call him, awkwardly enough, the 'Pretender to Wealth'.

That person, gentlemen, who thinks it grand to be described as a rich man—in the first place observe his expression as he looks at you. Is it not as if he were saying 'I might give you something, if you did not pester me'? When he rests his chin upon his left hand he is under the impression that he is dazzling you all with the brilliance of the gem and the glitter of the gold. When he looks round towards his solitary servant—I know him, though I dare say you don't—he addresses him by a wrong name. After doing this once or twice 'Hi you', he says, 'come, Sannio, and protect me from these rough, vulgar persons'. The effect on listeners who do not know their man is that they imagine Sannio to be one servant who is being chosen out of many. He whispers Sannio to see that the dining room couches are spread, or to ask his uncle as a favour to send the black boy to the hot baths, or arrange that his Spanish horse should be posted before his door, or that some other delicate and precious show-piece of his pretended grandeur should be got ready. After that he says in a voice loud enough for all to hear, 'See that the reckoning is carefully made—before night, if possible'. The servant, who by this time is familiar with his master's peculiarities, replies, 'You must send more than one there, if the reckoning is to be finished today'. 'Then', says the other, 'take Libanus and Sosia with you.' 'Very well, sir.' Next the man has a visit from some foreigners who had entertained him lavishly when he was abroad. Of course this upsets him frightfully, but he remains true to his instincts. 'Delighted to see you,' says he, 'but it would have been better if you had gone straight to me at my house.' 'So we would', they reply, 'if we had been acquainted with your house.' 'No difficulty about that; anybody could have told you. But come along.' They follow him, and as they go his entire conversation is devoted to showing off. He asks what crops are produced on their estates, remarking that he can't get to his own because the farms upon them have been burned and even now he won't take the risk of building more, though in his Tusculan domain he has begun to spend money regardless, building on the old foundations. In the course of this talk he comes to a

mansion where there was to be a private party that day. On the plea
of knowing the owner of the house he—the fellow you see before
you—marches in with his guests. 'This is where I live', quoth he. He
examines the silver, which had been laid out; he pays a visit to the
dining room, which had its couches properly spread, and approves.
Up comes the slave creature and whispers to him that the master of
the house is expected any moment, and had he not better clear out?
'Is that so?' says our man. 'Let's go, guests; it's my brother coming
from Salernum. I shall go and meet him; do you come here at four
p.m.' The guests take their departure, whereupon he makes a dash
for his own house. At four they turn up at the place to which he had
invited them, and ask for him. They discover whose house it is and
betake themselves to a hotel under a shower of ridicule. Catching
sight of the man next day, they tell him of their experience, heaping
charges and reproaches upon him. He assures them that they had
been misled by a resemblance in the topography and had strayed
out of their way the whole length of a lane. 'He himself had sat up
waiting for them, to the injury of his health, a good part of the
night.' He had instructed his servant Sannio to collect all the plate,
tapestries and slaves he could. The smart little fellow makes a good
job of it, and our gentleman conducts the guests to the house. His
most commodious residence he says he has lent to a friend for a
wedding. At this moment his servant brings him a message that the
plate is being asked back—the lender had got nervous about it.
'What the deuce,' says he, 'I have lent him a house, I have provided a
staff of servants. Does he want silver too? Well, though I have
guests, he may use the silver, and we shall do very well with
ordinary cups and plates.'—Need I tell you his subsequent proceedings?*

It should be understood that the character here depicted is
altogether fictitious. The author is simply giving an illustration
of what he calls *notatio* ('characterization'), a method by which
the prosecution or defence in a lawsuit attacks one of the
parties by making him seem ridiculous or odious or both,
so weakening the force of his pleadings. All that is needed for

Ad Herennium IV. 50–57.

the illustration is that the details should be 'in character'. And here they are; the thing could not be done better. But it is just like the elaboration of a sketch by Theophrastus.

Oratory is not confined to the law courts; there is, for example, pulpit oratory. Mediaeval sermons were full of characterizations of virtues and vices, while it is common to find in them a particular type of virtuous or vicious man described with touches of the kind we call 'realistic'. Bunyan's *Life and Death of Mr. Badman* continues this tradition; it is the biography of a type, a 'character' drawn with unusually vivid detail, some of it taken perhaps from observation of an actual person or persons. Now mediaeval writers probably learned the method from the *Rhetorica ad Herennium* more than from any other source. After the Middle Ages were over, or supposed to be over, we have Erasmus doing what the author of the *Rhetorica* did, and doing it even better. Erasmus was for so long the instructor of intelligent youth that his positive influence was unusually strong and deep. It has been observed that the *Colloquies* often recall Lucian. But a great deal of Lucian's work is very much in the vein of the passage quoted from the *Rhetorica*. And if Erasmus knew Lucian well, he had Cicero at his fingers' ends. At all events he was writing 'characters' in his Latin before it occurred to anyone to imitate Theophrastus in English.

When one comes to a German inn,

There is nobody to welcome you on your arrival, in case it should be thought that they are soliciting custom, a procedure which they regard as mean and contemptible, unworthy of the honest German nature. After you have been a long time shouting somebody at last sticks out his head, like a tortoise peering out of its shell, through a little window of the stove room, for in such rooms they live till almost the summer solstice. He has to be asked if you will be allowed to stay at that inn. If he doesn't shake his head, you gather that room is being granted you. If people ask him where the stable is he waves a hand in its direction. There you may curry your horse as you can, for no ostler lends you a hand. If the inn is rather full, the ostler shows you the stable, also a very inconvenient place for your horse; all the best places they reserve for expected guests, especially gentry. If you complain you are instantly told 'If you don't like it, look for another inn'. In the big towns there is a poor and limited supply of hay, costing not much less than oats itself. After you have seen to your horse you change quarters for the stove room, which you enter in full kit, boots, luggage, mud and all, for there is the common rendezvous. . . . In the stove room you take off your boots and put on slippers; change your shirt, if you like; hang up your rain-sodden garments beside the stove, and approach in person in order to get dry. Water is also provided, in case you should like to wash your hands, but as a rule so dirty that you have to look for other water afterwards to wash away the washing. . . . If you pull up at the inn as early as four in the afternoon, you will have to wait for dinner till nine or even ten. . . . They make no preparations for the meal until they see everybody present, so that all may be served at one time. . . . The consequence is that quite often there meet in the same stove room eighty or ninety humans—pedestrians, riders, travelling merchants, seamen, coachmen, farmers, children, women, sick and sound. . . . There one combs his head, another wipes off his sweat, a third cleans his boots or leggings, a fourth belches garlic. In a word there is no less confusion of tongues and persons than of old in the Tower of Babel. But if they catch sight of a foreigner whose dress indicates that he is a man of some eminence they all stare at him as if he were some animal of a new species that had been imported from Africa, and that so intently that even after they have sat down at table they turn their heads and never remove their eyes from him for a moment, regardless of their food . . . and in the meanwhile it is an offence to ask for anything. When it is already late in the evening and no more are expected, an elderly waiter makes his appearance with a grey beard, a shaven head and a dirty suit. . . . He casts an eye round the company and silently counts the number of those in the stove room. The more he sees there, the more vigorously is the stove heated, even if the day anyhow is oppressively warm. They consider it a principal part of hospitality to have everybody streaming with sweat. If anyone unaccustomed to this experience opens the window a little to avoid suffocation, he is told at once

'Shut that window!' If you answer 'I can't stand this', you are answered, 'Then find another inn.' . . . Afterwards back comes the bearded Ganymede and lays as many napkins on the tables as he considers enough for the company, but, Heavens, how far from being of Milesian quality! You would say they were of canvas from the rigging of ships. (He has fixed the number of guests at each table at a minimum of six.) Now everybody who knows the custom of the country takes whatever seat he likes. For they make no distinction between poor and rich, master and man. . . . After all are seated, again appears that grim Ganymede, counts his diners once more and presently returning sets before each guest a platter of wood and a spoon of the same precious material, then a glass rummer, then a good while after a piece of bread. This everyone cleans at his leisure while the porridge is cooking. In this way sometimes the guests sit for near an hour. . . . At last the wine is served. Lord, how it tastes of smoke! It should have been drunk by the Sophists, so thin and bitter is it. But if a guest, even with the offer of a tip, asks for a better sort of wine from some other vat, they first pretend not to understand, though looking as if they would murder him; press them and they answer, 'Any number of counts and marquises have stayed at this inn, and not one of them ever complained of my wine. If you don't like it, find some other inn.' It is only the gentry of their own country whom they regard as human beings, and their coats of arms are everywhere in evidence. They do in fact have a morsel to fling to a ravenous stomach, for presently in grand procession come the dishes. The first usually consists of lumps of bread soaked in beef juice or, if it is fish day, in vegetable juice. Then comes another soup and after that some re-cooked meat or warmed-up salt fish, then more porridge and presently some more solid food. Then after your appetite has been thoroughly subdued they put before you roast meat or boiled fish, which you cannot altogether despise; but they are not lavish with these courses and remove them quickly. In this way they manage the whole entertainment according to the usual method of the players who introduce dances into their scenes, offering you sops and porridge alternately, taking care however that the last act is the best. . . . At last forth steps our bearded friend or the landlord himself, whose dress differs very little from that of his servants, and asks if there is anything we should like. Soon afterwards a more generous wine is brought to us. Now they have an affection for deep drinkers, since the man who quaffs most wine pays no more than the man who takes least. . . . But before I conclude this entertainment let me say that it is extraordnary what a noise and confused clamour there is after all have begun to be warmed by their potations. . . . Last stage of all, when the cheese has been removed—they have little taste for it unless it is rotten and full of mites—the bearded one comes forward carrying a dinner plate on which he has drawn with chalk certain circles and semi-circles. This he lays on the table, uttering not a word all the time and look-ing glum; you would say he was a Charon. Those who are familiar with the meaning of the chalk drawings put down some money, then another does the same and another, until the plate is full. Then after noting those who have paid the money he silently counts it; if there is no deficit he nods. . . .*

Here is all the characterization you could desire. Hall and Earle, both men of some learning, must have known the *Colloquies* from end to end, and perhaps they got as many hints from Erasmus as from Theophrastus. What they got from the Greek was the descriptive title *Characters*, and this has diverted attention from the fact that they had other sources of inspir-ation than Theophrastus. After them the genre was established in England and developed there into a form in which it could be absorbed into the work of the essayists and novelists.

Coll. I. Diversoria.

CHAPTER FIFTEEN

THE PROSE OF SCIENCE

IT HAS come to be thought no part of a scientist's business to have a style. It is, however, his business to be accurate, and inaccurate writing—all bad writing is inaccurate—is in itself unscientific, for a distinct conception should be expressed distinctly. But the point does not require to be argued. There does in fact exist a literature of science, and the development of this literature is matter for the historian.

It appears to begin among the Ionian Greeks on the eastern shore of the Aegean, whence it spread to South Italy and to Sicily. I shall touch only on such phases of this development as may have had a positive, though indirect, influence on English prose. Thus it would be hard to prove that Heraclitus had any, even through the medium of his German imitator Nietzsche. In any case the style of Heraclitus is altogether personal and peculiar to him, and it is the norm that creates a standard. Such a standard may be found in what is called the Hippocratic Corpus, a body of writing produced by a medical school, first of its kind, which arose in the Aegean island of Cos. The Corpus gets its title from the most famous member of the school, Hippocrates, who was born about 460 B.C. Whether any of the surviving treatises comes from his hand is not certain, but all are written in more or less the same style, though the earliest contributors write in it best. It is perfectly adapted to its purpose of clear, exact and yet not excessively technical exposition. It is more, it is good prose by any standard. The style of the Corpus reflects its spirit, which is scientific in the modern way. It is not influenced by any prepossessions. Thus, whereas it was popularly believed that epilepsy was caused by some supernatural agency, the author of a little treatise on that malady quietly remarks that no disease is more supernatural than another, and goes on to the description of its symptoms. In such ways the habit of dispassionate observation recorded in clear untechnical language was started and a literature of science became possible. And it could be maintained that this, the first and most difficult step, was the most important.

Apart from this medical writing, only part of which belongs to the fifth century before Christ, we have not the materials which would enable us to pass judgment on scientific prose before Aristotle. Ancient critics (who had all his voluminous works before them) thought highly of the style of Democritus, and their opinion is confirmed by the fairly numerous sayings of his which have been preserved. They reveal an aphoristic quality, often with some touch of imagination or poetry. It was Democritus who developed, if he did not originate, the first 'atomic theory', which was later adopted by the Epicurean school of philosophy. About the same time the rival school of Stoicism adopted the physical theories of Heraclitus. In that way these two philosophers were rescued from something like oblivion and became immensely famous to later generations. A kind of mythology gathered about them which is worth our notice because it has left some mark upon our literature. Heraclitus was depicted as the 'weeping', Democritus as the 'laughing', philosopher, no one quite knows why. But the representation is at least as old as Horace. Indeed Latin authors often refer to it, as in the following brief quotation from Seneca (*Dial.* IX. 15. 2): Democritum potius imitemur quam Heraclitum. Hic enim, quotiens in publicum processerat, flebat, ille ridebat. 'Let us imitate Democritus rather than Heraclitus, for whenever the latter appeared in public, he used to weep, while the former used to laugh.' Mediaeval and Renaissance men refer to this contrast over and over again; in particular it led Burton to write his *Anatomy of Melancholy* under the pseudonym of 'Democritus Junior'.

We may come now at once to Aristotle; and at once we are

faced by a problem. The Aristotle known to us might be described as a writer without a style, although what he writes is never without character. Language is reduced to a kind of notation, relieved by phrases that are flashes of genius. This can hardly be called a style, but then it was not meant to be in any considered sense a style. What we have is the manuscript of Aristotle's lectures to his students at the Lyceum, of course a select audience of highly intelligent persons—by no means always young men—who were familar with his logic and terminology. It was enough if the Master could make out his own script. But this was not the Aristotle that was read in the specially 'classical' ages. In his younger days he had written dialogues and homilies intended for the 'general reader', and these he had published. Only fragments survive, but even these indicate that Aristotle did have a style and an excellent one. Cicero, who was in a better position to judge than we, admired its 'golden flow'. He did more, he took these earlier writings of Aristotle as the principal model of his own dialogues and disquisitions on philosophical, which for the ancients often meant what we should regard as scientific, subjects. We have therefore this curious result that, while the surviving works of Aristotle have had little effect on style, the lost works have, through Cicero, exerted a great deal.

Yet though the surviving works have had but little effect on style, it would be wrong to say that they have had none. Aristotle may be said to have invented technical language, and this was a great invention, though one ominous to literature. Here is his definition of the syllogism, which I give because of its singular importance for the study of our own philosophical literature, especially in its mediaeval period.

The syllogism is a form of speech in which, certain things being assumed, something different necessarily follows in virtue of them; and by 'in virtue of them' I mean that it follows in consequence of them, and by this I mean that it follows necessarily without any external term being necessary to make it follow. I call that a perfect syllogism in which the necessity of the result appears without the addition of anything to the original assumptions, and I call that an imperfect syllogism which requires one or more additions which are necessarily implied by the original terms but are not actually contained in them.*

This is obviously the right way to make definitions, but it is not the way to make literature. Something else is needed— some emotion or imagination—to turn a mere arrangement of words into language which is beautiful in itself. Aristotle, who wrote the first treatise on style, knew this well enough. But when he was lecturing on one of the exact sciences, with no immediate intention of publishing his views, he thought it best to sacrifice everything else to exactness of statement. On the other hand in subjects which he considered did not admit of great exactness, such as Politics and Ethics and Rhetoric, he allows himself at times a less formal and rigid manner of writing, often giving one the impression (from which regret cannot be entirely absent) that he could have been a great writer as such if he had cared. It is not only that he says striking things but that he says them in a way of his own, and that is what makes a great writer. But he drops these sayings almost casually, as if he attached no particular importance to them. Nevertheless his influence on literature has been very great, and this calls for some explanation.

The Peripatetic school of philosophy, which looked to Aristotle as its founder, had a special attraction for men with a native talent for research and scholarship. These steadily added to the sum of human knowledge and a good deal of this got into books which survived the eclipse of ancient learning. These books were prized and preserved through the Dark Ages, because men were then humbly aware of their ignorance and hoped to cure it. It was rather a long time before the work of

*Prior Analytics I, 2.

the Master himself was translated, although he was always a figure of legendary fame, chiefly as a 'magician' and tutor of Alexander the Great. But gradually it came to be better known and to exercise an authority such as no other secular writer has enjoyed in the whole course of history. This authority prevailed almost equally, though not with equal justice, in all the sciences which he had been the first to define and classify. But a special importance was assigned to his Logic, a science which he had himself created. Yet it was not exactly a science, it was rather the instrument which science must employ. The mediaeval Schoolmen perceived how useful it would be in the clarification and formulation of theology, which was their supreme interest, and they learned to apply it with a thoroughness and subtlety which has never been surpassed or perhaps equalled. From this flows a consequence. If one is to argue logically one must express oneself grammatically. Grammar in fact is a creation of the logicians. Aristotle was the first to 'analyse sentences' in a systematic way. But bad grammar is not only bad logic, it is bad writing; because when a man expresses himself ungrammatically he is saying what he does not mean. It is because of Aristotle chiefly that we feel it necessary to consider whether our sentences are grammatical or not.

It was, of course, the Latin Aristotle—that is Aristotle translated into Latin—who influenced the Middle Ages. It is worth while to give a brief illustration of how this influence operated, and I take it from the *Summa Theologica* of Thomas Aquinas, the greatest of the mediaeval Schoolmen. It answers the question whether there is one *summum malum* which is the cause of all evil, as there is one *summum bonum* which is the cause of all good.

I reply that we must say, as is evident from what has been said before, that there is no one first principle of evils, as there is one first principle of goods. For (1) the first principle of goods is essentially good, as was proved above. Now nothing can be evil in its essence.

For it has been shown that every entity, so far as it is an entity, is good; and that evil does not exist except in good as in its subject. (2) The first principle of goods is the supreme and perfect good, which already has in itself all goodness, as has been shown above. Now there cannot be a supreme evil; for, as has been shown, although evil always takes something from good, it can never utterly destroy it. And so, good always remaining, there cannot be something entirely and perfectly evil. Wherefore the Philosopher says in the fourth book of his *Ethics* that, if there is an entirely bad thing, it will destroy itself; because when all good has been destroyed (which is necessary for the entrance of evil) the evil itself is also withdrawn, having the good for its subject. (3) The rational ground of evil is opposed to the rational ground of a first principle both because every evil is caused by good, as has been shown above, and because evil cannot be a cause except *per accidens*. So it cannot be a first cause, because an accidental is posterior to an essential cause.*

'First principle', 'essential', 'accidental'—these are words we cannot do without. They and others come from Aristotle. That is but a reflection of the fact that during the later centuries of the Middle Ages Aristotle was the educator of Europe. And not only in logic. Thomas had studied the physical and metaphysical works of the Master, his psychology (the *De Anima*), his *Ethics* and the eloquent *De Caelo*, not actually from the hand of Aristotle but in the main a product of his school. The man who had studied these works was not just a logician or a theologian. Nor was Thomas singular in this range of interests. Thus, while it is true that the theologians dominated the mediaeval schools, it is also true that they saw to it that a liberal education was pursued in them.

Next to logic it is probable that the Middle Ages most revered the cosmology of Aristotle. The reason is stated by Seneca in a passage so well known to mediaeval readers that it may be put in evidence here.

*S. Th. Quaestio 49.

The difference, most excellent Lucilius, between philosophy and all other sciences is not greater in my opinion than the difference in philosophy itself between that which has regard to men and that which has regard to gods. The latter is more sublime and daring; it has expatiated at large; it has not been content with the evidence of the eyes. It has come to believe that there is something greater and more beautiful which nature placed beyond our seeing. In a word there is as great a difference between the two philosophies as there is between god and man. The one teaches what should be done on earth, the other what is done in heaven. The one dispels our errors and brings a light whereby the problems of life may be solved, the other soars far above this darkness in which we stumble and, rescuing us from its shades, leads us to the source of light. I render thanks to Nature when I behold her not from this common point of view but when I have penetrated into her deeper secrets; when I am learning what matter the universe is composed of; who is the author or guardian of that universe; what is God, whether he is wholly intent on the contemplation of himself or sometimes casts a benevolent look on us; whether he creates something every day or has created once for all; whether he is part of the cosmos or the cosmos itself, whether he may determine an issue today and make some encroachment on the law of Fate, or whether it detracts from his majesty and is an admission of error to have done things which had to be changed. For he who cannot be pleased except with the best must always be pleased with the same things; neither is he on this account less free and omnipotent, for he is his own necessity. Were I not admitted to the contemplation of these things, it were not worth while for me to have been born. For what reason would there have been for me to be glad that I have been placed among the company of the living? Was it to give a passage to meat and drink? Was it to cram this sickly and limp body, which would actually perish unless it were immediately stuffed again, and live in attendance upon an invalid? Was it to fear death, for which we all are born? Take away this inestimable boon, and life is not worth sweating and sweltering for. What a mean thing is a man unless he raises himself above the concerns of men! . . . A man enjoys the blessing of the human lot in full perfection when, trampling all evil beneath his feet, he seeks the heights and passes into the inner heart of nature. Then as he roams from star to star he has the joy of laughing at the marble floors of the rich and the whole earth with its gold.*

In these words is expressed a feeling, common to classical antiquity and the Middle Ages, that the starry heavens are divine. The constellations were regarded, even by Plato and Aristotle, as 'animals', that is to say living creatures, of far greater dignity and importance than man. Christianity so far opposed that as to uphold the transcendent value of the human soul, but it continued—think of Dante's *Paradiso*—to regard the stars as glorious creatures of God. On the other hand it tended to confuse astronomy with astrology. But in all essential respects the cosmology of Aristotle prevailed, with modifications, up to about the time of Shakespeare; and among poets (who are traditional in such matters) much longer. Without some knowledge of it a good deal of our literature up to and including Milton and even Dryden is not fully intelligible.

According to Aristotle the earth is a stationary ball in the exact centre of the universe. Round the earth the heavenly bodies revolve at various speeds and distances. This happens because they are fixed in a number of hollow concentric spheres of graduated size moving about the earth under the impulse of the outermost, largest sphere, which came to be called in Latin the *primum mobile* because, while it set in motion all the other spheres, it was itself first moved by God, the 'First Mover'. This theory was elaborated into the 'Ptolemaic System' by the Greek astronomer Ptolemy of Alexandria, and this (though itself undergoing some correction and revision) held the field until Copernicus revived another ancient theory, propounded by Aristarchus of Samos,† that the earth moved round the sun. It was not, however, from Aristotle that the average mediaeval writer got most of what he believed about the heavenly bodies. It was from Latin authors like Cicero and

N. Q. Praefatio.
†Third century B.C.

Seneca and the Elder Pliny. I have already quoted a passage from the *Dream of Scipio*. Here is another, short but concise, from Pliny, mainly about the sun.

With respect to the elements I cannot find it doubted by any authority that they are four. . . . Struggling with equal force in opposite directions they are kept each in its own place by the ceaseless rotation of the universe itself. As this keeps turning rapidly upon its axis the earth, which is the lowest element, is the centre of the universe, for which it provides a fixed hinge, suspended yet balancing its suspending elements. Thus it alone is motionless, with all else wheeling round it wherewith it is connected, while providing a support for all else. Between earth and sky, supported by air, are seven stars, at fixed distances from each other, which from their motions we call planets or wandering stars, though none wander less. In the midst of them the sun is carried along, mighty in size and influence, the ruler not only of seasons and lands but also of the very stars and the heavens. Him, when we contemplate his works, it is fit that we should believe to be the mind or, more definitely, the reasonable mind of the whole universe, the chief governor and divinity of nature. He furnishes light and takes away darkness from things, he conceals and he illuminates the other stars, he orders the changes of the seasons and the year as it is continually reborn in the course of nature, he dispels the gloom of the sky and even enlightens the cloudy thoughts of the human spirit; he lends his light to the other stars also, glorious, supreme, beholding all things, as Homer the prince of literature has, I see, been pleased to say of him and him alone.*

> The heavens themselves, the planets and this centre
> Observe degree, priority and place,
> Insisture, course, proportion, season, form,
> Office and custom, in all line of order;
> And therefore is the glorious planet Sol
> In noble eminence enthroned and sphered
> Amidst the other; whose medicinable eye

Nat. Hist. II. 1.

I

Corrects the ill aspects of planets evil,
And posts, like the commandment of a king,
Sans check to good and bad.*

There you have it all in Shakespeare.

What effect did it have on our prose? It led English writers,
when they discussed cosmology—as they often do in the
seventeenth century—to discuss it in the lofty style of Pliny
and the *Somnium*. For Pliny too can rise to a lofty style. It is
possible to adduce a highly instructive illustration. I draw it
from the *Telluris Theoria Sacra* of Thomas Burnet, published
in 1680, and an English version (not translation) of it called
The Sacred Theory of the Earth, published in 1684. Here we
actually see the formation of an English style upon the model
of the Latin. I will give a quotation from the Latin first.
Burnet had convinced himself that the earth was doomed to be
in the not distant future consumed with fire, and this is how
he describes that conflagration.

Ad caelorum phenomena iam pergimus. solis et lunae
obscuratio aut sanguineus color facile explicatur incepto iam
incendio. ubi enim fumo et ignibus repleta fuerit atmosphaera,
obscurabitur procul dubio et solis et lumae facies et totius caeli:
aliamque induent formam et colorem corpora caelestia. hoc in
Aetnaeis ignibus contingere solet, ut vidimus supra ex Dione
Cassio; cui adde verba Ciceronis: 'Nos autem tenebras cogite-
mus tantas quantae quondam eruptione Aetnaeorum ignium
finitimas regiones obscurasse dicuntur: ut per biduum nemo
hominem homo agnosceret; cum autem tertio die sol illuxisset,
tum ut revixisse sibi viderentur'. credo quidem solem et
lunam pendente incendio multas subituros esse mutationes
et formarum vices pro ratione ignium fumorum cinerum
fuliginum flammarum, quae aerem intermedium occupaver-
int; nec tam mundi luminaria iam referent quam nescio
quos turbidae lucis grumos. quandoque sol apparebit solito

Tr. and Cress. I. 3. 85f.

maior et iracundior instar sanguinei montis in caelo penduli; quandoque pallescet aut ferrugineus videbitur; et quandoque picea caligine interposita penitus abscondetur. immo fieri potest ad augendum rei horrorem per totum caelum et per omnes planetas ut sol obductis in faciem maculis re ipsa obscuretur et haereat in medio planetarum sine luce quasi mortuus. dirum hoc esset spectaculum circumpositis mundis, qui flammantem tellurem vice solis haberent et a sedibus nostris accensis omnem suam lucem et calorem accipiant.* 4

I give now a parallel account from the English version:

The countenance of the heavens will be dark and gloomy; and a veil drawn over the face of the sun. The earth in a disposition everywhere to break into open flames. The tops of the mountains smoking; the rivers dry, earthquakes in several places, the sea sunk and retired into its deepest channel, and roaring, as against some mighty storm. These things will make the day dead and melancholy; but the night scenes will have more of horror in them, when the blazing stars appear, like so many Furies with their lighted torches, threatening to set all on fire. For I do not doubt but the comets will bear a part in this tragedy, and have something extraordinary in them, at that time; either as to number, or bigness, or nearness to the earth. Besides, the air will be full of flaming meteors, of unusual forms and magnitudes; balls of fire rolling in the sky, and pointed lightnings darted against the earth; mixed with claps of thunder, and unusual noises from the clouds. The moon and the stars will be confused and irregular, both in their light and motions; as if the whole frame of the heavens was out of order, and all the laws of Nature were broken or expired.

Though Thomas Burnet is now forgotten, he was greatly admired—and obviously not without justice—by critics as influential as Addison. And it was on writers like Burnet, and not Addison or Swift, that Johnson built that style of his which for good and also no doubt for evil was to produce such an effect on the development of English prose.

*T. Th. Sacr. III. ii.

It is now agreed that Aristotle's finest work in the natural sciences was done, not in astronomy or physics, but in biology. Yet his biology has had nothing like the same effect on the history of literature as of science. Even in biology his influence has been almost confined to the theory of the subject, since his remarkable collection of material, for the most part zoological, is lost except in his descriptions of it. What a modern zoologist, examining these descriptions, notes is that some are based upon first-hand observation, while the rest is just traditional lore recorded by Aristotle in case there should be something in it. But the Middle Ages swallowed it all, the absurdest parts often with the greatest relish. They were not the first to do this. For some reason the science of zoology rather deteriorated than progressed after Aristotle, and the deterioration is shown in the number of silly stories about animals that were received as true. Listen to Pliny on the elephant:

Of land animals the largest is the elephant and, after man, it is the most intelligent. They understand the language of their native country, they obey orders, they remember the duties they have been taught, they find pleasure in love and in glory, nay more they possess virtues which are rare even among men—probity, prudence, a sense of justice, besides a religious awe of the constellations and a worship of the sun and moon. It is seriously reported that in the wadis of Morocco herds of them, when the moon is shining, march down to a great river called Amilus and there solemnly asperge themselves with water by way of purification, and then, after saluting the luminary, return to the bush carrying those of their calves that have tired themselves out. The first occasion of their being seen at Rome was when a team of them was yoked to the chariot of Pompey the Great in his triumph over Africa. According to legend this had previously been done when Bacchus celebrated his triumph over conquered India. At an exhibition of gladiators given by Germanicus some executed clumsy movements in the nature of a dance. It is certain that one elephant which was rather slow in comprehending its instructions, for which it was more than once whipped, was found at night practising those very instructions.

We have the authority of Mucianus for saying that one of them not only learned the Greek alphabet but had a trick of writing in Greek these words: 'I have written this myself and I have dedicated spoils won from the Celts.' He likewise assures us that at Puteoli he saw with his own eyes the following incident. When elephants that had been shipped there were being forced to disembark, they were seared by the length of the gangway, which stretched a long way from the shore. So turning round they proceeded tail first, that they might in this manner give themselves a false impression of the distance.*

Elephants at least exist. Some of the creatures dear to the Middle Ages could not have even this said of them. The unicorn is one, the phoenix another. The phoenix makes so great a figure not merely in mediaeval but also in Renaissance and Romantic literature that the description of it in Pliny, from which chiefly the mediaeval fantasies grew and spread, may be given.

Ethiopia and India produce variegated birds which almost defy description, in particular the famous phoenix of Arabia. Truth or perhaps rather fable describes it as unique and not much seen. It is said to be as large as an eagle, its neck a brilliant gold, its body a rich red, its tail a bright blue contrasting with rose-coloured wings. Its throat is adorned by a tuft of feathers and its head by a feathery crest. The first and most careful report of it by a Roman author comes from that self-educated savant, the senator Manilius. This is what he says.—No one has ever seen it feeding. In Arabia it is sacred to the Sun, lives 540 years, constructs a nest when it is getting old from twigs of cassia and frankincense, stuffs it with aromatic substances and dies upon it. There from its bones and marrow is born first of all something like a little worm, which gives birth to a chick. The first action of the new phoenix is to perform the obsequies of its pre-decessor, then to carry the whole nest (somewhere about Panchaea) to Heliopolis and lay it on the altar there. Manilius further reports the tradition that the life of this bird is coextensive with a revolution of the Great Year, when the significations of the seasons and stars

*N. H. VIII. 1.

repeat themselves, beginning about noon of the day when the sun
enters the sign of the Ram, and by his report that revolution was
completed in the consulship of Publius Licinius and Gnaeus
Cornelius on the 215th year from the foundation of Rome.
Cornelius Valerianus reports that a phoenix flew to Egypt in the
consulship of Quintus Plautius and Sextus Papinius. It was brought
to Rome when the emperor Claudius was censor in the year of the
city 800 and exhibited in the comitium, as is duly recorded in the
official proceedings. But nobody could be persuaded that it was a
genuine specimen.*

Extracts like these from Pliny's book could give a false
impression of the man. He was writing a kind of encyclopaedia
which was to summarize not merely the discoveries in what we
call natural history but what was known or believed about
many other matters which were of interest to his contemporaries. He does not engage for the truth of all that he sets down
—on the subject, for instance, of the phoenix—and he might
plead that like Aristotle he felt bound to assemble all the
material. But then Aristotle had an almost unexampled
sagacity in dealing with such material as he could control,
whereas Pliny is quite uncritical. This did not hurt him with
the Middle Ages, which in matters of physical science were,
generally speaking, more uncritical than himself. So with them
he had immense authority—not so much directly as through
abstracts and epitomes—and this was not at once destroyed by
the Renaissance. As late as 1601 his immense book was translated into English by Philemon Holland, attracting Shakespeare
among its readers. It was Pliny's matter which fascinated people,
but his way of writing had some influence too. It is highly
personal and therefore not well suited for the statement of
scientific results, for that ought to be strictly impersonal. A
book like Burton's *Anatomy of Melancholy* or Browne's
Vulgar Errors is really in the tradition of Pliny rather than
Hippocrates or Aristotle. Each is a collection of material

*N. H. X. 2.

drawn in the main from books—as Pliny drew his—accompanied by a highly personal commentary. We now expect a different style from a man of science, whose business it is to let the facts 'speak for themselves', so far as that is possible. It may be thought that, if he does this, he cannot have a style of his own or indeed a style of any kind. But this is a mistake. White's *Selborne*, Adam Smith's *Wealth of Nations*, Mill's *Logic*, even Darwin's *Origin of Species*, though genuinely in the Aristotelian tradition, belong to literature. An eloquent treatise on logic or political economy or even zoology is not what is needed. Nobody could be more eloquent than Plato on these and kindred subjects, but the future in the literature of science lay rather with Aristotle. For it was his school which trained the great collectors and systematizers of knowledge in antiquity, and it was they who settled the question of how scientific matters should be treated in their exposition. This is what I meant when I said that the influence of Aristotle on the prose of scientific literature had been very great.

CHAPTER SIXTEEN

THE THEORY OF PROSE STYLE

A<small>RISTOTLE</small> applied his 'method'—it is his own word—not only to the physical and mental but to the aesthetic sciences. In particular he composed a treatise on the art of poetry, which survives in a fragmentary state, and a considerable treatise on the art of prose, which survives entire. They are known as the *Poetics* and the *Rhetoric*. The *Poetics* hardly concerns us except so far as it established the literary criticism of poetry as a form of prose. There has been, of course, an incalculable amount of such criticism in modern times, and some of it has been fine literature in its own right. But it is not clear that Aristotle had much to do with its quality as literature, while his observations on the nature and form of poetic composition belong to the history of poetry. On the other hand the *Rhetoric* concerns us intimately.

Literature began as the writing down of the spoken word, and a very long time after books began to be written their writers continued to envisage an audience rather than a reading public. This is why Aristotle is able long after the chief masterpieces of Greek literature had been composed to include under 'rhetoric' the art of writing as well as speaking. He did not in fact think of them as different arts. It is not possible to go into that here; we must be content with a summary of his views. 'Good prose will reveal its quality both in its style and in its arrangement. The primary virtue of prose style is clearness. But clearness is not everything; style must have distinction. It must be natural, rising and falling with the subject. The worst vice of style is stale and meretricious ornament. Your sentences should be grammatical, alive, rhythmical, but on no account metrical. As for arrangements, you must not make a fetish of it.

But you ought at least to set out your case in a clear and orderly manner before going on to prove it.' All of which is sound and sensible, almost too sensible. But it is an admirable formula for a *standard* prose; and that is all that Aristotle sought to provide.

His work in this department was taken up by later Greek writers, who elaborated it in various ways. But it was not these, it was not even Aristotle, who influenced (except, of course, indirectly) the practice of modern literature; it was certain Latin writers, who adapted the Greek principles to Latin prose or expounded them to readers. Cicero did both; Quintilian became content to expound. These two between them may be said to have taught later ages the writing of prose as a conscious art. As their elaborate instructions cannot even be summarized in less than many pages, a specimen of them is all that can be given.

There remains the question of the special note or 'stamp', as it is called, of the oratorical style. What it ought to be like may be gathered from what has been already said. For we have already touched on the ornaments or 'lights' resulting from words used singly or in ordered phrases. A good style will be so rich in these that not one word will be uttered that is not choice or weighty. There will be very many metaphors of every kind because, owing to the likeness they involve, the mind of the listener is carried to another point and back again, and moved hither and thither, and such a rapid movement of thought is intrinsically delightful. But the other 'lights' too—those which come from the placing of words —are a great adornment to style, resembling as they do what in an elaborately staged play or when the forum is dressed for a great occasion are called 'decorations', not simply because they are decorative but because they stand out boldly. It is the same with the 'lights' and decorations of prose style, which you have when words are duplicated and repeated, or set down with a slight variation, or when a series of clauses begins with the same word or ends with it or does both, or when the same word is repeated at the beginning of a sentence or at its end, or one word is used throughout but not in the same sense, or when words have a like case or ending, or when a number of words are balanced by their contraries, or when the sentence moves to a climax, or when conjunctions are removed and there is a good deal of asyndeton, or when we explain why we are passing over something, or when we correct ourselves with an appearance of self-criticism, or when there is some ejaculation of surprise or indignation, or when the same noun is frequently used in different cases.*

That is a résumé of the stylistic devices which may be employed by the artist in ornate prose. Though we do not look for them, as we do not find them, in modern English, their effectiveness had been proved by centuries of ancient oratory. Cicero uses all of them. A little reflection on this fact will lead us to recognize that the ornate style is the child of oratory as certainly as the plain style is conversational. It is a fundamental difference, from which a great deal has resulted. For instance, ornate prose has a different rhythm from conversation. The ancients paid what may seem to us an excessive amount of attention to this. Yet all our own masters of ornate prose do, by instinct or design, pay very great attention to it. They are conscious or half-conscious of an audience, and the character or composition of the audience affects their style. It may be observed that they prefer an audience of some education, for some education is needed to appreciate the ornate style. Cicero was convinced that the orator—that is the composer as well as the speaker of ornate prose—should be a man of wide culture. Because of his authority, supported on this point by Quintilian, the ornate style and learning, or at least wide reading, came to be thought of as almost inseparable. Think of Hooker, Donne, Milton, Browne, Taylor, Johnson, Burke, De Quincey, Pater.

Cicero himself was saturated in literature, and quotations are lavishly scattered about his less political compositions. His example had great weight with succeeding writers. Thus many years later we find Quintilian including in his book a concise

*Cicero, *Orator* 39.

account of the Greek and Roman authors whom the student of oratory (and ornate prose) might read with most profit. It is indeed concise, but surprisingly wide and catholic in its taste; and what he does so briefly say appears to be just and discriminating, especially, as one would expect, on Latin authors. This is what he says on the epic poets:

It will be proper for us to follow the same arrangement in going through our Roman authors. As to Homer among the Greeks, so among our own writers we must give pride of place to Virgil, who of all Greek and Latin poets of that class undoubtedly comes next to Homer. I shall quote the actual words which I heard in my young days from the lips of Domitius Afer when I asked him who he thought came nearest to Homer. *Virgil is second, but he is nearer the first than the third.* And certainly, while we must yield to that celestial and immortal genius, yet Virgil is the more careful artist for the very reason that he had to work harder at his task, and while we are beaten in the splendour of separate passages we perhaps make up for that by keeping a more consistent level. All the other epic poets will be found to trail off behind. Certainly Macer and Lucretius are to be read, but not for their diction, for while each is master of the style appropriate to his subject, Macer lacks elevation and Lucretius is different. Although Atacinus Varro has won his reputation in the field of translation, he should not be disregarded; yet he has not much to give for the increase of the orator's resources. Ennius let us venerate as we reverence groves of ancient sanctity where the huge old trunks are more impressive than beautiful. Others are nearer our own times and more useful for the purpose of which we are speaking. Ovid lacks restraint even in his use of the heroic hexameter and is too much enamoured of his own native wit, yet now and again his epic poetry is quite good. Then Cornelius Severus, though a better versifier than poet, might fairly have claimed the next place to Virgil, if, as has been said, he had only written the whole of his *Sicilian War* as well as he wrote the first book. The premature death of Serranus did not permit the full development of his powers, but his youthful productions not only reveal a remarkable talent but a desire to follow the best models astonishing in so young a man. The recent loss of Valerius Flaccus has been a heavy one. There was passion and poetry in Saleius Bassus, but the passage of the years did not ripen his gifts. Rabirius and Pedo are worth reading, if you have the time. Lucan is all fire and energy, full of striking aphorisms and, in my personal opinion, a better model for orators than for poets.*

It will be observed that this is not literary criticism in the absolute sense but something like a *catalogue raisonné*. Before Aristotle poets were apt to be praised or blamed, even by Plato, for other reasons than the quality of their poetry. Aristotle was content to ask the question 'How do the poets produce their poetry?' and by this restriction founded at a stroke the whole art or science of literary criticism. Yet of literary criticism as it is now practised there is in Aristotle very little. He does not describe or analyse the qualities which distinguish a particular author or a particular book from others of the same kind. He is interested in poetry and prose, not in poets and prose-writers. And this is true of ancient criticism in general. The case of Cicero is in point. He writes at length on the subject of rhetoric, but what he writes amounts to a delineation of the ideal orator, who never existed. He does sometimes characterize particular orators, but he does it in terms so general that we get no sharp impressions. The reason was that he had not inherited the special vocabulary which would have enabled him to discriminate between the qualities which appeal to the preciser aesthetic sensibilities. What he did have was a name for every device of oratorical style. In contemporary criticism we find the exact opposite of this—the most refined and subtle analysis of a particular writer's qualities from critics who could not tell us the meaning of 'synecdoche' or 'enthymeme'.

Yet this kind of criticism also has its roots in antiquity. They lie in the book best known by its Latin title *De Sublimitate*. For long it was attributed to Longinus, who lived in the second half of the third century, but it is now thought to have been written

Inst. Orat. X. 85.

(by an unknown author) about the time of Augustus. Whoever wrote it, we must bear in mind that when a seventeenth- or eighteenth- or even a nineteenth-century author refers to 'Longinus', this is the book to which he is referring.

It contains some aesthetic terms not easy to translate. There is 'sublimity' itself—what does the author mean by that? Certainly not what is ordinarily understood by the word in modern English but some quality of a much wider scope. Hence in discussing the book it is probably least misleading to dismiss the notion of 'sublimity' from our minds altogether. (It is one of the difficulties which the historian must face in connexion with the *Poetics* and the *De Sublimitate* that, vast as the influence of both has been, they were very far from being well understood by those who felt their influence most.) But, as I have said, it is 'Longinus' and not Aristotle who is the father of modern literary criticism. I shall try to indicate this with the help of two quotations, both referring to Demosthenes, for between them they should give a not inadequate idea of his method when it is applied to a particular author.

If in judging how far an author has succeeded we were to go by points and not by the true criterion, Hyperides would get more than Demosthenes. He has more notes within his compass and more literary virtues; he is like the all-round athlete who just misses the first place in everything; he fails to get that in competition with the other athletes, but except among these professionals he is the leading man. Now Hyperides not only reproduces as far as he can all the elements in Demosthenes' style—except his composition—in which he surpasses all competitors, but he has included in his repertory the graces and good points of Lysias into the bargain. When he adopts a conversational tone it is when that is appropriate, and he keeps it simple; Demosthenes has none of this variety. When Hyperides introduces touches of character they have a delightful piquancy. He is perpetually amusing in a witty way, urbanely sarcastic but never caddish, a master of irony; his jokes do not smack of the Old Comedy with its coarseness but fit naturally into what he is speaking about;

he is an adept at making people look ridiculous; he has any amount
of humour, but there is a sting in the well aimed shafts of his raillery;
over all these is an inimitable charm. He has a fine natural gift for
pathos; he can tell a story with negligent grace; his pliant suscepti-
bility makes him exceedingly apt to enter upon digressions—witness
his rather too poetical version of the story of Leto—and he has
managed his show-piece, the Funeral Oration, incomparably well.
Now look at Demosthenes. He is not good at character-drawing, he
is without mobility of spirit or pliancy or brilliance, he is deficient
in all the qualities we have just ascribed to Hyperides. When he
tries to be funny or witty we laugh at him, not with him; all his
efforts to attain to charm end in his getting farther from it. If he had
attempted to write the little speech about Phryne, or the one about
Athenogenes, we should have seen how much better Hyperides could
do it.—Yes, but the excellences of Hyperides, numerous as they are,
have nothing grand about them; they find expression in the
language of a cool and sensible man to which one can listen quietly.
One's heart does not beat when one reads Hyperides. But what does
Demosthenes do? He draws upon a store of literary virtues, such as
belong to the most sublimely gifted nature and had been brought to
perfection—the accent of the great orator, heart-felt emotions,
copiousness, alert intelligence and (when justified) rapidity, together
with that unapproachable vehemence and power of the man—and
when he has incorporated all these heaven-sent and superhuman—
for we must not call them human—gifts, he thereby overpowers all
antagonists by means of this glorious endowment, even when the
call is for qualities he does not possess, overwhelming the orators of
every age by the thunder and the lightning of his genius. Yes, a man
would sooner look descending thunderbolts in the face than storm
after storm of his passion.*

Now here is the other passage. It is an analysis of the famous
apostrophe in which Demosthenes calls upon the glorious dead
of Athens to bear witness to the justice of his policy. *It cannot,
it cannot be, men of Athens, that you erred when you undertook the
perilous duty of fighting for the freedom and security of all—no, by*

*xxxiv.

those of your ancestors who faced the foe at Marathon and fought by sea at Salamis and Artemisium and stood together at Plataea, and many another lying in public sepulchres, heroic men, all of whom were deemed by the state equally worthy of the same honourable interment, Aeschines, and not only the successful and victorious. (De Corona 208.) That is the sentence which the great critic now proceeds to analyse.

Demosthenes is beginning an exposition of his policy. What was the natural way to do this? 'You did not err, you who undertook the struggle in defence of the liberties of Greece; you have precedents for that in Athenian history; for the men of Marathon and Salamis and Plataea did not err'. Not so Demosthenes. When like a man suddenly breathed upon by God and filled with inspiration he intoned that oath by the brave of Hellas: *It cannot be that you erred— no, by them that faced the foe at Marathon! . . .* he *deifies* their ancestors, suggesting that men who had died such a death ought to be sworn by as we swear by the gods, and implanting in the hearts of his judges the heroic spirit of those who fought that field, and transforming the natural way of stating his case into a sublime outburst of high emotion which the strangeness of the oath makes only more convincing, and at the same time infusing into the breasts of his hearers the soothing and healing reflection that—uplifted by these words of praise—they should be no less proud of their conduct in the war with Philip than of the trophies won at Marathon and Salamis— by all this he carries his auditors completely with him. . . . And since the objection presented itself, 'The policy you are expounding ended in defeat, yet what you swear by were victories', he consequently measures his words and makes no slip, showing that a speaker must keep his head even in the transports of his enthusiasm. For what he says is, *those who faced the foe at Marathon and fought by sea at Salamis and Artemisium, and stood together at Plataea.* Nowhere has he used the expression 'were victorious'; at every point he has avoided mention of the result, since that was fortunate, just as the battle of Chaeronea was not. The consequence is that when he does rush on he instantly sweeps the hearer off his feet, saying, *all of whom, Aeschines, were honoured by the state with a public funeral, and not only the successful.*★

No such criticism, at once discriminating and appreciative, is to be found in English until we come to Dryden. It was then that the impact of the *De Sublimitate* began to be felt. This was due, not entirely but in the main, to Boileau, who published in 1674 a kind of translation which produced an extraordinary impression, rather increasing than diminishing, till well into the eighteenth century. It might almost be said of this translation that it moulded the taste and set the critical standard of the age of Pope, who himself was under the deepest obligations to it. In this indirect way 'Longinus' taught the art of literary criticism to our eighteenth century. Horace could not do this because his judgments are summary and general; detailed criticism is not in his line. But Boileau, more or less in good faith, misrepresented 'Longinus'. While formally recognizing the Greek critic's insistence on the importance or rather necessity of genius and inspiration in the great writer, what his own criticism fastens upon are those chapters in the *De Sublimitate* which illustrate and condemn bad taste, over-emphasis, 'purple passages' and the like. This was grist to his mill as the prophet of correctness in writing. As for Pope, it is clear that he was struck by the enthusiasm of 'Longinus'— whom, of course, he read in Boileau, not in the original Greek —but in his practice he is all for correctness. One might have expected that when a new tone was given to criticism by the Romantic Movement the eloquent plea of the ancient critic that all faults are to be forgiven to native genius would have been heard with admiration. But this was hardly what happened. It may be that they were prejudiced against the *De Sublimitate* by the praises of Boileau and Pope, and therefore assumed that there could be nothing in it for them. Indeed it may be doubtful if Hazlitt or Lamb ever read 'Longinus', although it is probable that Coleridge did. However that may be, it is only within the last hundred years that the greatness of the book has been fully perceived.

There was no comparable Latin critic. What the Romans

learned in this field they learned from the Greeks. The excerpt which I propose to give from a letter of the Younger Pliny will be proof of this. It is an example of the method of illustrative quotation, which the Greek critics (including 'Longinus') had worked out for themselves. It is worth giving because for centuries Pliny was read when the *Poetics* and the *De Sublimitate* were not or not with the same intelligence. To that extent and in that way his criticism was important. The translation of the letter which follows is by Melmoth. It is accurate enough to serve our purpose and it has the advantage of catching the tone of Pliny better than an up-to-date version. For in almost everything but date Pliny was an eighteenth-century dilettante.

But it will be said, perhaps, there is a wide difference between orators and poets. As if, forsooth, Tully were not as bold in his figures as any of the poets! But not to mention particular cases from him, since in his case, I imagine, there can be no dispute; does Demosthenes himself, that model and standard of true oratory, does Demosthenes check and repress the fire of his genius, in that well-known passage which begins thus: 'Ye infamous flatterers, ye evil genii'?—And again, 'It is neither with stones nor bricks that I have fortified this city.' And afterwards: 'Was it not well done to throw the rampart of Euboea in front of Attica on the seaward side?' And in another place: 'O my Countrymen, I think, by the immortal gods, that he is intoxicated with the grandeur of his own actions.'

But what can be more daring and beautiful than that long digression, which begins in this manner: 'A terrible disease, O my countrymen, has seized upon all Greece'?—The following passage, likewise, though something shorter, is conceived in the same boldness of metaphor:—'Then it was I rose up in opposition to the daring Pytho, who *poured forth a torrent* of menaces against you'. The subsequent stricture is of the same stamp: 'When a man has strengthened himself, as Philip has, by avarice and wickedness, the first pretence that offers itself, the least false step, overthrows him and brings all to ruin'.

So in the same style with the foregoing is this: '*Railed off*, as it were, from all the privileges of the society, by the concurrent judgements of three tribunals in the city.' And in the same place: 'O Aristogiton! you have betrayed that mercy which used to be shewn to offences of this nature, or rather indeed, you have wholly exhausted it. In vain then would you *fly* for refuge to a port, which you have *shut up*, and *choked with piles*'.—He had said before: 'I am afraid you will appear in the judgement of some to be *setting up a public seminary* of faction'. And later on: 'I see *no footing for him in any of these places*; but all is *precipice, gulf*, and *profound abyss*.' And again: 'Nor do I imagine that our ancestors erected these courts of judicature, that men of his character should be *propagated* there;'— And afterwards: 'If he deals in, and retails, and peddles wickedness.' —And a thousand other passages which I might cite to the same purpose: not to mention those expressions which Aeschines says are not *words*, but *wonders*.

You will tell me I have lighted on an adverse instance, since Demosthenes is condemned by Aeschines for running into these figurative expressions. But observe, I intreat you, how far superior the former orator is to his criticizer, and superior, too, in virtue of these very passages: for in others, the strength of his genius discovers itself: in those above quoted, the sublimity of it shines out. But does Aeschines himself avoid what he reproves in Demosthenes? 'The orator', says he, 'Athenians, and the law ought to *speak* the same language; but when the *voice* of the law declares one thing, and that of the orator another'—And in another place: 'he afterwards manifestly discovered the design he had, of concealing his fraud under cover of the decree, having expressly declared there in, that the embassadors sent to the Oretae gave the five talents, not to you, but to Callias. And that you may be convinced what I say is the truth (after having *stripped* the decree of its *pomp*, its *galleys*, and *braggadocio*) read the clause itself.' And in another part: 'Suffer him not to *break cover* and *wander* out of the limits of the question': a metaphor he is so fond of that he repeats it again: 'But sitting firm and lying in ambush in the assembly *drive* him into the merits of the question, and observe well how he *doubles*.' Is his style more reserved and simple when he says: 'But you are *manufacturing wounds*', or, 'will you not seize and punish this political *pirate*, who *cruises* about the state?'—with many other passages of a like nature?*

Ep. IX. xxvi.

If this criticism is compared with that of 'Longinus' it will seem to be greatly inferior in power, insight and originality. But it is sound enough so far as it goes, and it is evident that Pliny has culled his own examples. In this way it escapes the charge that can be brought against so much ancient criticism, that of being too general. Pliny here is detailed and concrete. This was a valuable lesson for later ages, though they were slow in learning it. Indeed it was not learned until quite modern times.

But it should not be imagined that literary criticism as it is now pursued can be traced back in all its forms to ancient writers. No ancient critic known to us seeks to interpret the work of a writer as an expression of his life and character. That method does not seem to be in any systematic form older than Sainte Beuve.* It is a question whether by this time it has not been carried too far. At least a great deal of contemporary criticism appears to regard a writer's work as so much evidence for the kind of man he was—to turn literary criticism into a branch of psychology. Now it may be true that the man is more important than his work. But the work is literature, and the man is not.

*Something like it is sometimes attempted by Carlyle.

CHAPTER SEVENTEEN

THE LITERATURE OF TRAVEL

So MANY books of travel are now written, if we include, as surely we may, books of adventure and exploration, real or imaginary or partly both, that they may be thought to have become a distinguishable branch of literature. Some belong to science and are written in the prose of science. But many have, and many make, no pretensions to scientific qualities and are read only for their style or the interest of their matter. It seems therefore worth enquiring whether this literature of travel has any of its roots in the ancient classics.

Now I should be surprised if those who know it would not agree that the second book of the *Histories* of Herodotus is the best piece of travel literature ever written. The charm, the freshness, the brilliance, the novelty of it are incomparable. It is about Egypt, which he visited before the end of the fifth century B.C. Much of what he tells us is given on the authority of ignorant or mendacious guides—for even in the fifth century before Christ Egypt was a tourist country—and that, though always highly picturesque, is often quite untrue. But what he saw with his own eyes he reports with fidelity and delighted interest. Instead of quoting some more entertaining passage, I will translate for their scientific interest some of his observations on the Nile.

The greater part of Egypt, according to what the priests told me —and my own observations confirmed their view—is an accretion to the original country. I am of opinion that the whole stretch of land between the two ranges of hills south of Memphis which I mentioned was once an arm of the sea like the country round Ilium and Teuthrania, and like the Maeander valley—though this is to compare the small with the great. For none of the rivers which have silted up these districts is comparable in size to even one of the five mouths of the Nile. There are other rivers too, not so large as the Nile, which have done wonders in this way. I will only mention the Achelous, which, flowing through Acarnania to the sea, has joined half of the Echinades islands to the mainland.

In Arabia, not far from Egypt, is a gulf running inland from the sea called Red. . . . I believe that Egypt was another such gulf, running in from the Mediterranean in the direction of Ethiopia, while the Arabian Gulf* stretches north in the direction of Syria; the recesses which they bored were close and they missed each other by quite a narrow strip of land. Now if the Nile should decide to turn his current into this Arabian Gulf, what is to prevent it then from being filled up in less than twenty thousand years? My own estimate would be less than ten thousand. So in the time that had passed before I was born would not even a much larger gulf have been silted up by a river of such volume and such activity?

My own opinion then strongly agrees with this theory about Egypt, and I accept it as true. Moreover it is confirmed by what I saw with my own eyes. Egypt projects from the land with which it is connected, sea-shells are to be seen on the mountains, there is an efflorescence of salt which is gradually destroying the Pyramids, only one ridge—that south of Memphis—is formed of sand, while Egypt† bears no resemblance to the land bordering on Arabia, nor to Libya, nor to Syria either, but has a black, friable soil, which is in fact the silt that has been brought down in solution from Ethiopia by the river.‡

A modern geologist would, of course, have many corrections to make in this account of the formation of the Nile Delta. But, unless he were quite incapable of seeing things in historical perspective—think of the date of Herodotus—he could not but admire it. It is an excellent piece of scientific reasoning and the more remarkable because nothing so good of its kind is to be found until quite modern times. For the fact has to be

---

*The Gulf of Suez. †Herodotus means the Delta.
‡II. 10–12.

recorded that geology and even geography made very little progress for some time after Herodotus, and then proceeded to get worse and worse. The truth is that the ancients were not fond of travel for its own sake. The hero of the *Odyssey* liked to see new men and new cities, but he hated going to see them; the Ulysses of Tennyson's poem is quite unlike the Odysseus of Homer except in his thirst for knowledge. The Romans were worse in this matter than the Greeks. There is something discreditable to the Romans in the fact that they never made any concerted effort to settle the geography of their own empire. What they knew about it was nearly all got from Greek explorers and scientists, and as often as not this knowledge was misrepresented or misunderstood. And it was the misunderstandings that got into the mediaeval books.

There may be one Roman author who escapes this criticism. Julius Caesar had evidently some of the instinct of the explorer, although the *Gallic War* is singularly uninformative about some things on which a modern explorer would dwell. He tells us very little about his journeys, very little about the natural features of the countries he visited. Whereas the modern travel book is nothing if not picturesque, there is hardly a touch of that sort in Caesar, and what there is appears to be quite accidental. (Of course, he was not writing that kind of book.) His two invasions of Britain struck the imagination of his contemporaries but not—or so it would seem—his own. There is indeed a formal description of the island, but it is so inaccurate that editors are disposed to think it an interpolation. All that matters to us is that it was believed by our forefathers to be Caesar's.

The population is very large—how large, it is impossible to ascertain—and habitations (built mostly in the Gaulish style) are exceedingly numerous. Cattle may be seen in great numbers. Their currency is of copper or gold coins, or iron ingots of a standard weight. There are deposits of tin in the midlands and of iron ore in the maritime districts—the latter not rich. What bronze they use is imported. Trees of every species except the beech and the fir grow in Britain as in Gaul. They have some scruple about eating hare or chicken or goose, but this does not prevent them from breeding them for sport. The climate is milder than that of Gaul, frosts being less intense. The island forms a natural triangle, one side facing Gaul. One of the corners of this side is in Kent and has an eastern aspect; here nearly all ships from Gaul put in. The lower corner points to the south. The whole side is about 475 miles long. The second side trends towards Spain and the west, where lies Ireland, which is computed to be half the size of Britain, from which it is separated by the same distance as Gaul. Midway in the crossing to Ireland is the island called Mona. There are reputed to be many smaller islands adjacent, concerning which some have written that about mid-winter there are thirty days of unbroken darkness. We could get no satisfaction by asking questions, but by definite measurements, using a water clock, we determined by inspection that the nights are shorter than on the continent. This side, according to the prevailing estimate of the natives, is 665 miles in length. The third side fronts the north and has no land opposite it, but a corner of it looks in the general direction of Germany. The length of this side is taken to be 760 miles. Thus the whole island has a circumference of 1900 miles.

Of all its inhabitants by far the most civilised are those who live in the peninsula of Kent. Their way of life is much the same as that of the Gauls. Broadly speaking the tribes in the interior do not raise crops but live on milk and butcher's meat. They are dressed in skins. All Britons stain their bodies with woad (which produces a blue colour) giving them a more fearsome look in battle. They wear their hair long and shave every part of their person except the head and the upper lip. Groups of ten or twelve men have wives in common, the groups being composed generally of brothers, or of fathers and sons; children born in this society are accredited to the girl's first 'husband'.*

Little of this can be first-hand observation; the geography is wildly mistaken and the ethnology leaves the experts puzzled

*Bell. Gall. V. 12, 13, 14.

or sceptical. Nevertheless Caesar did add to our knowledge of Britain, and the romance of his British adventure lives on in spite of him. But what are we to say of Tacitus? Long after Caesar he writes a book, a very short book, the main substance of which is the penetration of Scotland by Agricola. Yet about Scotland itself he has only a few vague and perfunctory remarks. Evidently the 'unknown' did not excite his curiosity, nor apparently that of his readers. It cannot but seem strange to us. And what are we to say when we discover from the *Agricola* that Tacitus believes in a flat earth—a thing no educated Greek had believed for half a millennium? You may think these points are not worth mentioning. But they are, because it was the Romans and not the Greeks who taught the Middle Ages. These ages are often accused of being unscientific, but they are hardly more unscientific than the Romans, who had infinitely less excuse.

The discoveries of ancient travellers and explorers were epitomized along with other matters in Pliny's *Natural History*. He attempted the impossible, and his immense compilation could not fail to be often inaccurate. But his influence was so great and so long continued that we must give it some attention.

Even before Herodotus the west coast of Africa had been explored, evidently far along the Barbary Coast, by a Carthaginian admiral called Hanno. He made a report to his government which, some centuries later, was translated or partly translated into Greek. The passage which follows is based on the certainly inadequate Greek version of what a Phoenician sea-captain had written five centuries before. Such was Roman geographical science.

On the coast 50 Roman miles from Lixus is the river Sububus, which runs past the colony of Banasa, a grand navigable stream. At an equal distance from it is the town of Sala, situated on the river of the same name. It is quite close to the uninhabited country and is infested by herds of elephants, but has much more to fear from the raids of the Autololes, a nation on the route to the most romantic part of Africa, Mount Atlas. The Atlas rises, according to the accounts which have been handed down, from the middle of the sandy region, scaling the heavens; on the side which slopes to the shores of the ocean to which it has given its name it is rough and frowning, but on the side which faces Africa it is shady and wooded and watered with natural springs, and so rich in fruits of every kind coming to maturity in succession that the palate is perpetually gratified. By day none of its inhabitants are visible, there is an all-pervading silence, which thrills like that of the desert; as one draws nearer a speechless awe comes over one which is more than the shudder caused by the way it towers up above the clouds and into the neighbourhood of the moon's orbit. At night it flashes with many fires, is filled with the frolics of aegipans and satyrs, and re-sounds with the music of fifes and flutes and the noise of drums and cymbals. All this we have been told by celebrated authors, not to mention certain Labours of Hercules and Perseus. The distance to it is of uncertain, but vast, extent. Other authorities were the Observa-tions of the Carthaginian admiral Hanno, who in the most flourish-ing period of Punic history was ordered to explore the extent of Africa. He was followed by a number of Greek and Roman writers, who among other fables have preserved an account of many cities founded by him, of which there survives no trace or record. When Scipio Aemilianus was in command in Africa he gave the historian Polybius a fleet with which he sailed along that coast on a voyage of discovery. Polybius has left it on record that the distance from Mount Atlas on the west to the river Anatis in the direction of the forest lands full of the wild beasts which Africa produces is 496 Roman miles.*

The Greek version of Hanno is said to have been made about 130 B.C. Polybius, for whom it was made, evidently did something in the way of noting and charting sites, but nobody has suggested that he was a great and daring explorer like Hanno or like the Greek Pytheas, who three centuries before

*Nat. Hist. V. 1.

Caesar's landing sailed along the British coast as far as the Shetland Islands. Pytheas recorded his observations in a book which, because truth is stranger than fiction, was not believed and therefore not preserved. It was the fictions that survived. Because these were repeated by Latin authors they were received by the Middle Ages as true.

Nothing fascinated the mediaeval imagination more than the stories about India. Alexander the Great had invaded India in the fourth century before Christ, and after his early death more than one of his officers related their experiences there. But in a surprisingly short time their accounts were submerged under the vast Alexander myth, to which the oriental imagination largely contributed. India became a wonderland. The most sober account we now have is Arrian's; but Arrian wrote in Greek, and the Middle Ages, roughly speaking, read nothing in Greek. They went instead to a certain Curtius Rufus, who wrote a concise history of Alexander in Latin. It is quite good Latin, and Curtius is by no means a stupid person. But he was writing up his subject for a public which cared little for the facts and a great deal for the romance (as it is politely called) of Alexander's career. Curtius was not a serious historian, but he knew what his readers wanted, and he gave them that. There is no point in blaming either him or them.

Of India he says:

The land is prolific in flax, so that the dress of most Indians is linen. Their writing material is the bark, delicate as paper, of certain trees. They have birds that can be taught to imitate human speech. Their animals, unless imported, are strange to the rest of the world. India also breeds, though it does not produce, the rhinoceros. Their elephants are stronger than those which they tame in Africa, and their size corresponds to their strength. Gold is brought down by their rivers, which flow in a lazy and gentle current. Gems and pearls are cast by the sea upon their shores, and this is the chief source of their wealth, at least since they have begun to share their vices with foreign nations. Forsooth things washed up by the tides are valued at the price fixed by luxury. The character of the population, among the Indians as elsewhere, is formed by geography.

They cover their bodies with a linen robe reaching to the feet, their feet with sandals, their heads with a linen turban; from their ears hang jewels; their upper and lower arms are adorned with gold in the person of those who are notable among their fellow-countrymen for their rank or wealth. They are more given to combing than shaving their hair; their chin is always unshaven; they aim at giving an appearance of smoothness to the rest of their skin. In the case of rajahs however their luxury, which they call magnificence, exceeds the extravagance of all other races. When the rajah permits himself to be seen in public, silver censers are carried by attendants, who also drench with perfumes all the way over which he has resolved to be borne. He reclines in a golden palanquin hung with pearls; the fine linen which clothes him is variegated with gold and purple. The palanquin is attended by an armed bodyguard carrying birds (perched on branches) which have been trained by them to drown serious conversation with their song. The palace is open to visitors when he is combing and decking his hair; that is the time when he gives audience to embassies and delivers judgments to his subjects. When his slippers have been removed his feet are smeared with balsams. His greatest efforts are exerted in hunting, which takes the form of despatching arrows, amid the prayers and songs of his concubines, at animals which have been shut up in a park. Their arrows, two cubits long, are shot with more effort than effect, since the bolt, the merit of which consists wholly in its lightness, is made unhandy by its weight. His shorter journeys are performed on horseback; when a more distant expedition is made he rides in a carriage drawn by elephants, whose enormous bodies are covered from head to foot with gold. To complete this exhibition of degeneracy he is followed by a long train of concubines in golden palanquins, the troop being separate from the ranee's train, which it equals in expensiveness. The royal banquets are prepared by women, who also serve the wine, which all Indians drink freely. When the rajah has been stupefied by drink and sleep he is carried to his bedchamber by concubines invoking the gods of night in a traditional lullaby.*

*Vit. Alex. VIII. ix.

It was descriptions like this which fired the imaginations of the men who discovered America. Why should curiosity about India lead to the discovery—or rediscovery—of America? Because it was thought that anyone sailing from Europe across the Atlantic would come reasonably soon to India. This was the result of an exaggerated estimate of the land mass of Europe —Asia, which was believed to extend so far over the surface of the globe as to leave no vast space between Spain and the east of Asia, where India was supposed to lie. Columbus died in the belief that he had reached not America but India. He had read in Seneca: Quantum enim est quod ab ultimis litoribus Hispaniae usque ad Indos iacet? paucissimorum dierum spatium, si navem suus ferat ventus, implebit. 'How much is the distance from the western shores of Spain to India? A ship, if it is carried by a favouring wind, will cover it within a very few days.'* He had also read in Seneca's *Medea*:†

> venient annis
> secula seris quibus Oceanus
> vincula rerum laxet et ingens
> pateat tellus, Tiphysque novos
> detegat orbes; nec sit terris
> ultima Thule.

'A generation shall come as time draws late when Ocean will loosen the bonds of the world, and earth be revealed in all her vastness, and a new Tiphys discover new latitudes, and Thule will not be the farthest land.'

In his copy of Seneca's tragedies the son of Colombus wrote against this passage some words to this effect: 'My father fulfilled this prophecy.' The claim was justified.

But Columbus comes at the end of the Middle Ages. All through that long tract of time the interest in travel, stimulated no doubt by the Crusades and the habit of pilgrimage, and in

*Nat. Qu. I. 7.   †374–9.

what the ancients said about it, persisted and perhaps increased. The passages I have just been quoting from classical authors show a disposition to record, if not to believe, the strange rumour in preference to the known or ascertainable fact. This disposition is intensified as writers approach or fall within the mediaeval period. There was Solinus who, probably in the second half of the third century, conceived the notion of picking out the plums from the geographical part of Pliny's *Natural History*. Much of what he says would make a cat laugh, yet it was believed. A little less fabulous, but only a little, was the guide book of a Greek versifier called Dionysius. It was translated by Avienus and later by Priscian, and the Latin version had a great popularity. Even more popular were the works of the encyclopaedists Isidore of Seville in the seventh and 'Bartholomew the Englishman' in the thirteenth centuries. In them the picturesque old errors continue to flourish. Yet they were models of sober learning compared with the propagators of the Alexander Romance, which came to embody all the fantasies about India and the Orient which make it in its later forms look like something out of the *Arabian Nights*. Finally a writer of genius, supposed to be Jean d'Outremeuse, drew on this pseudo-geographical matter to compose what in its English dress is called *The Travels of Sir John Mandeville*, which has always been read with delight, first as truth and then as fiction.

Literature as such has nothing to do with the truth of history or science. Mistaken geography and natural history have often been the food of poetry and romance.

> Wherein of antres vast, and deserts idle,
> Rough quarries, rocks, hills, whose heads touch heaven,
> It was my hint to speak. Such was my process,
> And of the Cannibals that each other eat,
> The Anthropophagi, and men whose heads
> Do grow beneath their shoulders.

All that, Shakespeare found in Pliny, as translated by Philemon Holland. Many poets, even when they 'knew better', have found inspiration in such fancies, as Milton, Wordsworth, Coleridge, who were all lovers of travel books.

With the Age of Discovery the literature of travel took a new lease of life. But it can hardly be said to take a new form, for it is still in the tradition of Herodotus. It should not be forgotten that nearly all the explorers had some tincture of literature—which then meant Latin literature—and some were even learned. They had read their Pliny and their Pomponius Mela, a geographer who lived a little before Pliny. Here is part of a report made by Sir Walter Raleigh on his expedition to Guiana in 1595. 'Next unto Arui there are two rivers Atoica and Caora, and on that branch which is called Caora, are a nation of people, whose heads appear not above their shoulders . . . they are reported to have their eyes in their shoulders, and their mouths in the middle of their breasts.' Whoever 'reported' this was stealing from Pliny who says:* Blemmyis traduntur capita abesse ore et oculis pectori adfixis. 'It is reported of the Blemmyae that their heads are without mouth or eyes, which are fixed to their breast.' The English redaction of 'Mandeville' is full of such reports. It is strange to find even in Elizabethan literature how many of the old errors vigorously survive.

The stories of the English explorers are recorded in the great collection of Hakluyt. They lay stress on whatever was striking in the landscape or customs which they saw. In this they follow the tradition of Pliny but they make better reading because, though they write with less art, they write more fully and naturally. The world was almost as wide to them as it had been to Hanno or Pytheas. They sailed uncharted seas in ships not much larger or handier. Their mental outlook was therefore much the same, and they were interested in much the same things. But this is not the whole story. They felt it to be their

*V. 8.

business to confirm or disprove the theories about the unknown parts of the world which they found in the Latin books, and this knowledge permeates what they write. They do not think of themselves as creating a new literature of travel but as adding to the old. In fact they do not think very much about themselves at all. Now and again one finds an exhibitionist like Coryate or a Renaissance egotist like Raleigh, who have a turn for self-expression. But these are not typical. The Elizabethan seaman is a reporter, not a commentator. In this he is fortunate, because what he saw was interesting, whereas his comments would almost certainly have been trite.

The objective travel book continues to be written, sometimes very well, though it is apt to degenerate into a 'guide' of the Baedeker sort. That at least, it is natural to suppose, must be a modern thing. But no, there were exactly such books in ancient times. At least one has been preserved, the *Periegesis* or 'Guide' of Pausanias, who wrote (in Greek) about the middle of the second century. It is quite like Baedeker, full of directions to the tourist and paying special attention to the works of art and antiquities of each locality. It is written without grace, but that is not infrequently the case with guide-books.

It would seem that books of travel—they were nearly all in Greek—were very popular under the Roman Empire, and popular in the ratio of their picturesqueness. Very little of this literature has survived. Its very popularity may have been its undoing. The 'traveller's tale' easily lends itself to parody and satire on the one hand, as in *Gulliver's Travels*, or to fiction or romance on the other, as in *Robinson Crusoe*. The ancients were fully as well aware of this as the moderns, and the consequence has been that the satire and romance have largely survived, while the genuine narrative has suffered eclipse, as being more sober and less 'readable'. One of the pieces which has survived is Lucian's *True History*, which is a parody and a satire upon the more extravagant and mendacious type of travel book. This is how it begins.

I once set out from the Pillars of Hercules* and setting course for the Western Ocean† I began my voyage with the aid of a favouring wind. The reason and motive for my journey was intellectual curiosity, the love of novelty and the wish to discover the limits of the Ocean, and what people dwell on the other side of it. Such being my intention, I provisioned the ship very abundantly, took on board an adequate supply of water, and took with me fifty men of about my own age, who shared my ambition. I also provided myself with a stock of arms, and took on the best pilot at a high salary, and strengthened the ship—a brig—to face the buffeting of a long voyage. For a day and a night we sailed before the wind without losing sight of the land on a pretty smooth outward course. Next day however at sunrise the wind began to increase, the sea rose and darkness came on before we could brail the canvas. So we let her run before the wind and, leaving ourselves to the mercy of the gale, we were tempest-tossed for seventy nine days in succession. On the eightieth the sun suddenly shone out and we descried at no great distance an island, mountainous and wooded, with a moderate surf breaking; for by this time the swell had greatly subsided. So we put in there and landed and lay a long time on the shore, worn out as we were by our long struggle with the elements.'‡

We might be reading *Gulliver*. But, though Lucian was apparently the first to give the scientific romance this satirical turn, the scientific romance is older than Lucian. What else is the account of Atlantis in Plato? It is an account that has been almost too successful, not indeed with the ancients, who knew that Atlantis was invented by Plato, but with a surprising number of the moderns. A generation after Plato, the ingenious Euhemerus invented another island, Panchaea, in which he had 'found' evidence to support a theory he had evolved about the origin of religion. He convinced a good many of the ancients not perhaps of the existence of his island, but of the truth of his theory, which was all he really cared about. But that is another matter.

*The Straits of Gibraltar.   †The Atlantic.
‡*V. H.* I. 5, 6.

Now with the satire and the romance there creeps in a subjective element. We may observe it in that early satire of Horace (the fifth of the first book) which is often called *Iter ad Brundisium*, 'On the Road to Brindisi'. In this story of a journey, the reader will remember without my quoting it, we are more interested in the travellers than in the travel. We are particularly interested in the adventures or misadventures of Horace himself and in his way of meeting them. He meets them in a way which engages the amused sympathy of the reader. The delightfulness of the method has led countless imitators to follow it in their own narratives. It gives a special pleasure to English readers, who ever since the time of Chaucer, and no doubt before that, have been sympathetic to humorous self-depreciation. The extraordinary influence which Horace exerted upon the eighteenth century undoubtedly penetrated through its verse to its prose. Thus Addison very often reflects the tone of the Satires and still more of the Epistles of Horace. It is also reflected in our travel literature. The spirit of the *Iter ad Brundisium* is to a considerable degree that of Sterne's *Sentimental Journey* and its progeny, of which the best known is probably Stevenson's *Through the Cevennes on a Donkey*. *The Sentimental Journey* makes its effect by a combination of humorous self-criticism (of the Horatian kind) with what the eighteenth century knew as 'sensibility'. The combination is original, but hardly the elements of it. It is not difficult to find in ancient literature a disposition to idealize the 'simple life' in a way that might fairly be described as sentimental. We detect this for example in Dion of Prusa, who in the course of his career as a professional man of letters was converted about A.D. 100 to something like Cynicism. The Cynics believed that most of our sins—and consequent unhappiness—were due to unnecessary desires. What was the remedy? To reduce our wants to a minimum. When we had done that we should be healthy and happy—like the simple folk who live in the country. Whether the people who lived in the country were in

K

fact healthy and happy, or even very simple, was a question
which was not considered to require investigation. Yet Dion
was given a chance to investigate it. He was shipwrecked once
on a lonely part of Euboea, where he was lost until he found
a hunter who takes him to a tiny community, utterly poor,
extremely happy, and perfectly virtuous. 'I had no fear', says
Dion, 'of any design against me—I had only a cheap cloak.
But it was my experience then, as it has been my experience
on many similar occasions (for I have been a restless wanderer),
that poverty is indeed a holy and inviolate thing and the poor
man far safer from outrage than official persons with all their
paraphernalia.' At any rate in the hamlet Dion finds everyone
angelically good and kind. It is a charming picture he gives
and makes one think of Goldsmith in his most idyllic mood;
but it is too long to quote. I give the final sentences.

Meanwhile the girl rose and brought from the other cabin minced
service-berries and medlars and winter apples and swelling clusters
from the generous grape bunch, and set them on the table, wiping
it with leaves after the meat course and putting everything upon
clean ferns. Also the boys now came bringing the pig with laughter
and sport. With them came the lad's mother and his two small
brothers carrying loaves of pure wheat, and boiled eggs on wooden
platters, and roasted chick-peas. After embracing her brother and
her niece she sat down beside her husband and said, 'There's the
victim*; our son has been keeping it for quite a while against the
wedding. We have made all the other preparations, and the wheat
flour and barley meal are ready. The only other thing we shall need,
I think, is a drop of wine, and that can easily be got from the
village'. Her son stood close beside her with his eyes fixed on his
prospective father-in-law, who mischievously remarked, 'Here's
the one who can't make up his mind. No doubt he wants to go on
fattening his pig awhile'. 'She's bursting with fat', cried the lad; and
I, anxious to come to his rescue, said, 'Take care that the boy doesn't
get thin while the pig is getting fat'. 'Our guest speaks the truth',

---

*The pig.

said the mother. 'You would hardly know him just now, he is so thin. No longer ago than yesterday I saw him get up in the night and leave the cabin.' 'The dogs', said he, 'were barking, and I went out to see why.' 'Nothing of the sort. You were walking about like mad. —So don't let us allow him to suffer any more.' Here she put her arms round the neck of the girl's mother and kissed her; and the latter said to her husband, 'Let us do as they wish'. So the matter was settled, and they said, 'Let us have the wedding the day after tomorrow'. They invited me to stay, and I accepted with thanks.*

This is, of course, a sentimentalized picture; country life is not so idyllic as all that, especially among the very poor. It was such misrepresentations that evoked the protest of Crabbe. Before he protested English literature had for about a century been deluged with sentiment about the happy rustic felt by ladies and gentlemen who knew nothing about him and did not in the least desire to know the truth of the matter. Yet hypocrisy is not the right charge to bring against them. Most people come to think, more or less sincerely, what they would like to think. Dion does not strike one as insincere, or as any more insincere than Goldsmith in the *Deserted Village*. He was not a great original influence like the author of *Daphnis and Chloe*. But he contributed something to the enforcement of that influence, and, as he is probably earlier than Longus, may have been something of a model to the novelist. At any rate he is a type of the Sentimental Traveller. What Sterne added was wit and naughtiness.

*Venator ad fin.

CHAPTER EIGHTEEN

THE LETTER

THE art of letter-writing is now so little practised that we have almost ceased to believe that it exists. Yet we have only to imagine how our own literature would suffer if we lost the letters of Swift and Gray and Walpole and Cowper, of Byron and Shelley and Lamb and Keats and Fitzgerald and the Carlyles, not to mention the novels of Richardson, to see that the letter or epistle (Latin *epistola*) is an independent and delightful part of it. The reason why the art is now neglected —the facility of communications—did not exist until well into the nineteenth century. To our ancestors letters were worth taking trouble over because they were infrequent. It might be supposed that the farther back we travel in time the more effectively this cause would operate. But it is not so. The postal service was about as good in Cicero's time as in the early years of Queen Victoria. But then came the 'penny post', the post-card, the telegram, the telephone, and they have almost destroyed the letter as literature.

In ancient Greece nobody thought of publishing his own letters. Some might be preserved by their recipients for the interest or importance of their contents. In this way there have been preserved some letters of Plato and some of Epicurus, the founder of the Epicurean philosophy. The Platonic letters (especially the seventh in the collection) are of extreme interest for the light they throw on the life and character of the writer; but they are not contributions to literature like the Dialogues. The epistolary style of Epicurus has perhaps been treated by critics with greater harshness than it deserves, because if it has no grace it has character. But, as it has had no influence on other writers, we cannot discuss it in this book. In later centuries there was a considerable output of fictitious letters ascribed to famous men of the past. Such were the *Letters of Phalaris* which were so much discussed at the turn of the seventeenth and eighteenth centuries. The most famous of all letters, the Epistles of St. Paul, are in Greek; but we agreed not to count the New Testament among classical influences.

It was Cicero who, so far as we know, created (it would seem unconsciously) the *art* of letter-writing. We possess a mass of his correspondence, including a good many letters from his friends. It is probable that Cicero is the greatest of all letter-writers. The importance of his matter, the range of his public and private interests, the variety of his moods, his facility in expressing every shade of sense and feeling, the aptness of his quotations, above all his spontaneity have never in combination been excelled or equalled. Like all masters of this form he adapts his manner to his correspondent. If he is writing to a man like Julius Caesar he is careful about what he says and how he says it. Writing to an intimate friend, like Atticus, he expresses himself exactly as he would in conversation. But he never writes (as some of his correspondents do) in slangy or barely grammatical Latin. He had subjected himself to so long and rigorous a training in the arts of writing and speaking that it had become impossible for him to be guilty of that. With him to be literate had become second nature. But he can be colloquial, and his colloquialisms, mingling with the literature he loves and knows so well, have like those of Lamb and Stevenson a peculiar relish. A correspondent to whom he writes in this way is Paetus.

My dear Paetus, I am scribbling the draft of this letter in my notebook as I recline at table: time, about 3 p.m. 'Place?' you will ask.... The house of Volumnius *le spirituel*. Yes, and two friends of yours are here: Atticus, who has the place above me, and Varius, who has the place below. Are you surprised that my serfdom has turned so jolly? Well but what on earth am I to do? Advise me, you that are a student of philosophy. Am I to torment, to torture myself? What good would that do me? Question two: how long am I to do it? 'Give your life up to literature', say you. Well do you suppose I do anything else? Or could I live at all, if I did not give my life to literature? But although one never tires of literature one must draw the line somewhere. So when I have quitted my books—though dining (which you suggested to the philosopher Dion as the one subject worth discussing) does not seem to me terribly important— what else there is for me to do before I betake myself to bed, I cannot think.—I have more to tell you. Listen! In the place below *le spirituel* reclines . . . Cytheris! 'So', quoth you, 'it is come to this. Among those present was the well known Cicero

> *On whom men gazed, towards whose countenance*
> *The Grecians turned their own.'*

The fact is, I had no idea she would be there. And let me tell you that Aristippus, the famous Socratic philosopher, did not even blush when it was cast up against him that he had got Lais. 'I have got Lais', was his retort, 'but Lais has not got me'. It is better in Greek— you can make your own translation. Actually that kind of thing never appealed to me even when I was a young man, let alone now that I am old. But I do like a good dinner where I can say whatever the Lord puts in my mouth and can turn my sighs into shouts of laughter. Can *you* do better?—admitting that you succeeded in making an ass even of a philosopher. Didn't you say, when he asked if anybody would like to propose a subject for discussion, that you had been hoping since morning to discuss dinner? The solemn ass was expecting you to raise the question whether there was one world or an infinite number. 'What application has that to you?' Ah, but a dinner means a devil of a lot to *you*, above all in Naples.—Well, that's how life goes with me. Every day I read or write. Afterwards —because I hate being unsociable—I dine with my friends not only without breaking the law (if any law can now be said to exist) but even within, and well within, the letter of it. So you must not look forward with apprehension to my arrival. You will receive a guest with no great appetite for food but an enormous one for fun.*

*Fam. IX. 26.

If Cicero had an important letter to write, he would no doubt compose it carefully. But one of his most appealing qualities as a correspondent—it is shown in the letter I have just quoted—is a complete spontaneity. This has got him into trouble with people who evidently consider that you cannot be too careful what you say in your letters. Thus Mommsen, the great German historian, blames him—for what? For not taking a strong line in a civil war. But even if this were a sensible criticism, it would not affect the literary quality of his letters. Here is part of a political letter.

Pompey, of whom I am so fond, has, I am terribly sorry to say, done for himself. He and his colleagues are loved by nobody now, and I am afraid they will have to rule by threats of force. Personally I am prevented from offering any active opposition to their policy by my friendship with him, but neither do I say anything in favour of it, for that would mean going back on my whole political conduct. I steer right onwards. What the public feels about it is most clearly shown in the theatres and at the free spectacles. For instance. At an exhibition of gladiators the presiding spirit, and his backers as well, were unmercifully hissed; at the Apolline Games the actor Diphilus made an attack, in the worst of taste, on my Pompey:

Happy art thou through our unhappiness . . .

and was encored over and over again.

A time will come when thou shalt sore repent
The very valour that is now thy boast,

he went on amid the applause of the whole theatre, and so through the rest of that speech. To be sure you would think the verses had been written for the occasion by a personal enemy of Pompey:

If neither law nor wont have force for thee——

and the rest of it was received with thunders of applause, which died down when Caesar made his appearance. He was followed by young

Curio and *he* was hailed with such cheering as used to greet Pompey in the great days of the Republic. Caesar took it very ill. It is said that a letter sped by express to Pompey at Capua. They are feeling bitter against the Knights for standing up to applaud Curio. They are plotting mischief against all of us. They are threatening the Roscian law and the corn law too. Certainly it is a very bad state of affairs. The easiest course for me would be to say nothing and let them do what they like, but I fear this will scarcely be possible for me now. It is no good people saying they won't put up with it, they'll have to put up with it. On every hand you hear the same criticism, but it rests on nothing more solid than the universal dissatisfaction.*

These two letters—one humorous, urbane, humane, touched with persiflage, the other serious but intensely interesting—may be taken as fairly representative of Cicero's mastery in this kind. Who would not wish to write such letters? Nobody, so far as we can tell, had written such before, and they set a standard and provided a model for later writers. Of course, there are and were other styles. There has always been a more formal type of epistle which, at its best, must not be refused a place in literature. There is a celebrated example included in the body of Cicero's correspondence. It is the letter which the great lawyer Servius Sulpicius wrote from Greece to condole with Cicero on the death of his daughter Tullia, whom her father adored.

My dear friend, After I had been told the news of the death of your daughter Tullia I was, as I could not fail to be, terribly grieved and distressed about it. I felt as if the blow had fallen on me too, since, had I been on the spot, I would have been at your side to support you and tell you how sorry I was. Although such consolation is a pitiful and painful business because the relations and friends who have to offer it are themselves affected and cannot attempt it without many a tear, so that they seem themselves to need consolation rather than to be capable of performing that service to others, nevertheless I have decided to write a few words expressing the

Ad. Attic. II. xix. 2–4.

thoughts that have occurred to me at the moment, not because I think that they have not occurred to you too, but because your grief may prevent you from seeing the truth of them so clearly.—Why should your private sorrow trouble you so deeply? Think how Fortune has hitherto dealt with us: those things taken from us which ought to be no less dear to men than their children, namely country, honour, rank, all public distinctions. What addition can this single loss make to the sum of our miseries? Or what mind is there, that has had these experiences, which is not sure to be callous by this time and to set a lower value upon everything? You grieve for her? How often must the thought have come to you—it has often come to me —that in these times their fate is not the worst who have been permitted to exchange life for a painless death! What indeed was there that could greatly tempt her to go on living in the present age? What present or future blessing? What comforting thought? That of going through life united in marriage to a young man of the highest distinction? What chance were you given of selecting from among such young men a son in law, suited to your reputation, into whose protection you felt that you could safely entrust a child of yours? Was it hoped that she would bear sons whose successful careers she might follow with joy, who might hold securely the estate inherited from their father, who might be candidates for the offices of state in their due order, who might enjoy freedom of speech in all their dealings with their friends? What one of these advantages was not taken from you before it was granted? 'It is sad to lose a child.' Sad indeed, but perhaps it is sadder to undergo and to endure the things I have described.—Let me tell you something that brought me no small consolation; perhaps it may lessen *your* sorrow. On my way back from Asia I was sailing from Aegina towards Megara and I began to cast my eyes on the scenery about me. Behind me lay Aegina, before me Megara, on my right Piraeus, on my left Corinth, towns which were once most flourishing but now lie fallen in ruins before our eyes. I began to think to myself, 'Ah poor creatures that we are, do we think it hard if one of us is dead or killed, we whose lives cannot fail to be comparatively short, when the bodies of so many cities lie in one place fallen and dead? Will you not check yourself, Servius, and remember that you are a mortal man?' Believe me, that reflection strengthened me not a little. There is another thing which I should like you, if you please, to contemplate along with me. It is this. In the last year or two there has perished a large proportion of our most distinguished men, the prestige of the Roman people has suffered a grievous diminution, the provinces are all convulsed: and are you overwhelmed by the loss of one poor little lady's life? If she had not died now, she must have died a few years later, for she was only mortal. Like me withdraw your mind and thought from these considerations and dwell instead on such reflections as befit a man of your character and standing: that she lived as long as there was need, that she did not survive the liberties of her country, that she had seen you her father hold the offices of praetor, consul, augur, that she had been the wife of young men of the greatest distinction, that she enjoyed all the good things of life and departed from it in the hour when her fatherland was falling into servitude. What complaint can you or she make to Fortune on this account? Finally do not forget that you are Cicero—that Cicero who has been in the habit of instructing and advising others. Do not follow the example of bad physicians who profess medical science when they are treating the maladies of other people, but cannot manage their own. Rather suggest to your mind and set before it the precepts which you inculcate in others. . . .*

This is a fine example of consolatory eloquence in the Stoic vein. Echoes of it may be heard through the Renaissance and linger in the pulpit oratory of the seventeenth century. It is quoted in *Tristram Shandy* and paraphrased in *Childe Harold*. Indeed it was perhaps better known than any single letter from Cicero himself. Yet it is hardly what we should now call a letter, being little more than a homily couched in epistolary form. It is Cicero who gives us the true epistolary art, in which the writer passes 'from grave to gay, from lively to severe'. Cicero is as certainly the father of it as Homer is of the epic. Of his Roman successors the most industrious and variously interesting was the Younger Pliny. Being composed with an eye to publication, the letters of Pliny are self-conscious, therein resembling the letters of Horace Walpole, which are

Fam. IV. 5.

sprightlier but perhaps not better, if indeed so good. Walpole's immediate models were the great French letter-writers of his own and the seventeenth century. But we may be sure that he read Pliny, and when he did he must have felt the affinities between himself and the Roman author. It was in fact Pliny rather than Cicero who influenced the practice of correspondents in later times, the very artificiality of his letters making them easier to imitate, since artificiality is a matter of rules and fashions, whereas spontaneity comes by nature. We are apt to forget that how to write a letter was a part of English education till well into the nineteenth century; I imagine it is still a part of a commercial education. Now we can say with full assurance that the more literary type of letter is derived, through Renaissance intermediaries like Erasmus, from the Latin letter-writers, in effect from Cicero and Pliny, especially, for the reason I have suggested, from Pliny. To be sure the style of Pliny cannot be reproduced in English, but it was found that his selection and handling of epistolary commonplaces could.

It can hardly be doubted that the most interesting to us of Pliny's letters are the two which describe the great eruption of Vesuvius in A.D.79. They are interesting both for their contents and for the correspondent to whom they are addressed, who is the historian Tacitus. They are rather reports than letters, Pliny justly looking upon them as contributions to history. But they are good letters for all that. Only some excerpts can be given. To understand them it should be noted that at first he is speaking of his *uncle*—the 'Elder Pliny'—who was in command of the Roman fleet at Misenum, just north of the Bay of Naples.

About one o'clock in the afternoon of August 24th my mother drew his attention to an extraordinary cloud on the horizon. My uncle had followed his daily routine—a few steps in the sun, a cold bath, a quiet lunch—and was among his books when she told him about it.

He called for his slippers and went up to a place where he could get
the best view of the phenomenon. A cloud was rising—from
Vesuvius, it was afterwards learned, but this could not be perceived
from a distance. I cannot give you a better idea of its shape than by
saying that it resembled a pine tree with a stem that rose high into
the air with branches spreading from it. The explanation may have
been that it had been driven up by a puff of wind, which had
subsequently died away and left it unsupported, or even borne down
by its own weight, with the result that it began to spread out
laterally, growing thinner and thinner. It kept changing its colour,
being sometimes white and sometimes a dirty grey from the earth or
ashes it had carried up. . . . Hastening to the spot from which others
were in flight, my uncle kept the flagship on a straight course to the
scene of danger, so free from fear that he dictated a detailed
description of every change in the motion and shape of the horror as
observed by his own eyes. By this time ashes were falling on the
ships which, as they approached the shore, came more dense and
hot, being accompanied now by bits of pumice and stones blackened
and scorched and fretted with fire. Almost at once they found themselves in shallow water, where a landslip had come down on the
beach and made disembarkation impossible. All this time the sky
was lit up by great sheets of flame and towering columns of fire rising
from more than one part of Vesuvius, their glare thrown into relief
by the darkness of the night. To reassure his people my uncle maintained that these were fires which had been left behind by the rural
population in their flight or burning farms deserted by their
occupants. . . . It was now daylight—daylight elsewhere, but in that
place Egyptian darkness, relieved by many torches and improvised
lights. They decided to make their way to the shore and judge from
closer inspection if the sea now gave them a chance; but it was still
impossibly high. . . . There had been earth-tremors for many
days, but people were comparatively unalarmed because they are so
frequent in Campania. But that night there was such an earthquake
that everything was not merely shaken but, people believed, turned
upside down. . . . After we got clear of buildings we called a halt.
We had many strange and alarming experiences there. For instance
the carriages we had ordered, though standing on perfectly level
ground, were tossed backwards and forwards and could not be kept

steady even when stones were wedged under the wheels. Then we saw the sea retiring as if it were being driven back by the earthquake. The land had unmistakably risen above sea-level, leaving many marine creatures high and dry on the sand. On another side of us a horrible black cloud, through which the fiery breath of lightning burst in forked and quivering flashes, every now and again gaped and shot out long streamers of flame, like sheets of lightning but on a greater scale. . . . Not long afterwards the cloud descended upon the land and shrouded the sea; Capri was wrapped in its folds and could be seen no more; no more could the promontory of Misenum. My mother then began to beg and pray, even command me to make my escape in whatever way I could; a young man like myself would manage it; she was too old and inactive and would be glad enough to die, if she had not the thought that she had caused my death. I answered that we would be saved together or not at all, and clasping her hand I urged her to walk faster. She obeyed reluctantly, blaming herself all the time for keeping me back. Ashes were now falling, though not thickly as yet. I looked round. Gross darkness loomed behind us, poured over the ground like a river in flood, and came after us. 'Let us get out of the road while we can see', I said, 'in case we get knocked down by the crowd and be trampled to death in the darkness'. We had scarcely found a place to sit down when it was night—not the sort of night you get when there are clouds and no moon, but the darkness of a cellar when the door is locked and the lamp put out. You could hear women screaming, babies crying, men bawling. Parents, children, husbands and wives kept calling on one another, trying to find where they were. . . . Slowly light returned; we took it for the harbinger not of day but of an approaching conflagration. The conflagration was a fact, but it stopped a good way short of us; then darkness again and a heavy downpour of ashes. We kept getting up and shaking them off; otherwise we should have been buried or even crushed under the mass. I might take credit to myself that amid such dangers I never once let a groan or an expression of fear pass my lips. But the truth is I was convinced that the world was coming to an end, and I with it, and I found a sort of comfort for my own death in the thought that it was part of that universal tragedy. But at last the darkness thinned, turned into a sort of smoke or fog, and disappeared. Presently we had real daylight again; the sun actually shone out, but a dull yellow, as he usually is in an eclipse. As we gazed, not yet recovered from our terrors, we saw a changed world blanketed with ashes white as snow. We returned to Misenum. There, after such rest and refreshment as we could get, we spent an anxious night, in which our hopes contended with our fears. . . .*

There had happened to Pliny what every newspaper correspondent hopes may one day happen to himself—to be on the spot when some tremendous event takes place. He might have been excused if he had written up his material in a more exciting way. Yet his description is better as it is. Any exaggeration would have spoiled its value not only as history but as literature, for here the truth is more interesting than fiction. And how good and well chosen are the details he gives! It is a 'classical' description, and Pliny's reward is that he has become a classic, though a somewhat minor one. But it is also possible to discern in him without too much fancifulness the first faint glimmer of something else—a *romantic* feeling for scenery. Here he is, at the dawn of the second century, trying to do what Gray does in his letters from the Lake Country and Shelley in his letters from Italy. Consider how much modern writing is anticipated in this account of the sources of the river Clitumnus.

Dear Romanus, did you ever see the source of the Clitumnus? If not—and I fancy not, otherwise you would have told me all about it—do see it, as I did the other day; my one regret is that I did not see it long ago. There is a hill, covered with a dense wood of old cypresses, which rises to no great height; from the base of this hill issues the spring, which is forced out from several veins of different sizes, forming a swirling pool. It struggles through this and then spreads out into a broad expanse of glassy water so clear that you can count the coins that have been flung into it and the pebbles gleaming at the bottom. From there it dashes on, not because of the slope of the ground but simply because of the mass and weight of its own water—a spring so far but very soon to become a broad and even

*Ep. VI. 16 and 20.

navigable stream carrying along to their destinations even ships, which meet the current and fight against it. So powerful is it that, although its course takes it over level ground, ships going with the current get no advantage from using their oars, while it is a great struggle to make headway against it even by using both poles and oars. It is great fun for people sailing up and down for pleasure to exchange hard pulling for an easy, and an easy for hard pulling, according as they go up stream or down. The banks are thickly clad with ash and poplar, adding to the charms of the river, the clear waters of which reflect their green images as if they were submerged. The water rivals snow for coldness and colour. Nearby stands an old and venerable temple. Within, there is a statue of Clitumnus himself clad in a ceremonial toga with border of purple. That the god visits the shrine and even gives oracles is proved by the lots one sees there. Several smaller shrines, each containing its deity, are scattered about the neighbourhood. Each has its own form of worship and its own name; nay some have their own springs. For besides what you might call the parent spring there are lesser ones, each with an individual head of waters; but they all join the river. It is crossed by a bridge which marks the boundary between the consecrated and unconsecrated ground; above it only boats may pass, but below the bridge swimming also is allowed. A public bath has been provided by the townspeople of Hispellum, to whom the emperor Augustus made a grant of the locality, and a hostel as well. There is also a fair number of country residences standing along the banks wherever there is an attractive bit of the river.*

Of this letter it might be said that, while it shows a true feeling for the picturesque, it gives the impression that the writer had no appreciation of wild and mountain beauty. But that is not claimed for him. Nor can it be claimed for the eighteenth century (as a whole) when Pliny was much read in the original or in such an admirable translation as Melmoth's. Pliny would have admired the park of an English nobleman as laid out by Brown or some other of the landscape gardeners. He would have admired it because he had himself largely

*Ep. VIII. 8.

created the taste for it. Every eighteenth-century architect and landscape designer is likely to have read that letter about the sources of the Clitumnus and certain to have read the two letters in which Pliny describes his famous 'villa' with loving minuteness. By such descriptions he influenced taste and thereby literature. We may at least say that the cult of the picturesque, which began to be developed towards the end of the century in books like Gilpin's *Observations*, and lasted long enough to have some effect on the work of Scott, was not so entirely modern as has been supposed.

It would produce some disproportion to say much more about the Letter, which was never counted among the important literary forms. It does, however, seem necessary in a historical sketch to add a word about epistles written in 'modern Latin', that is Latin composed by modern authors in more or less successful imitation of classical Latin. They are little read now, except perhaps by historians in the way of business. Those of Erasmus have the most vitality as literature; like Cicero's they have spontaneity and humour, qualities apparently denied to the excellent Pliny. Though it is impossible to do justice to his versatility in this form, we may find room for a passage which has a special interest for English readers. It comes from a letter to Dr. Francis.

I often feel sorry and I wonder how it happens that Britain has been plagued all these years by constant ill-health, especially the sweating sickness, a malady which seems almost confined to it. We read of a city which freed itself from endemic plague by changing its houses on the advice of a philosopher. If I do not deceive myself, England may be freed by adopting a similar policy. For, in the first place, they never give a thought to the question whether their windows and doors are facing north, south, east or west. In the second place their rooms are generally constructed in such a way that they have no ventilation, the value of which is stressed by Galen. Thirdly the wall of an English house largely consists of lozenged casements of glass which admit the light but exclude the air in motion; what they do not exclude is a draught which percolates through the chinks—a draught which is the more dangerous to health because for a long time it has not been in circulation. Fourthly the floors are mostly of clay covered with rushes never renewed except in such a manner that a foundation is left, under which fester, not infrequently for a score of years, spittle, vomit, beer drippings, fish bones and unmentionable filth. From this, when the warm weather comes, there rises an exhalation which in my humble opinion is far from salubrious to the human frame. Add that England is not only surrounded by the sea but is marshy in many places and intersected by brackish streams. I feel sure that the island would be much healthier if the use of rushes were done away with and if rooms were so constructed that they are open to the sky on two or three sides, all the windows being made to open and shut in one piece, and so tightly shut that there would be no room for noxious air currents to enter through gaping chinks.

Such letters in modern Latin need some consideration because the art of writing them was taught in schools long before there was any teaching of English composition. The models set before the lads were chiefly Cicero, Pliny and Erasmus. It was natural that letters written in English should be influenced by these masters, who had so brilliantly shown how to handle the sort of topics that come into a letter. I am speaking of carefully composed letters, meant for publication; for the occasional communications of friends are literature only when one or both have a natural gift of expression. There has no doubt been a great deal of development and expansion. For instance, the 'open letter', though not unknown in antiquity, is almost a modern invention. Yet such things as the Letters of Junius and Burke's *Letter to a Noble Lord* would have been very different in form and method if their authors had not been bred in the study of Latin literature.

It is all part of what happened to the European spirit when it embodied itself in English prose.

APPENDIX

1. Meanwhile a certain Gaul, unarmed except for a shield and a pair of swords but adorned with circlets of gold about his neck and arms, stepped forward more than a match for all the rest in strength and stature, in youth combined with prowess. The battle had begun and both sides were furiously fighting when who but he proceeded to wave his hand as a signal to both armies to stop. A halt was made in the fighting, and as soon as there was silence he bawls out that, if anyone wished to fight him, he should step forward. None dared, all fearing the size and savage look of the man. Then began the Gaul to jeer at the Romans and to put out his tongue. A sudden pang of grief and rage shot through one Titus Manlius, a man of the noblest birth, to think that such a disgrace was befalling his country that no one in all that host came forward. He, I say, stepped forth and did not suffer the honour of Rome to be foully stained by a Gaul. Girt with a footsoldier's shield and a Spanish sword he took his stand against the alien. The fearful combat was fought out on the bridge itself in sight of both armies. Thus, as I said, they took their stand. The Gaul waited with his shield held out before him according to the military practice of his nation, but Manlius, trusting more to courage than skill, struck the other's shield with his own and threw him off his balance. While the Gaul was struggling to recover his former posture Manlius struck his shield a second time, and a second time knocked the man off his stance. This allowed him to get under the Gaul's sword and with his Spanish blade lay his breast open. Having brought him down he cut off his head, pulled off his collar and put it, all bloody as it was, about his own neck.

2. After publishing a decree ordering the suspension of public business in face of a rising of the Gauls the dictator conscripted all the men of military age and, marching from Rome with a very large army, pitched camp on the southern bank of the Anio. Crossing the river was a bridge, which neither army broke down, lest their action should be taken as a sign of fear. There were frequent skirmishes for possession of the bridge, but these were indecisive. Thereupon a gigantic Gaul strode on to the empty bridge and cried out at the top of his voice, 'Now is the time for the bravest man that Rome possesses to step forward—come now!—to do battle, that the issue of our duel may show whether your people or mine is better in war'. There was a long silence among the leaders of the Roman youth, ashamed to decline the contest and yet reluctant to claim the leading share in facing the peril. At last Manlius, the son of Lucius—that Manlius who had

rescued his father from the persecution of the tribunes—left his post and went to the dictator. He said, 'Without leave from you, sir, I should not fight out of my rank, even if I could see victory assured; if you allow me I wish to prove to that animal, since he is swaggering so proudly before the standards of the enemy, that I am come of that family which flung an army of Gauls down the Tarpeian Rock'. Then said the dictator, 'Well done, Titus Manlius, and dutifully towards your father and your fatherland! Forward, and with heaven's aid show that Rome cannot be conquered!' On this the young man is armed by his fellows. He takes an infantryman's shield and is girt with a Spanish sword adapted for close fighting. So armed and equipped he is led forward to encounter the Gaul, who was grinning like an idiot and—our ancestors thought even this worth mentioning—putting out his tongue in mockery. The companions of Manlius then withdrew to their posts and the two armed champions are left alone between the armies as if they were to provide a gladiatorial show rather than engage in a military combat. To judge by appearances they were very unevenly matched. One was of huge proportions, in parti-coloured dress, glittering with arms that were painted and inlaid with gold; the other was of the right build for a soldier, while his arms, which were serviceable rather than decorative, did not greatly catch the eye. No war-song for him, no idle war-dance or brandishing of arms; but a heart full of courage and silent rage had reserved its fury for the decisive moment of the fight. When they halted between the two lines of all those mortals on the rack of hope and fear, the Gaul, who loomed over his adversary like a tower, thrust forward his shield with his left arm to parry the blows of his advancing foe and brought down the edge of his sword with a tremendous clatter, though to no effect. The Roman, keeping the point of his blade up, after striking the lower part of his enemy's shield with his own and, at the risk of a wound, insinuating his whole body between the body and arms of the other, with one and then another blow wounded his belly and groin and, as he fell, stretched his giant length upon the ground. Then as he lay there, leaving his body untouched by any other injury, he stripped off nothing but his torque, which, bespattered as it was with blood, he put round his own neck. The Gauls were rooted to the spot between terror and admiration; the Romans joyfully advanced from their position to meet their soldier, and with praise and thanks conduct him to the dictator. In certain jocular songs of the artless kind which soldiers make up the nickname of *Torquatus* was heard. Being taken up and repeated it became even a title of honour to that family. The dictator presented him also with a golden crown and in a speech to the army praised his martial feat to the skies.

3. If it had been only private citizens who came forward to speak for or against our proposal, I too, when I thought enough had been said on this

side and on that, should have awaited the result of your voting in silence. As it is, since a man whose opinion we must value very highly, the consul Marcus Porcius, has attacked our proposal not only by the weight of his opinion which, even if not put in words, would have told very heavily, but also by a long set speech, I feel bound to make a short reply. I am compelled to say however that he used more words in castigating our matrons than in producing arguments against the bill, to such an extent in fact that he left it doubtful whether it was of their own volition or at our suggestion that the matrons had done that for which he took them to task. I intend to speak in support of the proposal, which does not proceed from us tribunes, against whom the consul hurled this accusation rather in general terms than in such a way as to make a definite charge. 'Cabal', 'sedition', occasionally 'rebellion on the part of our women' was his way of describing the fact that the matrons had openly suggested to you that a law passed against them in the course of a war with its harsh conditions should in time of peace and when the state is rich and prosperous be abolished by you. I know that there are the high-sounding words he used as well as others that may be brought together to lend impressiveness to a case, and we are all aware that the oratory of Cato is not only powerful but also on occasion uncompromising, though personally he is not unkindly. Yet after all what is unprecedented about the matrons' action in appearing in large numbers in public in a case which particularly concerns them? Have they never been seen in public till today?

4. We now proceed to appearances in the sky. When the conflagration has well begun the darkening or sanguine hue of the sun and moon is readily explained. For when the atmosphere shall have been filled with smoke and flames, undoubtedly the face of the sun and moon and the whole sky will be obscured, and the heavenly bodies will assume a new appearance and colour. This is wont to happen when Etna sends out her flames, as we saw above in Dio Cassius; to whom add the words of Cicero. *Let us imagine such a darkness as is said once to have obscured the regions near when Etna burst forth in fire, so that for two days no man could see another, and when on the third day the sun shone out again they thought that they had come back to life.* I believe that during the conflagration the sun and the moon will undergo many mutations and changes of form according to the prevalence of fire, smoke, ashes, reek, flames, which will have occupied the intervening air; nor will they presently restore the luminaries of the world so much as certain lumps of dusky light. Sometimes the sun will apear larger than usual and wrathful like a blood-red mountain hanging in the firmament, sometimes he will look pallid or orange-coloured; and sometimes he will completely disappear behind a curtain of pitchy gloom. Nay it may come to pass that, to increase

the horror of the thing throughout the sky and all the planets, the sun will gather spots upon his face and be really darkened and hang lightless among the planets as though he were dead. This would be a fearsome sight to the surrounding worlds, which would have a blazing earth instead of the sun and draw their own light and heat from our burning home.

INDEX

GEORGE ALLEN & UNWIN LTD
London: 40 Museum Street, W.C.1

Auckland: Haddon Hall, City Road
Sydney, N.S.W.: Bradbury House, 55 York Street
Cape Town: 58–60 Long Street
Bombay: 15 Graham Road, Ballard Estate, Bombay 1
Calcutta: 17 Chittaranjan Avenue, Calcutta 13
New Delhi: 13–14 Ajmere Gate Extension, New Delhi 1
Karachi: Haroon Chambers, South Napier Road, Karachi 2
Toronto: 91 Wellington Street West
São Paulo: Avenida 9 de Julho 1138-Ap. 51

J. A. K. Thomson

THE CLASSICAL INFLUENCE
ON ENGLISH POETRY

In his previous book *The Classical Background of English Literature* Professor Thomson made an estimate of the influence exerted upon our literature by the ancient classics. He found it impossible, within the limits of a single book, to illustrate by actual quotation the points made. In *Classical Influence on English Poetry* he sets out to remedy this deficiency, so far as the poets are concerned.

By a careful selection of typical passages the author gives a reasonably complete idea of what the classics have meant to a number of the most eminent English writers. The passages have been translated where necessary and a sufficiently full commentary added. The student and the lover of poetry will find here the materials they need for studying the literary influences of the classics on English Poetry.

A further volume is being planned to deal with the prose authors. The three volumes, when completed, will form a coherent whole, but each volume will be complete in itself.

Demy 8vo, 15s. net

THE ETHICS OF ARISTOTLE

"A smoothly flowing translation in which italic passages by Professor Thomson enable the reader to see quickly the drift of the argument. . . . Professor Thomson has embarked upon a daring experiment, but it is successful. The Oxford Aristotle—unmatched as an exact translation—is not light reading whereas Professor Thomson's—though it really is a translation and not a paraphrase—could almost be read by him who runs." *Times Literary Supplement*

"A brilliant piece of work." *Church Times*

"He has given us a translation which makes us feel that we ourselves are in the lecture-room listening to Aristotle himself, and he makes Aristotle our own contemporary. Could any praise for a translation be more relevant or pertinent than that?" *Christian World*

Demy 8vo, 18s. net

HELLENISM AND THE MODERN WORLD

by Gilbert Murray

In the Six Talks given on the B.B.C. Home Service and before that on the Radiodiffusion Française, Gilbert Murray tries to show the special value to the world of those nations which have in various degrees inherited the great "Hellenic" or "Christian tradition that comes from Rome, Jerusalem and Athens". He suggests that it is not true that all nations or all men are "equal". Some are specially privileged, and therefore have special duties and are exposed to special dangers. The long historical contest between the "Hellenic" and the "Barbarous" is still actively at work in human society, bringing both a hope and a danger.

"There is literally no one who writes on the Greeks with, at one and the same time, such charm and such authority as does Professor Gilbert Murray." *Expository Times*

Crown 8vo, 5s. net

THE ITALIAN INFLUENCE
IN ENGLISH POETRY

by A. Lytton Sells

If poetry was the fashionable mode of expression in Tudor England, "Great Italy", as Shakespeare called her, was the land of predilection for Englishmen. They looked to Italy for lessons in philosophy, good-breeding, in the art of civilization and the art of government. Englishmen travelled to Italy and lived as students in Padua; Italian protestants came to England—Vermigli, Gentili, Florio, Bruno. The commerce in politics, religion, court life, manners and the things of the intellect was immense.

In this volume the non-dramatic work of various poets is analysed to show how, beginning with Chaucer, Englishmen took from Italy many of the forms of their poetry, many of its techniques and much of its subject-matter. But their policy was not to annex; rather to naturalise. Spencer tries to surpass Ariosto; Sidney finds a pattern in Petrarch; Greville adapts Machiavelli; and so on, through the study of Shakespeare, Drayton and Southwell, and a host of minor poets. The results of scattered research are here for the first time drawn together to form a comprehensive picture.

Sm. Royal 8vo, 8 plates, 30s. net

LONDON: GEORGE ALLEN & UNWIN LTD